INTO THE ARMS OF STRANGERS

Greater German Reich, late 1930s

INTO THE ARMS OF STRANGERS

Stories of the Kindertransport

Mark Jonathan Harris and Deborah Oppenheimer

Preface by Lord Richard Attenborough
Introduction by David Cesarani

BLOOMSBURY

Published by Bloomsbury Publishing, New York and London.
Distributed to the trade by St. Martin's Press.

Library of Congress Cataloging-in-Publication Data has been applied for

ISBN 1-58234-101-X

First published in Great Britain in 2000 by Bloomsbury Publishing plc
38 Soho Square, London W1V 5DF

First US Edition
10 9 8 7 6 5 4 3 2 1

Typeset by Hewer Text Ltd, Edinburgh
Printed in Great Britain

in memory of my mother
Deborah Oppenheimer

for my children
Mark Jonathan Harris

A child is an orphan when he has no parents.
A nation is an orphan when it has no children.

Rabbi Joseph Cahaneman of Panevezys
1886–1969

CONTENTS

PREFACE
By Lord Richard Attenborough

Like the many people who speak in this book, my life was transformed by the outbreak of the Second World War.

My parents were radicals. My father was a very early member of the Labour Party. My mother campaigned for women's rights. In the late 1930s, my father was principal of Leicester University College, where he also chaired a committee devoted to bringing Jewish refugees out of Hitler's Germany. In most of the cases it meant housing them for a few days while their papers were put in order to go to relatives in the United States or Canada.

One day my mother went up to London to fetch two German girls, Irene, aged twelve, and Helga, nine. I said hello and expected them to leave within the next few days, like the other children who had passed through our house. But while they were with us, war broke out, ending all transport to America.

I was fourteen, my brother David was three years younger, and my brother Johnny a couple of years younger than that. We all came back from school one day and were told to see my father in his study. This was unusual – it was rather formal and not like our household. We went in, and my mother and father were there. My father explained that Irene and Helga had been planning to go to America, but now they were stranded and there was nowhere for them to go. Their mother was in a concentration camp and their father likely to be.

My father said, 'Mother and I have decided that what we ought to do is adopt them – not in terms of calling us "Mother" and "Father", of course, but "Aunt" and "Uncle" because we hope their parents will come out.' Since being the principal of University College was not exactly a highly paid position, however, we had a problem. What we had been able to do as a family of five, we could not afford as a family of seven. That meant that holidays, outings all had to be reduced.

My parents both said, 'This is what we would like. We think it is the correct thing to do, but we won't do it without the agreement of you boys, because they are going to become your sisters, and in every sense that they are your sisters, this must be your new family.'

We all said we thought it was a marvellous idea: for three boys suddenly to have two sisters in the family was very good luck. But the remark that I always remember more than any other was my mother's. She said, 'The problem, darlings, is this: your father and I love the three of you so much, but we are going to have to give perhaps even more love to these two girls than we give to you at this time, because, of course, they have none.' This remark has affected my whole life in terms of attitude towards those who are not as fortunate as my brothers and I have been.

For eight years Irene and Helga were our sisters. We did everything together. There were little jealousies, little quarrels, as with any kids, but we came to love each other very much. I am sure my brothers would agree it was one of the best decisions we ever made. After the war, which Helga's and Irene's parents did not survive, the girls went to America. Irene, sadly, has died of cancer. Helga is still alive. She has children, grandchildren. We still keep in touch and always see them when we go to America. And they quite often come here.

My parents' generosity represents only one of many acts of kindness of the British people in those dark days. Others are movingly recounted in this book. Although ours is a reserved nation, we do feel things very deeply. At a time when other countries were unwilling to alter their immigration quotas, Britain alone agreed to provide sanctuary for children fleeing Hitler. Unfortunately, no other nation matched this act of mercy, and nearly 1,500,000 children perished in the Holocaust.

My parents' attitude to life was always that there is such a thing as 'society', and that it involves obligations of concern, tolerance and compassion for those less fortunate than we are. But taking Helga and Irene into our family as sisters wasn't theory. It was first-hand experience. These were human beings whom we came to love. From the age of fourteen on, I have always believed that no man can live as an island. And I feel that very strongly.

I know that in the movies I direct, I want to make statements. I want to make a cry for compassion and a plea for tolerance. I suppose the most obvious example is *Cry Freedom*, an anti-apartheid movie about South Africa. If I had not had the beginning I did, if I had not known Irene and Helga, I doubt that I would have had the passion and the determination to demonstrate those feelings through my work.

As I read the compelling and inspiring accounts of the Kindertransport in this book, I am again grateful for the experience of taking two refugee children into our family. It certainly shaped my attitudes and development, much in the way it has shaped the lives of those who so eloquently reflect on that period in these pages. More than sixty years later, their stories of escape and exile, of kindness and cruelty, remind us that even in the worst of times people can still act with foresight and charity. In a world of Kosovos and Rwandas, it is a lesson that is still relevant to us all.

Lord Richard Attenborough
London, April 2000

INTRODUCTION
By David Cesarani

To Harold Waterman (né Hans Wassermann, born Frankfurt), my father-in-law, who was saved thanks to the Kindertransport, and Daniel Joseph Cesarani, his grandson, named in memory of Harold's adoptive father in Germany, who perished in the Warsaw Ghetto.

In January 1933 Hitler and his National Socialist German Workers Party came to power in Germany and a storm broke over the heads of German Jews. The lives of Jewish children, like those who tell their stories here, were among the first to be affected. As adults they have carried into our time the story of a political catastrophe that occurred over three-quarters of a century ago.

Jews had lived in the German lands since Roman times. Over the centuries their numbers and fortunes had waxed and waned, but by the middle of the nineteenth century German Jewry was embarked on a rising curve of security, status and prosperity. In 1870 they gained full civic equality in a united Germany. There were strong currents of anti-Jewish prejudice in German society, but anti-Semitic political parties met with failure. A substantial section of the German people valued their Jewish citizens and most at least tolerated them. When the First World War broke out in August 1914, German Jews flocked to serve the country they loved. The outcome of the war changed Germany for ever, although this was not immediately noticeable to those born in its aftermath.

During this period a maximum of 600,000 Jews lived in Germany, which was under 1 per cent of the total German population. However, they were heavily concentrated in a few cities. A third of the German Jews lived in Berlin, where they made up 4 per cent of the capital's population. Seventy per cent of Jews lived in large cities, with populations of over 100,000, whereas half of the Germans lived in small towns and villages. Even so, the urbanization of German Jews can be exaggerated. By 1933, in spite of years of demographic and economic decline, nearly one in five Jews still lived in small towns. Many children, like Jack Hellman and Ursula Rosenfeld, who were later evacuated from Germany on the Kindertransport, grew up in modest-sized towns or the country and were moved to the cities with large, secure Jewish communities, even before they were sent to live abroad.

Jews were also distinctive thanks to the nature of their social and economic profile. Three-quarters of all Jews in gainful employment were engaged in trade, commerce, the financial sector and the professions. This was three times the proportion among the general population. Jewish firms accounted for 80 per cent of the turnover of all German department stores, giving them a highly visible dominance in one area of trade. Jews owned 25 per cent of smaller retail outlets and 30 per cent of clothing stores, making them prominent in areas of business where there was extensive contact between the client and service-provider. It gave non-Jews the erroneous impression that Jews were 'everywhere'. For many Germans, particularly those in Berlin where Jewish representation in the professions was most concentrated, Jews were the face of commerce, medicine and the law. In reality, they represented only 11 per cent of all doctors and 16 per cent of all lawyers in Germany. The same deceptive effect was created in many rural areas. Jews handled a quarter of all wholesale agricultural trade and in some districts cattle dealing and grain marketing was largely in Jewish hands. Lorraine Allard's father – a dealer in hops – was typical of this stratum. These Jews were usually better off than the farmers and artisans around them and they often imported modern amenities and modern ideas into the countryside.

The impression that Jews were somehow associated with everything modern was fostered by their prominence in the arts and sciences. Several of the great publishing houses were Jewish-owned; Jews were over-represented among writers and journalists, in theatre and in the film industry. Some expressed radical cultural and political ideas, but they were hardly representative of the Jewish population. Whether they lived in the city or the country, German Jews were mainly middle class and rather conservative. In politics they overwhelmingly supported the liberal and democratic centre parties or the moderate socialist party.

A significant section of the German Jewish population was actually rather poor. During the depression unemployment hit the Jewish community too, and in 1932 over 31.5 per cent of Jewish employees in Berlin were out of work. One in four Jews was receiving charity. Most of these were the Jews who had immigrated from Poland and Russia between 1880 and the 1920s, derisively known by the German Jews as *Ostjuden* or Eastern Jews. In 1933, the *Ostjuden*, like Alexander Gordon's mother, made up about one-fifth of all German Jewry. They were small merchants, itinerant traders, shop-keepers, tailors, artisans and industrial workers. Many were Orthodox and religiously observant. In this respect they differed from the majority of Jews in Germany. For, although there was a notable minority that was Orthodox, represented here by the family of Bertha Leverton and her sister, Inge Sadan, most belonged to the Reform or Liberal movements that almost everywhere constituted the officially recognized community. Indeed, German Jews had become less and less religiously observant as they had become more and more integrated into German society. In the postwar years, 25 per cent of Jewish men and 16 per cent of Jewish women were marrying outside the faith. It was this sort of acculturation and assimilation that left Jews bemused by the persistence and strength of anti-Semitism.

Prejudice against Jews was rife in Germany before 1914, but the years of war, followed by defeat, political upheaval and economic distress, greatly enlarged the field of anti-Jewish activists. Politicians of Jewish origin played a leading role in the anti-war movement and in the progressive forces that finally swept aside the Kaiser's regime, replacing it with a parliamentary democracy in November 1918 – known as the Weimar Republic. A small number of Jews with even more radical ideas emerged as leaders of the Communist Party and the anarchists, and were involved in bloody civil unrest between 1920 and 1923. These Jewish figures never identified with their co-religionists, but military men, embittered soldiers, conservatives and nationalists of all kinds blamed the Jews for defeatism and revolution. They saw the Jews as one arm of a plot against the old order that was inspired by the Bolshevik regime in Russia.

From 1918 to 1924, Germany was in political and economic turmoil. As the value of German currency plummeted, the savings of the German middle class evaporated and unemployment soared. A clutch of parties on the far right sought to exploit the ensuing unrest. These parties were opposed to the Weimar Republic, hated democracy and socialism, resented the Versailles peace settlement which stripped Germany of territory, regarded modern culture as degenerate, and believed that the Jews were behind all these 'ills'. One of them was the German Workers' Party. In 1920, Adolf Hitler, who was then employed by the army as an undercover agent, joined it to spy on its members. Hitler liked its programme and soon rose to become its leader. He renamed it the National Socialist German Workers Party – NSDAP or Nazis.

From 1920 to 1923, the Nazis were a splinter group on the far right, based mainly in Bavaria. Hitler led the party in an unsuccessful coup against the Bavarian state government in 1923, as a result of which he spent a year in prison. On his release he pursued an electoral policy, building support for the Nazi Party among a range of discontented groups. In the 1928 elections for the Reichstag (the German parliament), the Nazis won just 800,000 votes or 2.6 per cent of the total poll. However, the Wall Street Crash in 1929 had a devastating effect on the German economy which was heavily dependent on loans from American banks. As these loans were called in, German businesses and banks folded, and unemployment spun out of control. In the elections of September 1930, Hitler's party obtained 6.4 million votes. The centrist government proved unable to alleviate the economic crisis and was forced to rule by decree when the work of parliament was paralysed by two large opposed blocs – the Nazis and the Communists. After elections in July 1932, the Nazis became the second largest party in the Reichstag with 13.7 million votes or 37.3 per cent of all votes cast. Hitler demanded that he be made chancellor, but the president, Field Marshal Hindenburg, resisted. In the elections held in September 1932 the Nazi vote fell to 11.7 million, but political intrigue led to Hitler being offered the post of chancellor in a coalition government. He seized his chance and became the ruler of Germany on 30 January 1933.

As Jack Hellman remembers, in cities, towns and villages around Germany the Nazi Party – spearheaded by the brown uniformed party militia, the SA (storm troopers) – celebrated its success by holding raucous torchlight parades and assaulting its political opponents. Four weeks later, an arson attack on the Reichstag building gave Hitler the excuse to demand sweeping powers from the parliament, ostensibly to protect state security. New elections were held in March 1933 in an intimidating atmosphere, yet the Nazis still could not obtain a majority of the votes and only commanded a majority of seats in the parliament by means of an alliance with a smaller far-right party. This was enough for Hitler to begin reconstructing Germany according to his ideology, with horrific consequences for the Jews and millions of other German citizens.

Hitler's politics were driven by a belief in so-called scientific racism and eugenics. The goal of his racial-biological politics was to strengthen the racially defined German people, the *Volk*. The *Volksgemeinschaft*, or racial community, had to be rid of alien elements and purified by eliminating carriers of physical and mental weakness. The Jews were considered racially alien and hostile. A stream of laws passed from April 1933 onwards excluded them from politics, culture, society and the economy.

Yet Hitler had to proceed cautiously at first. He was chancellor, but at the head of a government that included old-style conservatives who may have been anti-Jewish but not with the same viciousness that characterized Nazi thinking. President Hindenburg felt obliged to protect Jews who had fought in the trenches in 1914–18 or lost sons in the war. Hitler's finance minister warned him that measures against Jews would adversely affect Germany's image abroad and its trading position. Nor was the public united. Many people looked forward to shopping in Jewish-owned stores; peasants in the countryside might grumble about Jewish dealers, but they needed their services and valued their expertise.

To reward his loyal followers and show that he was in earnest, Hitler allowed a state-sponsored boycott of Jewish businesses on 1–2 April 1933. Jews who had not fought in the 1914–18 war, along with political opponents of the regime, were dismissed from the civil service. A succession of laws also pushed Jews from other areas of government employment, such as doctors working for state health schemes. Jews were systematically purged from cultural institutions, too, often after they were taken over by the Nazi Party.

In the early years of the regime, many Jews – like many other people

– thought that it would not last long. Hitler faced dissent within his own movement and in July 1934 instigated a bloody purge of the SA. Life for Jews in the big cities did not change that much. But in the small towns and villages, where Jews were few in number, visible, and vulnerable, there was constant harassment. As Jewish children like Jack Hellman who attended local schools faced more and more bullying from other children and Nazified teachers, their parents preferred to withdraw them and send them to newly established residential Jewish schools in nearby cities or to stay with relatives.

In 1933–4, about 12,700 Jewish children attended Jewish schools as compared to 58,000 in non-Jewish ones. The transfer of children like Lorraine Allard and Lory Cahn meant that a year later the number of Jews in Jewish-run educational establishments rose to 18,500, reaching 20,000 in 1935–6, and peaking at 23,600 in the school year 1936–7. Most of the teachers in these schools were Jewish. Many were young Jewish university lecturers and other professionals who had been found work after they were dismissed from their jobs. The official Jewish community – the *Reichsvereinigung der deutschen Juden* – created by Nazi decree in September 1933 and led by Dr Otto Hirsch, among others, tried as far as possible to preserve an air of normality. Paradoxically, as a result, Jewish cultural life flourished.

The creation of a racially organized state did not make existence impossible for Jews. In September 1935, Hitler announced at the Nazi Party rally in Nuremberg that the Jews would be stripped of civil rights and reduced to the status of second-class citizens. To many observers, including Jews, this was the nadir of the persecution: the worst, especially the random violence and chaotic administration of anti-Jewish laws, seemed to be over. For two years a sort of calm reigned over the Jews in Germany. During 1936 it was still possible for Jews to sit in cafés on the boulevards of Berlin, drinking coffee and reading Jewish newspapers. This peculiar normality, and the impossibility of predicting what might happen next, help to account for the relatively low rates of emigration. In 1933, 37,000 Jews left Germany in a panic. The number fell to 23,000 the following year. In 1935, about 10,000 of those who had fled to neighbouring countries actually went back. The figures for Jewish emigration to Palestine rose from 7,600 in 1933, to 9,800 in 1935, but fell back to around 8,500 for the next two years. After that the rate was artificially held down due to restrictions imposed by the British, who controlled Palestine.

From the start of 1938, Nazi policy towards the Jews underwent a radicalization. This was part of a general shift. The regime was secure, the economy was strong, and Hitler felt able to pursue more ambitious goals. He now sought the incorporation into Germany of ethnic Germans in adjacent countries, especially those who had been removed by border changes under the Versailles settlement. His first target was Austria, where an indigenous Nazi Party had long been agitating for a merger with Germany. The Austrian government had fended off these demands and in March 1938 planned a referendum to strengthen its position. Hitler moved first and sent his army to occupy the country. The Germans received a rapturous welcome, confirmed by their own referendum held a short while later.

Austria was home to around 185,000 Jews, of whom 170,000 lived in the capital, Vienna. Jews comprised just over 3 per cent of the country's total population, but nearly 10 per cent of Vienna's inhabitants. They were clustered in just eight districts and in some formed a distinct majority. They were even more concentrated in a few occupations than was the case in Germany: some 62 per cent of all Viennese lawyers, a similar percentage of those engaged in finance and commerce, and nearly half of the city's doctors were Jewish. The pre-eminence of Jews in trade – from corner shops to department stores – and their visibility in the world of culture made them easy targets for anti-Semites and the socially disaffected. In fact, anti-Semitism was a fundamental element of Austrian life. Vienna had been ruled by one of the first and most successful anti-Semitic politicians, Dr Karl Lueger, from 1897 to 1911.

It was hardly surprising, then, that the incorporation of Austria into the Reich – the Anschluss – was accompanied by a festival of hatred directed at the Jews. Over the days and weeks following the annexation, Jews were assaulted in the streets and ritually humiliated. The anti-Jewish laws, which had been passed steadily over a period of five years in Germany, were promulgated and enforced at breakneck speed. Jewish businesses were shut down and sold off. Apartments, like those of Kurt Fuchel and Robert Sugar's parents, were seized and their occupants evicted. In August 1938, Adolf Eichmann, an SS lieutenant-colonel, was dispatched by the headquarters of the SS-Gestapo apparatus in Berlin, to organize the rapid, mass emigration of Jews. He set up a central emigration office and in just eighteen months 150,000 Jews, stripped of their rights, their property and their wealth but glad just to be alive, passed through it on their way to other countries.

In Germany itself the Nazi-led clamour to get rid of the Jews mounted again. Acts of violence escalated and more pressure was put on Jewish businessmen to sell up and leave. In the autumn of 1938, partly in response to the request of Switzerland – fearful of an influx of impoverished Jewish immigrants – the passports held by Jews were marked with a 'J' stamp. Jews were also forced to add Israel and Sarah to their names on all personal documents. This made it easier for Nazi officials, and immigration officers in other countries, to identify Jews.

In October 1938 the German authorities moved against the Jews of Polish nationality or Polish origin who resided in Germany. Thousands, like Alexander Gordon's mother, were rounded up and expelled to Poland. However, the Polish government – which wanted to reduce its own Jewish population and stripped expatriate Jewish Poles of their passports – refused to admit them. They were left to rot in the frontier zone. Herschel Grynszpan, a young Polish Jew living in Paris whose parents were among those who had been deported, was so incensed that he obtained a revolver, marched into the German Embassy on 7 November, and shot the first official he encountered – Ernst vom Rath, the third secretary. Vom Rath died two days later.

The shooting gave Josef Goebbels, Hitler's propaganda minister and party boss of Berlin, the pretext to organize a nationwide pogrom against the Jews. During 9 November disturbances occurred all over Germany and Austria. In the evening, Reinhardt Heydrich, the commander of the security police, authorized the mass arrest of Jewish men. During night-time, SA and SS men pretending to be outraged citizens set fire to 1,000 synagogues, smashed up 7,500 Jewish-owned businesses, invaded and ransacked the homes where Jewish people lived, and fatally assaulted over 90 Jewish men. The police herded 30,000 male Jews into concentration camps until they could be ransomed out by their terrified families. Ursula Rosenfeld's

father was taken to Buchenwald concentration camp where he was
beaten to death. Jack Hellman's father was luckier: he got out of the
camp alive.

German people were taken aback by the scale of the destruction.
The pogrom was known by the Nazis as Kristallnacht, night of
crystal, because the next day the main streets of cities and towns
were littered with fragments from broken shop windows – as Jack
Hellman vividly testifies. Hermann Goering, Hitler's deputy, who
had not been consulted by Goebbels, was furious at the disruption it
caused to the economy. Nevertheless, he cynically used the havoc as
a way to deepen Jewish misery and signal that the Jews had no
future in Germany. The Jewish community was subjected to a
massive fine as a penalty for vom Rath's death and forced to
compensate for the ensuing damage. A rush of laws in the following
months eliminated all Jewish economic activity. Jews who had no
capital or savings, like Bertha Leverton and Inge Sadan's parents,
now subsisted on work or welfare provided by their community. An
emigration office, modelled on the one in Vienna, was set up to
speed the departure of Jews lucky enough to find a country that
would have them.

Sadly, the opportunities were all too few. Every modern, indus-
trialized country in Western Europe, North America and Australasia
was still suffering from the global recession and rates of unemployment were high. Social distress fuelled powerful currents of xeno-
phobia and anti-Semitism; in several countries there were substantial
pro-German Fascist movements. A conference on the world refugee
problem that had convened in Evian, France, in July 1938, was a
dismal failure. It had been called by President Roosevelt in response to
the terrible scenes that followed the Anschluss, but of the thirty-two
countries that sent delegates not one said it could accept more than a
tiny number of refugees. This was the background to the initiative to
take children from Germany and Austria.

After Kristallnacht public opinion in Europe and America was
shocked by the newspaper reports of burning synagogues and the
spectacle of ransacked shops. President Roosevelt recalled the US
ambassador in Berlin. Neville Chamberlain, the British Prime Minister, wrote to his sister that he was 'horrified by the German
behaviour to the Jews'. On 15 November 1938, the Prime Minister

received a deputation of eminent British Jews, including Viscount Samuel, Lord Bearsted, the Chief Rabbi Dr J. H. Hertz, and the Zionist leader, Dr Chaim Weizmann. In addition to other measures they asked him to permit the temporary admission of young children and teenagers who might re-emigrate after retraining. The Jewish community promised to pay guarantees for the refugee children, emulating a successful proposal by Dutch refugee workers to the Dutch government. Weizmann specifically mentioned teenagers who were in concentration camps or threatened with incarceration, and asked that they be allowed into Palestine.

The cabinet discussed the question the next day. The Home Secretary, Sir Samuel Hoare, said that the country could not admit more refugees without provoking a backlash. But the Foreign Secretary, Lord Halifax, thought that an act of generosity might have a knock-on effect and cause the United States to open its doors wider. (A plan to allow refugee children into the United States – where quotas for immigration from Germany and Austria were already filled – came to Congress in early 1939. The bill, sponsored by Sen. Robert Wagner and Rep. Edith Nourse Rogers, was resisted by the powerful anti-immigration lobby which depicted the entry of unaccompanied children as the 'thin end of the wedge'. The bill died in committee.) The cabinet committee on refugees subsequently decided that Britain could accept unaccompanied refugee children under the age of seventeen years. No limit to the numbers of children was ever publicly announced. The Jewish refugee agencies initially saw 5,000 as a realistic target, but after the British Colonial Office turned down a request from the Jewish Agency to allow the admission of 10,000 children into Palestine, this number seems to have been adopted informally as an appropriate goal for Britain herself to meet.

On the eve of a major House of Commons debate on refugees on 21 November, Sir Samuel Hoare met a large delegation representing the Jewish and non-Jewish bodies working for refugees, including the Quakers and Inter-Aid, a Christian organization headed by Sir Wyndham Deedes. These groups had now combined forces under the banner of the Movement for the Care of Children from Germany, a non-denominational body. The Home Secretary agreed that to speed up the emigration process travel documents would be issued on the basis of group lists rather than individual applications. But strict conditions were placed upon the entry of the children. The refugee agencies promised to fund the operation and ensure that none of the refugees became a burden on the public purse. Every child would have a £50 (approximately £1,000 today) guarantee paid against their subsequent re-emigration. Hoare announced the initiative to MPs in the House of Commons later that day and it was broadly welcomed. It was undoubtedly a great humanitarian gesture, although it was difficult to object to helping children and they could hardly be accused of taking the jobs of Englishmen. In any case, their stay was to be strictly temporary. Moreover, even if at this stage their parents were not confronted by genocide, there were few illusions about the poverty, discrimination and physical danger they were being left to face.

Within a very short time the Movement for the Care of Children from Germany (later called the Refugee Children's Movement – RCM) sent representatives to Germany and Austria to set up the mechanisms for selecting, processing and transporting the children. It was able to build on a series of existing schemes, such as the Inter-Aid Committee for Children from Germany (associated with the Save the Children Fund), the Quaker German Emergency Committee and the Jewish Refugees Committee. Wilfred Israel, scion of a wealthy Anglo-German family, provided an early rallying point for refugee workers. He was already busy in Germany organizing Youth Aliyah – a scheme to train young Jews in agriculture so they would qualify for emigration to Palestine – via the Zionist movement. Israel, who had sent to London a proposal to evacuate children on a larger scale, helped lay the infrastructure.

On 25 November, Viscount Samuel broadcast on the BBC Home Service an appeal for foster homes. Soon there were 500 offers, but they needed to be checked before they could be accepted. Volunteer committees around Britain started visiting the homes and reporting on conditions. These volunteers reflected the multi-denominational composition of the RCM. Because it drew on the experience of Christian aid groups, all of its branches were a mixture of Jews and non-Jews. They did not insist that prospective homes for Jewish children should be Jewish homes. Nor did they probe too carefully into the motives and character of the foster families: if the houses looked clean and the family seemed respectable, that sufficed.

Norman Bentwich, an executive of the Jewish refugee agencies, travelled to Berlin to meet leaders of the battered Jewish community. They issued a call for organizers and soon a national network was set up, drawing on young people like Norbert Wollheim. These volunteers worked round the clock to compile lists of those most imperilled: teenagers who were in concentration camps or in danger of arrest, Polish children or teenagers threatened with deportation, children in Jewish orphanages and those whose parents were too impoverished to keep them, or those with parents in a concentration camp. About seventy volunteers at Bloomsbury House in London processed individual applications which arrived at the rate of several hundred per week.

Once the children were identified and grouped by list, their guardians or parents were issued with a travel date and departure details. For those who were chosen for a Kindertransport the last days and hours were unimaginably stressful and distressing. Parents tried to cram a lifetime of care and advice into a few moments. They agonized over what to pack for their children, smuggling valuables into their luggage in defiance of the Nazi edict that the diminutive emigrants could take only a token sum with them. All the while, they reassured their children (and themselves) that the parting was only temporary. Many children, like Hedy Epstein, who could not fully appreciate what was happening, felt rejected and angry. Others, especially the younger ones, were filled with excitement at the prospect of a journey. These feelings of anger or excitement would leave a residue of guilt about parting on the wrong terms.

The scenes at the stations, or the discreet places of last farewell dictated by the Nazis to avoid a public spectacle, were terrible. Parents and children came face to face with the reality of separation. No one could know how long it would last – if it would be ended at all. For some parents, like Lory Cahn's, it proved literally impossible to let go and allow their loved ones to pass into the arms of strangers.

The first train left from Berlin on 1 December 1938. The first from Vienna, assembled at great speed, departed on 10 December. The trains passed through Germany and crossed into the Netherlands because the German government decreed that the evacuations should not clog up German ports. The Nazi authorities could not resist a final torment: officials at the border frequently rifled through luggage, disturbing clothes and toys that had been lovingly arranged by parents, and terrifying the children. From the Hook of Holland the children travelled by ferry to Harwich or Southampton. They were accompanied en route by a few adults, usually volunteers like Norbert Wollheim. Under the arrangements between the British and the Germans the adults had to return once their mission was completed.

For the first three months the Kindertransports came mainly from Germany. Then the emphasis shifted to Austria. When the German army rolled into the Czech lands in March 1939 to establish a 'protectorate' under the Third Reich, frantic arrangements had to be made to get children out of Prague, too. The city was the home to most of the 118,000 Jews who lived in the Czech-speaking area of Czechoslovakia. There were also thousands of German and Austrian Jewish refugees, and Jews who had fled from the Sudeten border region which was annexed to Germany under the Munich Agreement in October 1938. In addition, three trainloads of Polish Jewish children were arranged in February and August 1939, including one from the dismal camp at Zbaszyn, which had been home to the Polish-Jewish expellees since October 1938, and one from Danzig, the Free City which was Hitler's next target.

By the end of 1938, children were pouring into Britain and straining the resources of the RCM. The earliest arrivals tended to be older teenagers who were at risk of arrest, but most families wanted to take in young children. So there was urgent need to find a temporary holding centre. Two summer holiday camps were located, one at Dovercourt near Harwich and the other at Pakefield near Lowestoft, both situated on the wind-swept, low-lying coast of East Anglia. Due to flooding, Pakefield had to be abandoned shortly after it was opened. Dovercourt was quickly filled to capacity with some 1,000 Jewish children and teenagers of all ages and backgrounds. Conditions at first were chaotic.

The children were assigned beds and bedding in the huts. They were served warm meals in the camp canteen, although often not what the well-bred German and Austrian youngsters necessarily recognized as food. They were bewildered by the practice of putting milk in tea; soft, white English bread looked like cake to their eyes (and didn't taste much different, some thought). Kippers (smoked herring) tasted as odd as it sounded. Initially they were more or less left to their own devices. Teenagers acted as informal group leaders, while older siblings shepherded younger ones. They used the leisure facilities to play table tennis, but the lack of organized activity led to boredom which, in turn, bred fractiousness. Fights occasionally broke out between teenage boys who were continuing home country feuds. All the children, like Lore Segal, remember the bitter cold in the camp that winter. Since it was intended for summer inhabitation it had no heating whatsoever. The children wore (and often slept in) every available piece of clothing and ate their meals wearing gloves.

Despite an appeal for funds by Earl Baldwin, a former prime minister, money was constantly a problem. To obtain more homes for the children, and reduce the numbers piling up in Dovercourt, the BBC Home Service was invited to make a broadcast from the camp. In the new year, Anna Essinger was brought in by the RCM to improve conditions. Essinger had run an outstanding Jewish school in Germany which she arranged to be evacuated en masse to England by the Quakers in 1933. At Dovercourt she set up language classes, group singing, exercises and boosted morale. Yet it was difficult to soften the effects of what Bertha Leverton recalls as the 'cattle market' which took place every Sunday. It was then that prospective foster parents arrived to look over the children and select those that caught their fancy. Inevitably, the cutest and youngest children were picked first. Brothers and sisters were separated. Teenagers who were overlooked were left feeling even more rejected. In the end, many of them had to be placed in hostels run by the RCM.

However, being selected for a home was not necessarily the end of discomfort or distress. Children who had been fixed up with homes while they were still in Germany or Austria – either through relatives, or thanks to the advertised appeals – went direct by train from Harwich to Liverpool Street Station in London. Some were taken in by relatives whose kindness was not matched by their resources. In Britain, many Jews of East European origin were working class or lower middle class and lived modestly. German children were stunned by the 'primitive' way they lived, in houses without central heating and sometimes not even equipped with indoor toilets. As Bertha Leverton discovered, both Jewish and non-Jewish families took in teenage girls as a way of acquiring a maidservant. This was indignity enough, but girls faced greater peril at the hands of predatory males: Bertha had to fend off the unwanted attentions of her 'uncle', a not uncommon experience. Lorraine Allard found that she had been selected by her foster parents as a prospective daughter-in-law for their way-ward son.

There was little sensitivity towards the cultural and religious needs of the children. Jews in Britain who originally hailed from Poland and Russia remembered that their German co-religionists once looked down on them: they relished the reversal of fortunes. Instead of respecting the emotional trauma and cultural disorientation the children were experiencing, foster-families often disparaged and erased the youngsters' German-Jewish heritage. A few, mainly the youngest, were given new names, new identities and even a new religion. Although the Jewish workers in the RCM did their best to find Jewish homes for Jewish children, there were not enough offers. In any case, they did not regard this as a priority: few workers were Orthodox or alert to the needs of observant Jews. It did not even occur to them to provide kosher food at Dovercourt, much to the ire of Chief Rabbi Dr Hertz who demanded that greater attention be paid to religious requirements.

Dr Hertz patronized his own Emergency Committee, really a one-man operation carried out by Rabbi Solomon Schonfeld (his son-in-law), which specialized in bringing over Orthodox children. It was almost impossible to find homes for them and they would have been utterly neglected if not for Schonfeld's efforts. To complicate matters still further, Youth Aliyah ran its own programme to bring youngsters through the Zionist movement in Germany. The result was in-fighting, competition for funds and lack of co-ordination between the various branches of the evacuation effort.

A separate operation followed the German occupation of the Czech lands. Nicholas Winton, a left-wing stockbroker of Jewish origin, was invited to Prague in the winter of 1938–9 by a friend who was working with refugees from the Sudetenland. He was so moved by the plight of the children, he returned to London and began an energetic campaign to obtain sponsors for them. Sensing the urgency of the crisis, Winton got impatient with Home Office red tape and gave instructions for trains to be dispatched before the children had the necessary papers. Due to the desperate shortage of guarantors, about 100 Jewish children ended up in the care of the Barbican Mission, an organization devoted to converting Jews to Christianity. This step perturbed some Orthodox Jews who feared for the children's religious identity. Winton, however, believed it was more important to save their lives.

The Christadelphians, a Christian group, worked in complete harmony with the Jewish community and ran several hostels in the Midlands. Lord Sainsbury, whose family had Jewish connections, provided accommodation for twenty-five children. As the supply of foster-families fell behind the flood of children, and entire institutions were evacuated, such gestures became invaluable. In March 1939 Baron James de Rothschild offered a large house on the estate of Waddesdon Manor, his palatial country house, for twenty-six boys plucked out of a Jewish school in Frankfurt. They included Jack Hellman who ended his journey to England in the fairy-tale splendour of a Rothschild residence.

At the end of August 1939, the RCM ran out of money and said it could not take more children. The outbreak of war a few days later negated the dilemma. Hundreds of children, some literally waiting on the trains, were trapped. So were the parents of those who had made it to safety. This makes even more extraordinary the achievement of Jack Hellman, Lore Segal and Bertha Leverton who had managed to help their parents or siblings reach Britain. Added to the emotional burdens of separation and caring for younger siblings, youngsters like these also took it on themselves to find sponsors and jobs for their mothers and fathers. They wrote letters, knocked on doors and pleaded with relatives. In a unique inversion of normal affairs, in such cases it was the children who rescued the parents.

But the declaration of war ended such hopes and entailed still more disruption. In anticipation of devastating bombing raids on the major British cities, the government set in motion plans to evacuate children and pregnant women to 'safe areas'. Children from the Kindertransport were caught up in this great migration and were hastily moved to new homes in the countryside. Those who went with their schools benefited from a degree of organization and care. Others found themselves totally isolated, living with uncomprehending families in remote areas: it took years for the refugee organizations to establish links with the scattered children.

The older ones suffered a different hardship when, in June 1940, the British government ordered the internment of refugees aged between sixteen and seventy who came from enemy countries. Approximately 27,000 men and women were held in makeshift camps on the mainland and the Isle of Man, including 1,000 from the Kindertransport. Around 6,000 were transported overseas to Canada and Australia, among whom were 400 of the recently arrived teenagers. Hundreds of internees (mainly Italians) perished when the ship carrying them to Canada, the *Arandora Star*, was torpedoed in the Irish Sea on 1 July 1940. Those like Alexander Gordon who were shipped to Australia on the HMT *Dunera* were mistreated during the long voyage. The scandal that followed revelations about the mishandling of internment led to a programme of releases in late 1940. Men, in particular, were offered the chance to do war work or enter the Alien Pioneer Corps. About 1,000 German and Austrian teenagers jumped at the chance to put on an Allied uniform – even if their only mission was digging gun emplacements. As the war progressed they were able to transfer to other branches of the armed services, including combat units. Several dozen joined elite formations such as the Special Forces where their language skills could be put to good use.

For the younger children and most of the women the war years were marked by the struggle for education and then work. The RCM could not pay for the children to have any schooling beyond the statutory minimum, so at sixteen, with few qualifications, they entered the job market. Many were confined to unskilled menial or white-collar jobs until conditions made it possible for them to obtain vocational qualifications or get degrees through arduous evening courses. In spite of this many battled their way through to colleges and universities and made up for the years of lost education. Two, Arno Penzias and Walter Kohn, went on to win Nobel prizes.

From the moment of their arrival and throughout the war years the children (those old enough to write, of course) struggled to remain in touch with their parents. Letters flowed back and forth fairly easily for the first few months, but from September 1939 communication was only possible through intermediaries or the Red Cross. For as long as emigration was possible, letters from home contained pleas for help and news of rebuffs. Once all the doors were closed, the short Red Cross messages became unbearably heavy with significance. In the spring of 1942, the British press and the radio reported the deportation of Jews from Germany and Austria to Poland. By the end of the year it was clear that the deportations ended in mass murder: Nazi policy had made the quantum leap from removing the Jews to annihilating them. Older Jews and war veterans were sent to the fortress town of Theresienstadt, north-west of Prague, which the Germans converted into a ghetto. It was a concentration camp by any other name and little more than an antechamber for Auschwitz, though it suited the Nazis to use it as a showcase when the Red Cross looked into the treatment of the Jews. Red Cross messages continued to reach children from Theresienstadt well into 1944. Then there was a deathly silence. For all bar a few, the end of the war brought confirmation of the worst: their parents had perished or been murdered.

In a handful of astonishing cases, such as that of Kurt Fuchel, parents survived in hiding, endured the camps, or emerged unscathed from far-flung havens such as Shanghai. It often took years for them to re-establish contact with their children, and just as long to organize their reunion. Often, these were awkward encounters. The children were no longer children. Sometimes they had forgotten how to speak German. Their parents were also changed, exhausted by the horrors of war, hiding or flight. The majority of children, however, had to face the reality that home and family were lost for ever.

It took decades for the world to come to terms with the Holocaust, a delayed reaction that hardly helped the children of the Kindertransport to confront their past. Instead, they erected barriers against the pain of loss and separation and busied themselves building successful, prosperous and productive lives. When the first reunion organized by Bertha Leverton took place in June 1989, and the media began to take an interest in the stories of the refugee children, several felt as though it was someone else's past that was being described. Yet, on reflection, the *Kinder* (sing. *Kind*), as they have come to call themselves, began to understand how the tragedy had shaped them.

It is hard to generalize in view of the age range and varied backgrounds of the children, but certain common experiences do stand out. While only a tiny percentage succumbed to ill health or psychological illness, none was wholly unscathed. They all felt that they had lost the innocence of childhood too soon. The uprooting had left them without a clear-cut sense of belonging and a feeling that all attachments were precarious. They recognized the fortuitous nature of their survival and felt obliged to do something good with their lives; yet they also felt a residue of guilt that so many others – including their parents – had not been so lucky. Many invested hugely in children and grandchildren, seeking to make up for the losses inflicted on the Jews by Hitler. But perhaps they expected too much of their offspring and found it too hard to 'let go' of them when the time came.

They differed also in the extent to which they informed their children of what they had endured. Some found it extremely painful to recover the memory of what they had suffered, let alone articulate it, while others who felt it only too keenly did not want to 'burden' their sons and daughters with a horrific story. Others believed it was their duty to pass on the tale of the Kindertransport, to ensure that the hatred and the generosity would never be forgotten and that lessons would be learned. This is perhaps the greatest legacy of the Kindertransport experience. It shows that racial discrimination and ideologies which lead to mass murder do not draw the line at the persecution of innocent children. Their plight can be the trigger that finally stirs bystanders to action, but such help too often comes too late and benefits too few. The Kindertransport was a great, if flawed, humanitarian gesture which should inspire us to do more and do it better when such emergencies arise again.

Austria, 1938

Chapter One

WHEN THE BOUGH BREAKS

*'I still have nightmares sometimes . . . It comes
back to me in dreams, the terror which you felt at
the time.'*

URSULA ROSENFELD

LORRAINE ALLARD
Kind, Fürth, Bavaria, Germany

Looking back, I had a wonderful childhood. The only not wonderful
part was my experiences outside the home, after Hitler. I was born on 8
December 1924 – an afterthought. I have a very-much-older sister,
fourteen years older, and I had a sister in between, but she died as a baby
and I didn't know her. As an afterthought, I was very spoiled – not
materially because there was no material to spoil me with, but spoiled
with love and with affection. I was overprotected because of the Hitler
dangers outside the home, but very much loved in the home.

My parents had an extremely happy marriage. My mother sitting
on my father's knee for a cuddle was an everyday occurrence. I had to
join in because otherwise I would have been jealous. He had to have
both of us on his lap. Although he was fifty when I was born, he was a
very young father at heart. I remember doing lots of nonsense with
him, which possibly younger men wouldn't do, like Sunday morning
playtime in bed, tickling and acrobatics, things like that. I was the
apple of his eye.

It was at school that I had my first personal experience with anti-
Semitism. Even today, if I talk about it or think about it, I can still feel
the pain. I had a friend, a boy who was in nursery school with me and
later went to the primary school next door because the boys and girls
were separated then. Our parents were very friendly and we used to
play 'mums and dads' and 'doctors' as little children. One fine day, I

Lorraine Allard, age 14, with parents in Germany

was eight or nine, he chased me in the streets, throwing stones and calling me 'Juden stinker', which means 'you smelly Jew'. That's my first personal pain, which I will never forget.

I came home and told my parents about it. His parents sent him to apologize. His father was an orthopaedic surgeon in the town, and he made his son apologize because it was not what he'd learned at home, it was what he'd learned at school.

Then, of course, I had to leave the German school in 1934. I had already been through the experience of not being allowed to go to a theatre, or a cinema, or a swimming pool, or anything where we might have contact with German children, in case, I suppose, we contaminated them with Jewish blood. At the beginning it was very painful that we were excluded, but you came to accept it in time. Although I may have felt left out of certain things, I wasn't on my own. All the other Jewish children were going through the same thing. After a few years someone in the town opened a Jewish sports club. That gave us somewhere to go on Sunday. They had a field which they flooded, and we could skate in the winter.

The other memory I have is my father losing his business because of Hitler. He was a hop merchant and he would come home from business trips to breweries desperately depressed because one after the other used to say, 'Sully,' that was his nickname, 'I've known you for years and I want to buy from you, but if I do, my brewery will be closed. I'm not allowed to.' This is how he slowly lost his business. He wasn't forced to close it, but there was no business left.

Afterwards he started to sell insurance, which was of some help, but it didn't solve everything. We had to move out of the large apartment we lived in, where I was born, the apartment where my parents had lived since their marriage in 1910. I must have been nine or ten when we had to leave. Instead of ten or twelve rooms, we suddenly had four. It wasn't the end of the world.

As money got shorter and shorter, I remember my mother actually started to sell soap, which she sold to friends. As a little girl I delivered the soap, probably objecting, but I did. My mother was a very economical person. Things got repaired. Clothes-wise, something was made out of nothing. We had a maid who had been with us since I was born. My mother certainly couldn't afford her any more, but she still used to come once a week. I have a feeling that my mother paid her in kind rather than in money.

Other people around us were trying to leave Germany, but my father used to say, 'I'm too old to start anew.' The other comment he would make – because his father and grandfather and so on had been born in Germany – was that this has got to change, that this madman Hitler can't possibly last, and this is all just going to pass over and things will be all right again.

LORY CAHN
Kind, Breslau, Germany

Lory Cahn, age 6, in Breslau with mother and father

I was a very happy little girl growing up. My father was a lawyer and we lived in a very nice house. We always had a maid, which was nothing unusual in Germany. We weren't Orthodox, but we kept all the holidays and our house was strictly kosher.

My father was in the First World War, where he received injuries leaving him disabled. He had a very hard time breathing sometimes, and he was partly paralyzed on the left side. When you talked to him, you always had to go to his right side. If you came from the left, he would get scared because he wasn't able to notice you.

My father absolutely adored me. I mean, there was never anything that I could have possibly done wrong. My father used to go out shopping with me. And I always used to admire this one suit, which was for ladies. I always said, 'Oh, Daddy, I would love to wear that suit.'

One day he said, 'Should we go in there?' And I said, 'That's for big ladies.' 'Well, let's go in there.' They took my measurements and that suit was made for me. I came home and my mother was devastated. 'What are you buying this little girl all this stuff for? She doesn't need that.' And my father said, 'She is my pride and joy, and she needs everything I can get for her.'

Despite his war injuries, my father had a very good business. One day in 1934 he went into court and was sitting in a chair, when two of the legs broke off and he fell on his back, breaking it. By the time they got him to the hospital, he was one or two millimetres from being completely paralyzed.

He had many, many operations and a long, long rehabilitation. He was in that hospital two to three years, continuously. Fortunately, our house was only a block away. It was a terrible time for us, particularly my mother. We never thought my father would be able to do anything, but somehow he muddled along, walking on two canes, still able to work.

My father was never harassed. After 1935, Jews were not allowed to have domestic help any more. My father immediately objected and was told, 'Of course, you can keep your maid because you're one hundred per cent disabled from the World War.' My father was supposed to have gotten a great big pension for his disability, but he was so proud he was working and making good money, he felt it was better not to take the pension. Let others take it.

Around 1937 my parents started trying desperately to leave Germany. We applied for a quota number for the United States, but they weren't letting many people into the country. My mother had two sisters, who sent us papers to come to South America. We were all set to go. We sold our house and had all new furniture built because my parents thought the old furniture was too big for a South American country. We shipped a lift, a huge container with everything we owned – furniture, carpeting, silver and linen. We had our tickets and reservations for a hotel at the port in Bremerhaven.

A couple of days prior to our departure, my parents received a call from the Argentine consulate, informing us that Hitler had eliminated the rules allowing brothers and sisters to sponsor each other for emigration. We were not allowed to leave. My parents tried desperately, but there was nothing they could do. We were stuck; our things were long gone, and that was it.

My parents were devastated. We had nothing. At that time Jews weren't able to buy anything. We still had money, but there weren't many people who wanted to sell to us. We had no place to live because my father had given notice, so we went to a hotel in Breslau and started from scratch: dishes, clothing, furniture – everything, everything, everything.

We were living near the trolley car station and I had transferred to the Jewish school all the way in town. There was a newspaper kiosk at my bus stop where they sold *Der Stürmer*, which used caricatures to make fun of Jews. All Jews were portrayed with black hair and long beards and funny-looking noses, and I always looked at myself and said, 'That's funny, I don't look anything like that. I'm blonde. I don't have a funny-looking nose.' As I stood looking at the newspaper, people would say to me, 'Is that what the Jews look like?' I didn't dare say, 'I don't think that's what they look like; look at me.'

My brother, who was four years older than I, graduated school in 1937, three years ahead of his time. My parents were afraid to keep him home, so they sent him for safety to a small university across the border in Czechoslovakia, not far away. He only stayed one semester because he was so smart the headmaster felt there wasn't much he could be taught there.

He was supposed to come home for summer vacation in 1938, but my mother said, 'We cannot possibly keep him here. We have to do something with him.' My mother contacted her brother, who was a professor of old languages who taught at Cambridge and Oxford. She said, 'I'm sending him to you – let him be there for the vacation. By September, we'll see what to do with him.'

I remember my brother getting ready to go away. The last couple of days there was a terrible mood in our house. The day came and we went to the railroad and stood there at the train. It was terribly, terribly sad. My mother was crying, my brother was crying, and I was crying – we're all crying. My mother was holding me real, real tight, saying, 'Well, thank God I have you yet.' I kept saying, 'It's nothing. He's going to be home.' Little did we know he would never come back.

URSULA ROSENFELD
Kind, Quakenbrück, Germany

We lived in north-west Germany, in a very small town called Quakenbrück. The name denotes a lot of frogs under the bridges. It was the market town for a large number of villages and had about 5,000 inhabitants. Quakenbrück was also the centre for Jews who were spread over that area. It had a synagogue, and on holidays it would have quite a congregation. Normally, though, it was quite difficult to get a *minyan*.*

As a child, I remember my grandmother always peeling her potatoes very thickly because people would collect the peelings, ostensibly to feed their pig or whatever they were fattening. But my grandmother used to say she knew for a fact that was going to be their meal for the day because they just didn't have enough food to feed the family.

My mother always packed several extra rolls or sandwiches to take to school and she told me which children to give them to because, she said, 'I'm sure they've come to school without breakfast.' I found it quite embarrassing to do at the age of six or seven.

Strangely enough, a boy to whom I regularly had to take a sandwich eventually became the greatest Nazi in the town. I can understand his feelings of resentment. We stood out as Jews – we had enough to eat, but his family didn't. Taking charity is a very difficult thing to do, even for a child. It was sobering, eventually, to find so much resentment towards people who were doing all right from people who had nothing. It was a fertile area for National Socialism and for Hitler to sow his diabolical creed.

When the National Socialists came to power, the town became

* Quorum of ten adult male Jews needed for communal worship.

intensively anti-Semitic. Of course, everybody knew everyone else, and we stood out probably more than in a city where there are a lot of people and Jews are not so easily identified. My father had a lot of old school friends in the town who used to come regularly to our house. After January 1933, gradually, they came less and less or didn't even contact us. We became increasingly isolated.

I was just under eight years old when Hitler came to power. I was already at school then and had some friends there. My mother always tried to make a birthday party for us, which was the usual thing for Germans. The table was set. I was very excited. Nobody came. Not a single child came to this birthday party.

That was the first terrible blow to me. I know it sounds trivial, but it was the first sort of comprehension for a child that you're ostracized, that there's something different about you. I found that very hard. I can still vividly experience that disappointment. My mother tried to explain it to my older sister Hella and me, to make us understand that it was not our fault.

Ursula Rosenfeld

We were not a very religious family. We went to synagogue on the Jewish holidays, but we were not Orthodox in any way; we didn't keep a kosher home. After Hitler came to power, we became conscious of our religion. My mother started to light candles on Friday night and tried to compensate, perhaps, to give us a feeling of belonging within the family unit, which we didn't find outside.

At the same time, my parents also felt that this was all a passing aberration. My father had been a soldier in the First World War – in fact, he had volunteered – and he was very proud of his country, very loyal, patriotic. He was a leading person in the association of Jewish ex-servicemen in Germany. He felt that he fought for the country, that he belonged there. Whenever there was any talk of emigration, he would say, 'This is my country. I was born here, and this is where I want to die.' He had so much faith in the German people that he said,

'This will not last. They will see through it. It's a temporary thing.'

Of course, things gradually got worse and he withdrew more into his Jewishness. He came to think that what was happening to us was a punishment for his having lapsed his religious birthright. Eventually he had a nervous breakdown. Hella and I were about seven and eight years old at the time, and my mother tried to shield us. I have very little recollection except that he was away in a psychiatric hospital. He tried to jump out of the window and commit suicide because he couldn't cope with this sudden antagonism.

When he came back, he said, 'We've got to have a kosher household now. I think it was God punishing us and telling us that we've gone in the wrong direction.' Because it was forbidden to slaughter meat in a kosher way by then, or very soon after, we became vegetarians at home. It was very rare that we had meat. We had chickens in the garden – we had quite a piece of ground – and occasionally, for Jewish holidays, we would have a chicken at night. Father would kill it himself in the ritual way, but he hated doing it, and it didn't happen very often.

Because of all this I became more self-conscious and introverted at school. The children were very unfriendly, to say the least. We used to have twin desks to sit at, but nobody would share a desk with me. So I had a desk in the corner, right at the back – all by myself.

Whenever they had lessons on racial teachings – which I wasn't allowed to join – I had to stand outside in the corridor for the whole hour. The children and teachers who were walking by always gave me a funny look. It was quite frightening to be there on your own.

At the end of the hour, I had to go back into the class, and you could feel the tension. You could feel their eyes on you. They would look at you as if you were some sort of vermin. I found it very difficult to cope with.

I remember once the teacher had been teaching the children to measure skulls. There was a typical Germanic type of skull and I think the Jews were supposed to have very low, reclining foreheads – I can't remember exactly. The teacher made the children all measure each other, and when I came in at the end of the lesson he said, 'Now you go and measure Ursula.' I didn't dare to say anything, and the teacher was very disappointed because I didn't measure up to his expectations.

I can't remember how he explained this, but on top of that, I didn't have dark hair, I had blonde hair, and long plaits, and I didn't really conform to the caricature of what the Germans thought the Jews should look like. Perhaps only my nose.

I just hated school. I was terrified every day. But my mother made us go. She said we should be proud because we were Jewish, and this was the yoke we had to bear. We should do just a little bit better, we should work that little bit harder and we would get through in the end. She gave us a lot of encouragement, but it was very hard.

Playtime was an absolute nightmare for me. At least in class I could sit at my desk, and even though the children used to throw ink over my work, on the whole it wasn't too bad. I could cope. But after each lesson you had to go into the playground; they wouldn't let me stay in the classroom. In the playground you had to deal not only with your own class, but with the other children as well. I would have liked to have been invisible, to have disappeared into the ground.

I still have nightmares sometimes about it today. It comes back to me in dreams, the terror which you felt at the time, because you never knew what was going to happen, who was going to trip you up. If you fell, they just burst out laughing, they thought that was very funny.

Later, in the girls' high school, which I attended when I was ten, I had a gym teacher: Fraulein Maus. I still remember her very well – she was such a Nazi. She was also our history teacher and, of course, had her angle on history. I never learned any real German history. Her gym classes were worse. One particular instance: we used to have a vault horse, and we'd have to take a run to jump over it. She'd be standing at the other end to catch you. When it was my turn to go – I tried all kinds of excuses to get out of it, but nothing helped – I'd start to jump across, and the moment when she was about to catch me, she'd step aside. Of course, I'd crash. I tried not to jump too hard or run too fast, and then she'd shout at me, 'You're not doing it right', and I had to repeat it. It was terrifying really.

Hella and I were both very conscious, though, that our parents were going through tremendous problems themselves. There was very little laughter in the house. So gradually we told fewer and fewer tales about what was happening to us at school.

Now, my mother had a trained voice. In fact, she had studied at a music conservatory and she used to sing for functions. But for years we hardly heard any song in the house any more. I remember, though, in 1938, the Jewish Society of Culture from Berlin arranged a tour of some opera singers to go to various country areas. Two or three of the singers stayed in our house. And suddenly there was music, there was singing in the house again. That was the only time I ever remember my mother laughing and being happy. I thought she was such a stern person, but it was because life was so very hard for them. My mother had lost all her contacts, all her friends. Her life consisted of just work and making the home as comfortable for all of us as she possibly could.

CHARLOTTE LEVY
Mother of *Kind*, Leipzig, Germany

I was born in Leipzig, in 1900, the first woman of the century in my family. Both my parents came from very respected Jewish families who had been living in Germany for generations.

My father was a wonderful man, way ahead of his time. He ran a factory which produced fine knitted outerware, 'Marke Hammer', almost unparalleled in quality on the European continent. At its best times, the factory had 1,000 workers and employees.

In 1928 I married Berthold Levy, an apprentice in my father's factory. My father liked him and encouraged me to invite him to one of our parties. I did and we started a friendship, a very long friendship, before we really got close to each other.

After our marriage Berthold and I found a lovely, modern apartment in Leipzig. In 1929 our son was born, Hans Richard Levy. It was the greatest single joy of my life. Then in 1933 the Hitler calamity started, which was to grow into a full-blown tragedy and to end prematurely Berthold's life and my life in Germany.

From the turmoil of those years, much has sunk down in my mind, but some events stand out clearly in all detail: 30 January 1933, when, walking through the streets in the afternoon with Hans, I suddenly saw Nazi flags appearing in all the windows. 1 April 1933, the day of the boycott. Boycott has become a household word in our days. Then it was unheard of for us. We met in a family council that evening to discuss what to do. I was a Cassandra and wanted us to leave for

Paris, but my father and my husband had more sense than I had, because what would we live on? Many people had money outside Germany, which was forbidden. We didn't, and there was nothing we could do. Of course, we didn't fully realize what the danger was. Unfortunately, we had not read *Mein Kampf*, a big mistake, but even many of those who had could not believe it until it was too late.

Then what constituted our life began to crumble away. The Jews were guilty of everything. People who had been in school with you for years didn't greet you any more. They turned their back when they saw you on the train. You were just outcasts. Friends and relatives left the country – some never said goodbye. We were all scared to the last minute – would we make it? The noose around our necks got tighter. No more voting rights, no more membership in organizations, no more theatre, concerts, lectures, eating out. No more public schools for your children, no household help under forty-five. Denunciations. I remember the day when both my father and Berthold were summoned to the Gestapo and Finance Office, respectively. The fear, the sigh of relief, when they both returned.

On 19 January 1938, our daughter Elisabeth was born into our world out of joint. The only hospital where I could deliver my baby was a small, private Jewish orthopaedic clinic. Jewish women were encouraged to have abortions, otherwise forbidden in Germany. Some of my friends did.

Fortunately, Elisabeth made it easy for me. She was a plump, rosy baby with Oriental eyes, placid in her ways and a joy to look after. Hans was overjoyed and overexcited. He was extremely proud of his sister. There never was a tinge of jealousy. She was 'our' baby, the only beam of sunshine in those gloomy days.

NORBERT WOLLHEIM
Kindertransport Organizer, Berlin, Germany

Berlin, before the Hitler time, was a wonderful city, one of the centres of so-called 'European Civilization'. There was music, opera houses, theatres, literature. Jews participated in all of it. Jewish life was very active in our community; there were Jewish organizations for your care from the cradle to the grave.

After my bar mitzvah I joined the Jewish Youth Movement, a non-Zionist organization which believed strongly in teaching Jewish values and Jewish heritage. I would say that was an important turning point in my life. The group was very idealistic. We used to sing songs like '*Der Mensch ist Gut*', which means 'The Human Being is Good'. We all hoped to create a new and better world, and we tried to contribute to that by doing social work, which meant taking care of young people our own age who were in danger. These were children who came from broken homes, who had a brush with the law, and so on. On weekends we met with them, we ate with them, we played with them. We tried to alleviate their problems by showing that we were there for them.

In 1931 I graduated from high school and entered the University of Berlin to study law and political science, hoping to become a lawyer. This was my dream, also my parents' dream for me, because many parents wanted their children to have it better than they had. Then Hitler came to power on 30 January 1933. I remember that day very well.

I was at the university, listening to lectures as usual, and somebody came and said Hitler has been appointed chancellor by Hindenburg. It was a shock for those of us who had read his writings and listened to his speeches. Yet not only I, but the majority of Jews of Germany, still believed this was a transitory situation.

We had deep roots in Germany. For hundreds of years my family had settled here. Both of my grandfathers had been soldiers in the Prussian army and my father, bless his memory, was a conscript during the First World War and had served from the beginning to the end. So you don't just say, 'Now we pick up and go.'

It was very, very difficult, especially for professionals, for doctors and lawyers. To start completely anew was an idea which was not appealing. We all lived with the hope that sooner or later the allies around us would come to terms with Hitler's Germany, and he would have to go.

In April 1933, the Nazis promulgated very stringent laws depriving Jewish doctors and lawyers of their licences. Even though I could have continued studying at the university because my father was a veteran, I realized it would probably become impossible to be a lawyer in Nazi Germany. So I stopped my studies and volunteered to continue the kind of Jewish community work I had done in the Jewish Youth Movement.

In 1935, we in our group who had believed in our future in Germany came to the conclusion that we had to change our approach, that we should do whatever we could to help people get out of Germany. I joined a Jewish firm which was active in the export–import business, especially in metals and manganese ore. This firm had excellent business contacts with England, Sweden, France and the eastern countries, so it was my hope that I could also establish some kind of a contact in order to find a way out for myself and my family. I didn't love the work too much, and I still remained active in Jewish community affairs.

I lost my position with that firm around September 1938 because the firm was forced to change ownership and all Jewish employees lost their positions. By then I was already trying my best to get out of Germany. I was married that summer to a woman I met in the youth movement and we tried all kinds of things to leave Germany, but it was difficult to find a place to go.

In Berlin, at that time, you could find telephone books from New York and Chicago and people were racing to see if they could find people with the same last name as theirs. Very often they would write to them then and tell them they were relatives and ask for their help. I found relatives in Chicago. They were in the coal business, but by the time I got an affidavit from them and a quota number from the American Consulate, it was too late.

JACK HELLMAN
Kind, Tann, Germany

I grew up a happy child in Tann, a village of fifteen hundred people, where the Jewish population was nearly 8 per cent of the community. My father had what you would call a general store. We had feathers and down, piece goods, ready-to-wear. My father went on the road to sell to the farmers, and my mother stayed in the store. We were a religious family and the store was closed from Friday afternoon until Monday morning. My parents only ate the strictest kosher meals and, of course, observed all holidays. My father went to temple every

Jack Hellman, age 6, first day of school, Tann, Germany

morning and was president of the synagogue during the last years of its existence.

Most of my friends were non-Jewish children, but anti-Semitism was already rumbling in the late 1920s. The unemployment in the district where I lived was considerably high, and that caused even more anti-Semitism. When Hitler came to power, they would have torchlight parades at night. I lived on the second floor of our house, and I would lie in the dark, seeing the shadows of the torchlights and hearing them sing, 'When Jewish blood flows off the knife, we feel twice as good . . .' I was always tremendously frightened.

At the beginning of 1933, before Hitler became chancellor, as we were sitting down for Sunday dinner, the SS came into the house, beat my father unconscious and said, 'Karl Hellmann, you had your store open on Sunday.' Nothing was further from the truth.

I was extremely close to my father as a child, and to see him lying motionless, in a pool of blood on the floor . . . This left a tremendous imprint on me. It has been a constant trauma, a recurrent nightmare in my life.

The anti-Semitism grew worse. The local schoolmaster was a sadist and a fervent follower of Hitler. School was five and a half days a week, but on the Shabbat, when we had only a half-day of school, Jewish children were excused from writing. After Hitler came to power, the teacher insisted that Jewish children had to write on the Shabbat just like anybody else. This was very painful for my parents.

The teacher used to beat the Jewish children, unmercifully, with a cane. I was beaten, I would say, every other day. The teacher would walk through the class, and if you had your hands on the table, he would take a cane and hit you on the hands very hard, or you had to bend over and you got ten strokes across your bottom. I feared every day at school.

The children I'd been friendly with – I went to their house, they

Berlin, 1938

came to mine – they didn't talk to us any more, didn't talk to my parents, didn't talk to me. One winter day I was walking on the street. Six or seven boys came and called me 'Jew Bastard' and then attacked me and threw me through a plate-glass window. I was cut severely and had to go to the hospital for stitching. After that I didn't want to go to the school. I just felt that I was threatened constantly. Most of the young people in our little town went away.

At the beginning of 1935, my sister, who was five years older than I and also beaten, was sent to Hamburg, which had a large Jewish population. In August of 1935, my parents sent me to Frankfurt. I had an uncle who was a physician there and he told my parents, 'I have a place for him to go, a children's home where he can be in totally Jewish surroundings.'

I was the youngest in the home, and so I had to clean everybody else's shoes, and clean the showers, and do all sorts of menial things because I was being bullied by the older boys. My first months there, I felt utterly alone. The headmaster, even though he was Jewish, was no less sadistic than the schoolmaster in Tann. It seems to have been a German trait. I was so miserable in the Frankfurt school that I had a timetable in my notebook of when the next train would go back to Tann – regardless of how bad it was there. I was terribly unhappy and terribly homesick.

HEDY EPSTEIN
Kind, Kippenheim, Germany

Kippenheim, the village where I was born, is about forty kilometres north of Freiburg, Germany. My parents, as well as some of my paternal ancestors, had lived there for generations.

My parents only went to Jewish services twice a year, on the High Holy Days in the fall, and it was always a battle between them. My father would say, 'I'm not going.' My mother would say, 'You have to go.' They would argue back and forth and, in the end, they both went and I went with them.

On occasion, though, I also went to church with our housekeeper. I really didn't know what the difference between the two was, except it seemed to be more fun to go with the housekeeper, especially since the ceiling of the church had all these beautiful paintings on it and I could slide down on the bench and look at them.

When I was in first grade – it must have been the first week – the teacher said, 'The next hour is going to be religious instruction, and I don't know everyone's denomination. Would all the Catholic children raise their hands?' A lot of children raised their hands, so mine went up also.

The teacher knew who I was and said, 'No, put your hand down. You're not a Catholic.' Then she said, 'All the Lutheran children raise your hands.' A smaller number raised their hands. And mine went up again. She said, 'No, you're not Lutheran either.'

'Well, what am I?' I asked. She said, 'You're Jewish.' I must have heard somewhere that being Jewish was not a good thing because I said to her, 'No, I'm not, and I'm going to tell my mother, and she's going to straighten all this out.'

I came home and said, 'I don't like the teacher.' My mother wanted to know why and I told her. She said, 'But you are Jewish.'

I said, 'No, I'm not. Why? Are you?'

She said, 'Yes, I am.'

'Is father Jewish?' I went through every family member, and they were all Jewish. Even then I maintained that I wasn't. 'Maybe all of you are, but I'm not.'

When Hitler came to power, I began to realize what it meant to be Jewish. Before he became chancellor, my parents and other adults would talk about him and say they hoped he wouldn't come to power. Afterwards, they said they hoped he wouldn't remain in power very long. I heard all of that, but I didn't really think it had much to do with me.

Then, just two months later, on Saturday 1 April 1933, I realized it did have something to do with me because on that day there was a boycott of all Jewish businesses in Germany. My father and his brother had a business that my great-grandfather started in 1857, and there was an SA man standing in front of our store, in front of the Jewish hardware store, the Jewish bakery and the Jewish butcher.

I was almost nine at the time and I asked my parents, 'What is this all about? What is this man doing there?' I was told (I think my parents were trying to protect me), 'Don't worry about it, it's going to go away. It's just today.' I wanted to believe that, and indeed, the day

Nazi boycott of Jewish businesses, April 1933. Sign reads 'Germans don't buy from Jews'

after there was no SA man standing in front of Jewish stores. However, I hadn't grasped the boycott's long-range effects because afterwards Christians were afraid to be seen going to a Jewish store.

The first four years I was in grade school, I suffered no anti-Semitism. Once I changed to the *gymnasium** in a neighbouring community, gradually I began to experience it myself.

First of all, when my father and I went to enrol in the school, the principal said, 'I'm sorry, but Hedy can't come to school here because you're Jewish.' My father didn't say a word, but he pointed to a pin that he always wore very proudly in the lapel of his jacket. The principal said, 'Oh, I'm sorry. I didn't realize that you are a wounded veteran of World War One. In that case, Hedy can come.'

By the following year, the number of Jewish children had decreased considerably because their families had been able to leave Germany. At the same time, the anti-Semitism seemed to increase among my classmates, to the point where they no longer talked to me or played with me during recess.

Recess was the worst time of the day for me. I used to lean up against one of the pillars in front of the school and stand there all by myself and watch, longingly, how the other children were talking and playing with each other. If they did say something to me, it was to call me a dirty Jew or some other such name.

Then I also had the great misfortune to have a math teacher who was an SS man. He came to class almost every day wearing his black SS uniform, knee-high black boots. In his right boot, he usually carried a revolver. When he asked me questions, he would have his hand on the revolver. A couple of times, he actually pointed it at me.

No matter what my answers were, whether they were right or wrong, he'd ridicule me in front of my classmates and say, 'That's a Jewish answer. And we all know Jewish answers are no good.' As a result of what this teacher has done to me, to this day, when I have to calculate something, he walks across the paper or across the calculator, and I have difficulty with anything that has to do with arithmetic.

* German secondary-school.

Soon after Hitler came to power, my parents began to try to get out of Germany. I remember they registered at the American consulate in Stuttgart and, after a long time, their quota number was finally called, but we didn't have an affidavit, and so we had to re-register, start all over again. My parents also tried to go to Cuba, but I think by the time they found out about it, the doors were closed. There was also an effort made to go to Lima, Peru, because we found some distant relatives there.

Then we found a cousin, probably ten times removed, in Chicago, and my parents wrote desperate letters to this man, asking that either he help, or if he couldn't, that he ask his employer, or if that failed, maybe he could go to the Jewish community and ask them to help.

We had a box at the post office and I used to go there sometimes to pick up the mail. I remember finding a letter from this man and running all the way home, already dreaming what it was going to be like to live in Chicago. Then my father translated the letter – he knew some English – and this man said he couldn't help because it was the Depression in America and he was fortunate to have a job with which he could support himself and his elderly mother, and he didn't feel he could ask his employer because that might jeopardize his job. And he didn't want to go to the Jewish community either, because he didn't want to make a fool of himself. So he encouraged my parents to wait, and things would get better.

BERTHA LEVERTON
Kind, Munich, Germany

I grew up in a loving Orthodox Jewish family in Munich, the first of three children born to my parents, both of whom came to Germany from Poland. I was ten in 1933 when the restrictions against the Jews began.

Around 1935 my parents lost their business. They had a small leather goods company, manufacturing sports articles like rucksacks, which sold very well in Munich because it is near the Alps. But the Germans were greatly discouraged from buying from the Jews, so the business collapsed.

Then my mother had a great idea. She said, 'Let's do something that gets us Jewish customers. What can we do? We'll open a laundry.' They took lessons in a children's home, where they had laundry equipment, and then they set up a laundry. We had Jewish customers and it went very well.

I went to the Jewish school and we didn't suffer as much as the children who went to non-Jewish schools because they *really* had a difficult time. Our school swelled quite a lot in 1937. We doubled the number of pupils because they had to leave the German schools.

A lot of German Jews were very hard hit. They were first German, and then Jews. Those children felt it far more than we did. We Polish children knew that our parents were persecuted and so were our grandparents in Poland, so we half expected it. But for the German-Jewish children it was a tremendous shock to find that their *Heimatland*, the country that they loved and where their parents and grandparents were born, rejected them. They found it very difficult to bear, especially the ones who were hardly Jewish or hardly knew they were Jews. This shock didn't apply as much to us.

Bertha Leverton (*right*), with sister Inge, brother Theo and parents in Munich, 1935

Unfortunately, my parents, like a lot of other parents, thought, the Nazis don't mean us. We're just ordinary people, small people, working people. They just mean the rich Jews with the big firms and the big, big businesses. We'll stay put. It'll all blow over.

During this time I remember my family and most Jewish people were very careful not to attract attention. We tried to keep our heads down. We tried not to be noticed so much. I remember the rabbi begging the ladies to dress very modestly on the High Holy Days in order not to attract attention. Most people complied, but we didn't go in sackcloth and ashes. Everybody likes a new hat for *yontef*.* Some ladies, really, just couldn't help it.

Our synagogue in Munich was on an ordinary public street, and I remember on the High Holy Days in 1938, the rabbi stood at the door

* Yiddish for a Jewish holiday or festival.

and he would only let about five or six people exit at a time, because he did not want the well-dressed women to be out in the streets. It took ages and ages to get home.

Not long after the holidays, in October 1938, my parents heard a rumour that the Polish Jews were going to be deported from Germany. We had Hungarian friends and my parents took the younger children, Theo and Inge, to stay with them for a few nights. The Nazis didn't touch anyone with a Hungarian passport.

We left our flat, and we walked to the *Hauptbahnhof*, the train station, and we mingled with the crowds. It was a major train station and it was alive with people. We stayed there all night, and in the morning we came home, and we had escaped that transportation to Poland. We lived in a block of flats with no other Jewish people, and they didn't come back to look for us. But the experience was devastating.

INGE SADAN

Kind, Sister of Bertha Leverton, Munich, Germany

I was born in 1930, the youngest of three children, and brought up in the Hitler era. When the big children had a school holiday, they used to come to the kindergarten to play with the little children, and they always took me to the toilets and bashed me up. I thought, that's not a very nice thing to do, but I never told my parents. I think I was scared that they couldn't do anything about it. So I accepted it. 'They' were the Hitler youth and I was a very small child for my age. That was life.

At the age of six, I went to a Jewish school, and suddenly the bullying stopped, at least from the other children. My family came from Poland and the teachers, who were German-Jewish, didn't like the Polish or Eastern European children. They used to bully us quite a lot. But we accepted that, too. You just got on with life.

There was quite a large Jewish community in Munich – German Jews, Polish Jews. They all had their own synagogues, their own activities, their own friends. We, of course, went to the Polish synagogue and had Polish-Jewish friends. Only at school did I mix with all the other children.

In October 1938, suddenly a lot of the Polish Jews vanished. My uncle and aunt were taken. In fact, my aunt didn't even have time to put her false teeth in, which amused some people. But after about a week or so, they came back.

Other families weren't so lucky. All this created a great feeling of insecurity among the Polish Jews. The parents talked about it, and we children listened.

ALEXANDER GORDON
Kind, Hamburg, Germany

I was born in 1922, to a Polish family in Bergedof, Germany, which is a suburb of Hamburg. My father came to Germany from Grodno, Poland, after the Russian Revolution. In Germany he was what you call a 'Werkmeister', a manager of a factory which produced boxes.

In Bergedof we lived in an apartment house which was next to the factory. I had one brother who was about nine and a half years older than I was. My father died in 1925 when I was three years old. I can't remember his face or anything. My mother was left with two children, in a financially very precarious condition, so she had to go out to work. She was a seamstress.

Eventually in 1929, we moved to Hamburg. I started school there at Talmud-Torah, but my mother found it impossible to cope. She

Alexander Gordon, age 13, with his mother in Hamburg

had to go to work and my brother had to go to school, so at the age of seven I wound up in a Jewish orphanage.

Life in the orphanage was not particularly pleasant. We were about thirty boys. Nobody treated us badly; we were just neglected. 'Get the children downstairs!' whenever there was too much noise. We had a teacher who watched us doing our homework after school, but then we were on our own. They didn't provide us with any books or play or games. The food was sufficient, although not particularly good.

I was in the orphanage from 1929 until 1938. I graduated high school, even though it was a little bit abbreviated because conditions became worse from one year to another. After my graduation, I could not stay at the orphanage. Since my brother had already emigrated to Israel – in those days it was Palestine – it was thought it would be a good idea if I went to Palestine, too. My mother wanted to go anyway.

An Orthodox Zionist organization, the Mizrachi, had a training programme for Palestine in a suburb of Hamburg, where they assembled about fifty or sixty children, mostly 16-, 17-, 18-year-olds. Since the British restricted immigration to Palestine, there were only a limited number of affidavits, and they had to make a choice of whom they would send for *aliyah*.*

We took courses in Hebrew and other Jewish subjects, which I didn't particularly care for. The result was that they rejected me, not because of anything personal, but simply because my attitude towards religion was not what they expected. This depressed me greatly because they accepted children from wealthy homes, who had parents, and I was in an orphanage. They didn't give that any consideration. Their only thought was 'What is your attitude towards Orthodox Judaism?' So what could I do?

I had to go back to the orphanage in Hamburg, but they could not keep me because I had graduated and so didn't go to school any more. I said, 'What's going to happen now?' They had another idea: to send me on Hachshara, a farm where you worked and learned for about two years, and then you would be eligible to get an affidavit to go to Palestine.

I got to the farm in April 1938. It was about seventy or eighty miles

---

* Hebrew for 'ascent': refers to immigration of Jews to Palestine or Israel.

west of Berlin. It was run by the Mizrachi again – morning prayer, evening prayer, all this. Everything there I more or less adjusted to. I got along very well. There was a trial period and they accepted me.

Everything went along normally until 28 October 1938. Early in the afternoon we were suddenly summoned to the main office building, and everybody lined up – there must have been thirty of us: boys and girls. The funny thing was we were all born in Germany, but with a Polish background.

In front of us were two cars with two or three Gestapo agents standing in front, talking to each other. And they were looking at their watches. I didn't know what the whole thing was about or what was going to happen.

Suddenly they said, 'All those over eighteen on one side, and all the ones under eighteen on the other side.' Then they counted and the ones under eighteen, which included me, were told to go back to whatever we were doing. To the ones over eighteen they said, 'Get into the cars.' And they took them away.

What actually happened was that a train was coming from western Germany, going through different towns, picking up Polish Jews who were being sent to Berlin, and then on to the Polish border. The Gestapo were looking at their watches all this time because they didn't have enough transportation to get us all to the train on time. Either they took the people whom they could get into two cars or else none of us would have gone on the train.

So the ones over eighteen were taken away, and we never saw them again. And we were left alone. I found out a couple of days later that the same thing happened in Hamburg. They came to my mother's apartment at five o'clock in the morning. The Gestapo liked to do things early in the morning when it was very quiet on the street so nobody would notice. They told her to get dressed, come outside, and bingo, she was taken away. I found out afterwards when I came back to Hamburg; there was a seal on the apartment that nobody was allowed to touch.

LORE SEGAL
Kind, Vienna, Austria

I had my tenth birthday on 8 March 1938, with the usual Viennese child's birthday party – every child had to do a little dance or a song or a poem – and everything was as it ought to be. Four days later Hitler took Austria.

We were all at dinner: my father, my mother and I; my Uncle Paul, who was a medical student at the University of Vienna and was living with us; and there were visiting relatives, distant cousins of my father. The radio was on, which makes me think that there must have been something in the air that made us want to listen. It was a musical programme, and it was interrupted in the middle when we were told there was going to be a speech by President Schuschnigg.

Everybody around the table fell silent as Schuschnigg announced that he was resigning his post in favour of Hitler, who was in the process of marching in. I remember the depth of silence with which people listened to a disaster, to their own disaster.

Then my Tante Erna turned to my mother, who was a pianist, and said, 'Franzi, don't you think they're playing the national anthem more slowly?'

My mother said, 'I'm sure they're using the record they always use.'

'No,' said Tante Erna. 'Listen, Franzi, you're a musician. You don't hear that they're playing it slower?'

And my mother said, 'Erna, you're a cow. You're worrying about the speed of a song. Don't you understand what has happened?'

Tante Erna rose and said to her husband, 'Ernst, we're going home. Did you hear what she said to me, and in front of the child?'

My mother said, 'Erna, please don't be angry. I apologize. Our nerves are on edge.'

In a child's memory, or maybe in human memory, large events bring up these irrelevancies. It's wonderful to me that my memory of the entrance of Hitler into Vienna was my mother calling Tante Erna a cow.

The first thing that happens when a disaster strikes is nothing changes. You think there's going to be some great drama, and you put your nightgown on, and you say the *Shema** to your mother, and then you go to bed and you think, oh, this isn't so terrible.

But the next morning my parents took me downstairs into the street and, along with all our neighbours, we lined up at the bank to take out whatever money we could still take out. Except the bank didn't open.

The other thing I remember is that the streets were full of new uniforms I'd never seen – very smart, crisp new uniforms. And the young people wore the red bands around their arms, with the swastika – I didn't know what that meant – and they were stretching out their arms in the Hitler salute. There were flags everywhere, these new red flags, with the white circle and the black swastika.

My main sense of something wrong was the haste with which my parents got me back into the house. They rushed me up the stairs and into our apartment.

The next thing that happened was that I went back to school, and the Jewish children were organized into the two back rows, with two rows left empty between us and the Aryan children in front. Then, within the week, all the Aryan children had been removed from this particular school, and it became the school where the neighbourhood's Jewish children now congregated.

I also remember the teacher who was assigned to us telling us to get our books out and to read. She went to the window, opened it, leaned her elbows on the window ledge, and you could see her back, sobbing. That was another one of those silences. The children understood that here was somebody who was upset about having to be our teacher.

Then there was a series of events – I'm telling what I know now, not what I remember experiencing: our maid had to leave because Aryans were not allowed to work for Jewish employers; my father was fired from his job as head accountant in a bank; and a Nazi officer came into our apartment and told us to get out within twenty-four hours.

What I personally remember next is being on a train to Fischamend, a village some thirty minutes by train from Vienna. We moved in with my grandparents, into their large, very old house with immensely thick walls, which was situated at one corner of the village

---

* The Jewish prayer which affirms God's Oneness.

square. But I had the time of my life in Fischamend because my grandfather's shop was a delicious place for a child to play in.

There were cards from the First World War. There was a violin without a bow. There were gumboots. There was my grandfather's sixteen-year-old shop assistant, who came out and played with me in the yard. I had a lovely time.

But even one's cheerfulness and enjoyment as a child was clouded by the horror. I remember the day Uncle Paul came home from the university, where he had gotten into a fight with some Nazis. One of his ears was practically dangling. He said to me, 'Ask your mother to come to my room and help me. Don't tell your grandmother.'

By the time I got upstairs, my grandmother was already there, tying up his ear and scolding him for getting into street fights with Nazis.

Then there was the morning my grandfather came down to open the store and discovered that in the night somebody had written 'Jew' in thick red paint across the windows and the walls of the house. Also, painted in white letters that were so large they spanned the whole street, it said: KAUFT NICHT BEI JUDEN ('Don't Buy from the Jews'). The adults and grown-ups went out with buckets and wiped out the red lettering. You could get rid of the letters, but you couldn't get rid of the colour. There were red blotches on the stone that were there as long as we stayed.

The other thing that I remember very vividly was sitting under the table in the living room, which was on the second floor, over the store. My grandparents were there, my parents, my uncle, and I was playing with their shoelaces under the table. The windows were open – it was high summer by this time – and outside the house ladders were put up against the windows and young Nazis climbed into the room where we were sitting. They took away the radio on which we had been listening to broadcasts from England, they took away books by Grosz, whose caricatures of the Nazis were very brutal, and a whole lot of other things.

From then on, things were rough. My bed had been pushed way over to the wall side of the room because they kept throwing stones through the windows and every single window on the top floor was broken. At one point, they backed a truck up against the front door of the store, opened it, and took out everything inside. Then they made my grandfather sign a form declaring that he had given it to charity.

You have to understand, this was a small village where everybody knew everybody else. These were people who had bought from my grandfather. These were people who had been my uncle's and my mother's schoolmates at the village school. They were village folk. They took my uncle, my father and grandfather to the police station, beat them up a little bit, broke my father's glasses, and sent them back. I remember my mother waking me in the middle of the night and saying, 'You have to get dressed now. You are going to Vienna.'

My grandfather and my mother stayed behind to close up the store and the house, and my grandmother, father and my uncle and I went back to Vienna, where we billeted ourselves with cousins. This is the time when I remember there being no conversation among the grown-ups except how to get out of Vienna. It's interesting because we are now asked, 'How come you didn't leave?' But when I think of what it meant to leave – how impossible it was to leave.

First of all, you had to have a sponsor in the country you were going to, who would promise that one would not become a burden on the government. You would have to get a visa from the State Department or the government to be allowed in. Then you had to get an exit permit from the Nazis. All these things had to come together because they were all bureaucratic measures and they had a time span after which they would expire. You had to collect all these things together so they would all be operative at the same time. And it usually didn't happen.

The hardest thing, though, was to find a country to go to. The places under discussion were Argentina, Uruguay, Paraguay, Venezuela, Palestine, Shanghai, Cuba. I remember going with my father to the American consulate. There was a queue around the block, up the stairs, around the room, to put one's name on the list for a quota. This was in the late summer of 1938. I got to the United States 1 May 1951. It was a thirteen-year wait for us.

KURT FUCHEL
Kind, Vienna, Austria

I was seven in 1938 when life in Vienna fell apart. My parents were middle-class people. My father was a middle-level bank manager and my mother a lady of leisure. I was a much-desired first child.

We had one of those very nice apartments in Vienna, with a high ceiling, lots of light as I remember it, big windows. My father kept parakeets in a large cage, and he often showed them to me. There was a little spy-hole in the nest where they raised their young.

I guess I was spoiled. In addition to my parents, there was, of course, the inevitable maid – nursemaid in those days. My grandmother looked in often and lived nearby. My mother, in later years, used to boast that I was toilet-trained at nine months, which meant, of course, I was always followed around by a retinue of females. It was, in many ways, a rather idyllic life, and I was, indeed, sort of the centre of the universe.

After the Nazis occupied Austria, suddenly I couldn't go to my normal school any more. I was sent off to a makeshift school at the end of the tram line. I did it alone, even at the age of seven, and went to the end of the line, and then I would just walk on till I came to this house.

Kurt Fuchel, age 6, Vienna

Word got back to my parents that while on the tram I was a very talkative little boy. I told the other passengers all the bad things that Herr Hitler was doing. I thought that 'Herr' was his first name, of course. When my parents heard that, they decided I shouldn't be travelling alone. My father then came with me. He didn't say much, as he hardly ever did, but he let it be known that it's not wise to go around saying bad things about Herr Hitler.

Around that time my father lost his job. His manager called him in and said, 'You're a good worker, but, unfortunately, you have a "birth defect".' My father was so furious he almost killed him.

My mother then started to make artificial flowers at home, where she had to heat up special tools and bend the wire and canvas or whatever material she was using into shapes of flowers. One day something went wrong and she got severely burned. I remember the flames and the fear and the uproar over it. Her hands and arms were covered with burns. It was frightening.

As a child, I knew something serious was going on, but I really couldn't understand it. In all likelihood, my parents couldn't explain it to me either, especially as things were so uncertain. They were up late at night making phone calls, they had maps out, and my father was always out visiting various consulates. There were also things they whispered about and they weren't paying as much attention to me as before.

I remember there was this constant atmosphere of tension. One of the few really bad things I did as a child, and I was actually spanked for it, was to pull the tablecloth off the table with dishes on it. I suspect it was because I wasn't getting enough attention at this time.

ROBERT SUGAR
Kind, Vienna, Austria

I was eight years old when Hitler marched into Austria. For anyone coming from Vienna, it was very dramatic. I was an only child, and we were not exactly a fun family. We were not wealthy at all. I didn't know that because we had everything we needed. Thinking back, it was a very ordinary life; the only unordinary thing was that I was the only child in this whole extended family. Even this wasn't remarkable to me until later, when I met other children.

As far as anti-Semitism went, I had no notion of it. Half of these childhood memories are things you reconstruct later. They are not things that strike you at the time. I did notice that the adults, when they said the word 'Juden' – Jews – would lower their voices, that it was a fearful thing to be. But in terms of attacks or being beaten up, or even teased, I had no experience of it whatsoever.

Robert Sugar, age 8, Vienna

In the second grade there was a boy who always fought with me after school. Actually, I always thought I won those fights. They were

PERFECT Jewish cook seeks post in strictly Kasher household: long service testimonials: good references. — Ilona Steiner, Vienna 2, Odeong., 10/1.

URGENT APPEAL! Would noble-minded people assist Viennese couple to come to London: capable for every kind of housework: knowledge of English, French, and Italian: wife, excellent cook and good dressmaker: both in best health.—Apply for all English references, 62, Donnington-road, N.W.10.

VIENNESE couple: woman, former sanatorium manager, excellent cook: man, perfect butler: both fond of children and willing to do any housework: seek posts. — Schwartz, Vienna, 4, Margaretenstrasse, 22.

VIENNESE seeks position: perfect cook or as housemaid.—Write, Helene Schlesinger, Annagasse, 3/31, Vienna, 1.

VIENNESE lady, waiting to migrate, seeks position in household: London recommendations.—Write R.T., 35, Compayne-gardens, N.W.6.

MARRIED couple wants situation for household, London or provinces.— Address, 4,722, Jewish Chronicle.

MARRIED couple, Jewish, middle-aged, in Austria, urgently seek situation: wife, perfect cook and housekeeper: husband, gardener, handyman, chauffeur, or valet: excellent London references.— Write, Binder, 4, Clorane - gardens, London, N.W.3.

MARRIED couple, reliable, conscientious, experienced in all housework, wife, first-class cook, wait table, manicure: husband can drive car, clean plate and silver, wait at table, etc: perfect English. — Particulars, Ind. Deutsch, 56, Wymering-mans., Elgin-avenue, W.9. 'Phone: Abercorn 4334.

MARRIED couple, cook and footman, Jews, seek position in household, boarding house.—Write to Karl Beck, 19, Kreindlgasse, 27, Vienna.

MARRIED couple, Austrian Jews, excellent cook, needlework, laundry, gardening, valeting: efficient, faithful service: English references.—M. Frankel, Vienna, 2, Patzmanitengasse, 24.

MIDDLE - AGED woman, still in Germany, first-class cook-house-keeper, accustomed to hard work.—T.B., 124, Highbury New-park, N.5.

POSITION wanted by German Jewess (still in Germany), aged 20, as organiser in school, gymnastics, and games, or as mother's, nursery, or domestic help.—T.B., 124, Highbury New-park, N.5.

VIENNESE pastrycook, Jewish, seeks position in business or private: very urgent.—Roth, Vienna, 2, Wehlistrasse, 220/29.

Classified advertisements in the *Jewish Chronicle*, 1938

not very serious. Only later did it occur to me he must have been fighting with me because I was a Jew. To me, he was just a kid. After Hitler came, our teacher stopped those fights. Not to protect me, I realized later, but because it wouldn't have seemed right for a Jewish kid to beat up a Nazi kid.

The reality of the German annexation struck me when my parents talked about giving up the apartment, saying that we had to leave. That was something, you know, the bottom just falls out. Everything falls out of you. This is easy to say in retrospect, but this was all I knew, and we had to give it up. That probably was the biggest blow I had, just the idea that our life as we knew it would all end – that we had to give it up.

We didn't do it right away. First, I had a dog. I don't want to make a children's story out of this – I was not in love with that dog, I was getting used to it. But the dog had to go. Then, that summer, the apartment was dissolved. I don't know what the financial arrangement was, but there were people there and they gave my mother some money for some furniture or something.

My mother was an activist, and she knew something had to be done. The decision was to go to England, to be hired as a domestic because the English would take young women who would not interfere with the labour market. The plan was, she would go ahead, she would try and get me and my father out. My father did not appear to be perturbed by the events, and he was not going to take the initiative. Also it was more difficult for men to leave Austria.

After my mother left, I lived with my father – which was what I wanted – in a rented room. But that didn't work out. I don't think he liked the arrangement too much, so I went to my grandmother and he came and visited, which was better.

By this time, I had already been thrown out of my school. For the third grade I went to a school in the old ghetto district, the Jewish district. There the school was so overcrowded that they had three shifts. The Hitler Youth were constantly throwing stink bombs into the school, and the atmosphere was absolutely hectic. Nobody learned anything.

We formed gangs there to fight among each other, which in later years I also understood was to prepare ourselves for the real revolt to come. My uncle was a commercial artist who lived with my grandmother at that time. I remember that I took a ruler of his to use in one of the fights, and I broke it, for which he slapped me. Everyone was aghast at this. He didn't understand I was preparing myself for the revolt – for the uprising, which never came.

VERA GISSING
Kind, Čelákovice, Czechoslovakia

We were a very happy family living in pre-war Czechoslovakia We lived in a small town outside Prague – my mother and father, my sister, Eva, who was four-and-a-half years my senior. In 1938 I was just ten years old. There wasn't a single cloud on my horizon.

There were very few Jewish families living in Čelákovice. Religion did not play a major role in my life. Often at Christmas I went to the midnight mass because I enjoyed the singing. Although we were Jews, we were not an observant family. In my little town it didn't matter that I was Jewish, that my best friend was Catholic. The only thing which mattered was that you were Czech, and proud to be so because Czechoslovakia had only been founded in 1918. We were the children of the first generation of the Republic. And that was the most important thing.

I loved my parents equally, but I was closer to my mother. She was so soft and so warm, and I was such an awful tomboy who always got into scrapes. She was the one who always defended me to Father, who was a little bit more strict than she.

My sister had a special relationship with Father. They were not just father and daughter, they were best friends, both very serious and deep-thinking. I didn't have to envy her that relationship because of my closeness to my mother.

Although rumours of what was happening in Germany filtered through pretty sharply into our lives, my parents, particularly my father, were fairly optimistic – until 15 March 1939 when the German troops marched into Czechoslovakia and occupied our little town.

EVA HAYMAN
Kind: Sister of Vera Gissing, Čelákovice, Czechoslovakia

We had a very happy, carefree childhood. Ours was a very loving family. My father owned and managed a wine and liquor import–

export business and was always busy during the week, but when he was home, he often took me for walks, by the river mostly. We talked about everything. And that brought us closer. I don't remember having many secrets from my father, the kind of secrets that a teenager of thirteen or fourteen would have from others.

I loved my mother, but I probably had a greater understanding with my father. I always felt Father and I were protecting my mother and my sister. I don't know what we were protecting them from.

Looking back, I think I tried not to think about Hitler until he marched into the Sudetenland. I had such a narrow escape.

Eva Hayman (left) and Vera Gissing with their father in Czechoslovakia

I had been sent to the Sudetenland to learn German and I came back only a fortnight before it was taken over by the Nazis. That probably means that my parents were also unaware of the almost immediate danger there.

From then on people were wondering, what's going to happen next? Are England and France going to come to our rescue? Or are they going to believe that Hitler is not going to invade the rest of the country?

Father was an optimist. He did business with people in France, who wrote and said, 'It's going to be bad, get out.' But for Father, things like that wouldn't happen. His was a greater faith in mankind. Father always used to say that he would rather trust people and be disappointed than go through life not trusting anybody.

I don't remember being frightened after the Sudetenland, but I remember being apprehensive. Our parents didn't talk much about it to us. All I remember is that we had a big store room where mother used to put food, and she filled it with everything imaginable, so there would be plenty of food in case war broke out. Plus a big box of chocolates for us, which, when Vera and I knew we had to go to England, we were allowed to eat.

There was a Jewish family who lived next to us, and I remember that one of their relatives, I think it was an uncle, disappeared for a few months. He was a very young man, but when he returned, his hair was grey and he looked about fifty years old. He had been in a concentration camp. How he got out, I can't remember now, but that brought back how awful things were.

The big impact, though, was when Hitler marched into Prague on 15 March 1939. Father was in Prague, and we were at home. I remember sitting on the window ledge, watching the soldiers march through Čelákovice, and wondering when Father was going to come home. I can't remember when he came, but he was very, very late when he did arrive and very scared about what was going on. From that moment on, what our fate would be we did not know.

Berlin, 10 November 1938

Chapter Two
THE 9TH OF NOVEMBER

*'I remember the sense of everything turned upside down,
everything wrong, no one where they were supposed to be,
including me. This was the first time in all this period where
I remember sitting down and howling, but nobody had
much time or paid attention to this one howling child.'*

LORE SEGAL

LORRAINE ALLARD

I was woken up at two o'clock in the morning, a terrible banging on
the door, and there were two uniformed Nazis shouting, 'You're all
under arrest. Put some clothes on and come with us.'

I remember it was a very cold, very dark night, and we all went off to
an assembly point, which was like a big square. And there were just
thousands of other Jews, and I mean thousands. There were people I
knew and people I didn't know, and people getting beaten up, and people
crying. I think everyone was petrified. My main memory is of the cold,
and the dark, and my mother crying. Everybody was in a terrible state.

I remember, also very vividly, that they were beating up the rabbi
and he was bleeding. They had fetched the Torahs out of the
synagogue. And I think they were trampling on them.

It's a long time ago, but everything was just horrific. I did not know
while we were there, that they'd set fire to the two synagogues in Fürth.

We were taken to a theatre, and we sat there as if we were going to
watch a performance. The performance was that they fetched the men
out on the stage and made them jump over the chairs and over the
tables. If they couldn't do it, they whipped them. It's a sight you don't
forget, one of the worst I experienced.

My father did not take part in that because he was over sixty, and they
did make a distinction between people over and under sixty. Everyone
under was sent to Dachau, which was the nearest concentration camp.
My mother and I were allowed to go home. It must have been about

57

Destroyed altar and Torah scrolls, Herzog Rudolfstrasse Synagogue, Munich, 10 November 1938

two, three o'clock. My father was sent home later. When my mother and I got home, we found out that this lovely person who used to be our maid had stood in the streets, screaming how dare they arrest her beloved family, and they threatened her with arrest as well.

ALEXANDER GORDON

At eleven o'clock that night, there were bullets being shot through the windows and all kinds of noise. I said, 'What's going on? Everybody get dressed.' I knew we had to get out of the building.

The farm was behind our building, so we all went into the fields and hid in between the rows of asparagus. Twenty of us were sitting there in the cold, all spread out, and we didn't know what to do.

I said the first thing we should do is go and call the police. Somebody finally got through, but when the police heard 'We're being attacked' and where the call was coming from, they started laughing and hung up.

At five or six o'clock the next morning, when it started to get light and we thought things had quietened down, we went back to the house and saw that the windows had been smashed and everything was all messed up.

But one of the attackers had remained and he said, 'All of you, make sure that by this afternoon you're gone. Out! If you don't – can you see that tree? We'll hang you all up there.'

We went inside, got dressed, and shared whatever money was in the till. Where would I go? I was all by myself. I had nobody, no one, nothing.

LORE SEGAL

I was staying in the apartment of my friend Ditta, and her parents and her grandmother. Towards evening the Nazis forced every one of the Jewish families in the building to move into this flat. It was a brutal prank, because there must have been four or five families who were forced to move into the apartment with their furniture.

Now good Jewish-Viennese bourgeois furniture is not like the furniture we have today. It's this heavy, well-made, immense European furniture. I remember this elderly couple trying to get their huge dresser up the stairs. You could hear it squeaking along the tiles of the hallway.

By this time the apartment looked like a junk shop, with tables stacked on tables or cupboards. And one of the old couples sat on a bed and cried. I remember the sense of everything turned upside down, everything wrong, no one where they were supposed to be, including me. This was the first time in all this period where I remember sitting down and howling, but nobody had much time or paid attention to this one howling child.

The other thing I remember about that night is my friend Ditta's mother standing in the doorway, weeping because her brother had come to take what he thought was refuge in this apartment, and he had been promptly taken away by the Nazis. He was taken to a concentration camp. In November 1938, concentration camps were not the death camps we now know them to be. At that time they were used more for harassment than slave labour, although the system was already under way. I don't think the Nazis knew yet what they were capable of. They themselves had to learn their own brutality by degrees. Even that doesn't come naturally: you have to learn how to torture.

CHARLOTTE LEVY

We were awakened at dawn on 10 November by our faithful maid, Anne, all upset, stuttering. SA men had banged at our door and shouted, 'Get out, you Jew swine, and go to such-and-such a place.'

We did get up and dressed. It was a dismal day. I got Elisabeth ready, had her already in the baby carriage, but at the last minute we did not have the heart to take her out in that raw morning and left her with Anne.

Warmly dressed, we walked to the meeting place, Berthold and I holding our little boy of nine – so bewildered – between us. No one was at that place: it was a hoax, one of the many devices to torture Jews. Relieved, we wanted to turn back when we met a friend and he told us that during the night the synagogue had been burned down and Jewish stores robbed and burned. He was on the way to the train station and would travel between Leipzig and Berlin, never getting off, till this had blown over.

We thought that would be a good idea for my husband, too, but he wanted first to go to the factory and see if everything was OK there. We went to our home. When we got there, our nameplates had been taken off. We had become non-persons.

My husband didn't want to come in the apartment. We had a big field behind our house and he went there and waited to see if my father was safe, because they were beginning to arrest all the Jewish men. I called and found that nothing had happened to him so far, so I gave Berthold the sign we had agreed on that all was well. He told me that before going to the station he would stop at the factory and call me from there. No phone call came. I waited a while and then called the factory only to hear that Berthold had been arrested outside the gate and taken away. At that time he was quite a sick man, and I was terribly, terribly worried what could happen to him.

From then on, for the next ten days, I tried to find out where he was and what I could do. Luckily, my sister came with her little girl so I could leave my two children with her. Meanwhile I had found out which police station Berthold had been taken to and took the tramway out there – of course, in vain. Then I went to the main police station. A kind policeman there told me in strict confidence that next morning at 5 a.m., Berthold would be sent from some barracks to Buchenwald. I had never heard that name before. Next morning, before 5 a.m., I went out to those faraway barracks hoping I could catch a glimpse of Berthold – there was not a soul.

I tried to find out how I could help my husband. He had recently had a very dangerous surgery for cancer, so I called his surgeon, who was a very fine man, and who was horrified about the arrest. He called the Gestapo to inform them about Berthold's condition. They told him in no uncertain terms to keep out or he would be the next one to be picked up.

Day after day I tried what I could think of, with no result. Then, after ten days, I came home and my sister was already waving at the window and I knew something good had happened. My husband had come back and was just shaving. The fact was that Berthold never went to Buchenwald. All the men the Nazis had rounded up were checked. When they saw that big fresh scar from Berthold's recent operation, they kept him in prison. They feared he would not survive the transport. At that time they did not want such casualties.

LORY CAHN

I got up in the morning and the maid made me breakfast. My parents were still in bed, and I went off to the trolley car to go to school. At the first corner we came to there was a big Jewish café that had outside patio seating. The chairs, the terrace and everything was all smashed. I thought, gee, I wonder what happened there.

Then we came down another street, and I saw stores smashed, windows smashed. I said, 'God Almighty, they're all Jewish people.' I didn't know what to do, but I thought I might as well go to school and find out something.

The further I got into the centre of the city, no matter where I looked, there was nothing there any more. The merchandise was thrown out of all the Jewish stores, and everybody stood outside. I was so scared to get out of the trolley car. When I did, all I could see was the top of our synagogue: the flames were just coming out. And I was frozen.

I almost thought the trolley car was going to have to run me over because I could not move. I went across the street, waited for the trolley car, and went back home. I sat in my seat and I didn't look left and I didn't look right. I was afraid to look on the other side to see how bad it was. I didn't want to see anything.

I got out of the trolley car, and my house was three steps away. I ran into the house through our open front door. Our maid was standing there, taking me, holding me, crying. I said, 'What's the matter?' They had just come for my dad . . . maybe ten minutes before.

My mother was crying and carrying on, but she had the nerve to pick up that phone and call England, and she told her brother, 'For God's sake keep my son', but she didn't go into any detail because we didn't know whether the wires were tapped. It was so horrible.

About three or four hours later, our maid happened to be looking out the window, and a great big police car was coming, bringing my father home again. We thought that would never, ever, ever have happened.

It was because the only thing they respected until the day we left was that my father was 100 per cent disabled from the war, with an Iron Cross. My father thought nothing would happen to us since they let him go. And we were one of the very, very few families to whom that happened. A lot of men didn't ever come back.

JACK HELLMAN

I took my bicycle, went to school as always. As I got closer to school, I saw huge pillars of smoke coming from the sections where the two big synagogues in Frankfurt were, and I saw that they were on fire. I also saw that all the Jewish shops had broken windows. The merchandise was either on the street or looted completely. There was no Jewish business that I passed that wasn't broken into, windows broken and looted.

When I got to school, they told me, 'Go home. School is closed.' My parents had come to Frankfurt to visit me. I had said goodbye to them already the day before. When I got back to the children's home, there was a call for me from my uncle: 'Tell your parents not to come home. The store is in ruins, the car was pushed down a hill, there's nothing left of the apartment either – all the furniture is lying on the street.'

I knew what time my parents were leaving Frankfurt, and what track they were on. I took my bicycle and I pedalled as fast as I could. I knew I had very, very little time. Still I got to the railroad station with about seven, eight minutes to spare, no more than that, and found my parents. I said, 'You can't go home. Uncle Leo has called. He said everything is in ruins. There's nothing left to go to.'

My parents didn't even hesitate. They said, 'We're going to go home.' And they did. I went back to the children's home. We boys had a council and we took the knives and forks that we could get our hands on and put them in the plumbing pipes in order to defend ourselves, in case the Nazis would come.

In the evening, the Nazis broke the windows in the children's home, came in, took my house father, and marched him off. Everybody from the age of sixteen to sixty-five was taken. We did not, of course, use the utensils, but at least the will was there.

As soon as my father got back to Tann, he was immediately arrested and sent to Buchenwald. It was a tremendously traumatic time, a time when, even as a twelve-year-old, I realized there was no future for Jews in Germany any more.

BERTHA LEVERTON

Possibly because we lived in a building occupied by non-Jews, and the entrance wasn't very noticeable, the stormtroopers passed us by on the night of 9 November. But when we went to school the next morning, the synagogue was burning.

We stood there, absolutely terrified and thunderstruck. The fire engines came, not to help extinguish the fires of the synagogue and the school, which was right next to it, but to prevent it from spreading to the neighbouring houses. We ran home, past smashed windows of Jewish shops, past stores and warehouses cleared out and plundered. I can't recall all the details of that day. You try and block something out that is so horrible.

I went back to our laundry and I found some Nazis there. They actually didn't smash up anything, they just said they were going to close it down. I asked them quite politely, 'May I take my school-books home?' I used to do homework at the laundry after school and had some schoolbooks there. They said, yes, you can do that. So I opened the drawer and I didn't only pick up the schoolbooks, I picked up the address book with our customers' names in it, and I put that in my school satchel as well.

They also allowed my father to take the laundry parcels, which were ready for delivery, and to deliver them to his customers. Those

Burning synagogue, Baden-Baden, 10 November 1938

Nazis seemed to be a little bit more humane than others. They just sealed the store and that was the end of our business.

Later that day my father came home ashen-faced, because one of the customers he had gone to deliver laundry to had committed suicide, both he and his wife.

NORBERT WOLLHEIM

On the morning when I went out, somebody said, 'The synagogues are burning.' I couldn't believe it. I went to the synagogue where I was bar mitzvahed, and where I'd been married, and I saw the flames coming from the roof, from the cupola of this beautiful edifice. The fire engines were standing by doing nothing, only protecting the buildings next to it. I still couldn't believe it. I thought, maybe it's the only one, so I went to another major synagogue in West Berlin, and it, too, was burning and already partly in ruins.

I thought, this is the people you were brought up with, this is the poets and the thinkers. What happened to German civilization? The people standing with me in front of the burning synagogues didn't dare to say a word. They may have felt ashamed, but they didn't dare to say so, because this was one of the principles the Nazis had established: they had concentration camps for anybody who said something against them.

There were also quite a number who made very nasty remarks. There was glee among them. They said the Jews got what they deserve and so on. That really gave me the shock of my life. I saw it, but I couldn't digest it, not intellectually and not emotionally.

Then my wife came to me and said, 'Norbert, you're not going home.' I asked why. She said that the police were going around taking men into custody and she'd arranged for me to stay with the mother of a friend who had just left for America. She was alone and would feel more protected if I stayed with her. Arrangements had also been made for my father to take shelter in the apartment of a sister who was a widow. That's what we did, unaware of what the next step would be.

I spent a couple of nights away from my apartment – I was still free to roam around – and I saw what had happened in the main streets of

Berlin, the Jewish stores that had been smashed and vandalized and looted. Then I realized that Rabbi Leo Baeck, who was my teacher and spiritual mentor, was right when he said that the historical hour of German Jewry had come to an end.

ROBERT SUGAR

I was living with my grandmother in a set of workers' flats. She was very poor. She had one room, a kitchen, and a small room where my uncle lived. Bathrooms were in the hallway. We were so poor that nobody bothered us on Kristallnacht.

On the night of the 10th, my father came to pick me up. He took me for a walk because he was working, I guess, for a Christian client. My father built window displays in the stores, and he was working for someone for whom he shouldn't have been working any more, and he was collecting the money for his work.

I remember we walked through the shards, through the broken glass in the streets. To me my father was a war hero. He was in the First World War, and I felt no fear, and he didn't feel any fear. I thought he was very strong.

But when he brought me home to my grandmother, she said, 'Where were you, Sandor?' He said, 'Oh, we went to collect the debts.'

'Are you insane?' she said. 'Are you *meshugge*?* To be out to-night?'

He said in his Hungarian accent, 'Nothing will happen.'

He wasn't insane exactly, but he was in a sort of denial. And I went with him. So, in my family anyway, we went through the pogrom very safely.

KURT FUCHEL

After the Anschluss, a law had been promulgated which effectively allowed anyone in good standing with the Nazis to expropriate an apartment occupied by Jews. On the infamous Kristallnacht, my

* Yiddish for 'crazy'.

Kurt Fuchel's parents, Rudolf and Olga, in Vienna apartment, early 1930s

family was evicted from our apartment with only a few hours' notice. What happened, as recounted to me by Mother, was that an interior decorator had taken a picture of our beautiful living room and displayed this picture of our apartment in his shop window. A Frau Januba saw the picture and heard that we were Jewish. She came around to the apartment and asked if it was for sale. She was told it wasn't, but a few days later, on the morning of Kristallnacht, she came back with some officers and said, 'This apartment is now mine.' She showed a piece of paper with a swastika stamped on it and told us that we'd have to leave by six that evening.

My mother protested to the officers who were accompanying her that she had a sick child at home who was already asleep. They said, 'All right, but you have to get out by six in the morning.'

Next morning, when Frau Januba showed up, my father told her that she was stealing what he and my mother had worked for. She said, 'Stop talking like that, or I'll have you sent to a concentration camp.' I had seen this Frau Januba when she first came to look at the apartment, and when I saw what was happening now, I dashed in and yelled at her, 'You lied to us when you were here last time. You're a bad woman!'

She was terrifed at this onslaught and said, 'Get the child out of here!' And that's what happened. We packed up what we could, left the rest, and moved in with a neighbour.

HEDY EPSTEIN

Before I went to bed, my father, in a rather stern voice, said to me, 'If you hear any strange noises during the night, immediately get out of bed and go into the wardrobe in the hallway. Don't look for us, we'll probably hear it, too, and we'll join you there.'

I said, 'I don't understand.' And quite differently than my father would normally answer my questions, he said, 'Don't ask any questions, just do as you're told.'

I went to bed and I fell asleep. The next morning I got up and I'd heard nothing. I'd forgotten all about it. I left for school early in the morning, just like any other day. I remember it was a very sunny, but extremely cold day. Classes started punctually at eight. About eight-thirty, the principal walked in and he talked to all of us.

Then he suddenly stopped and he pointed his finger at me and he said, 'Get out, you dirty Jew.' I just couldn't believe what I heard because I thought the principal was a good, decent person, and his daughter was one of my classmates. So I asked him to repeat it. And he did. He also came over, and he took me by the elbow and shoved me out the door.

As I was standing in the hall, all kinds of thoughts ran through my head: what did I do? Did I fall asleep? Did I not pay attention? What am I going to tell my parents? While I was standing there, the children came running out of the classroom, and they put on their coats or jackets. Some of them pushed or shoved me, others called me 'dirty Jew' and other names. And then they all left.

I had no idea where they were going, so I went back into my classroom, sat at my desk, got out a book and attempted to study when there was a soft knock on the door. In came the only other Jewish child in school, a boy by the name of Hans Durlacher who also came from Kippenheim. He asked me, 'What are we going to do?'

I said, 'Hans, go back into your classroom, sit at your desk, get out a book and study. That's what I'm doing.'

But Hans said, 'No, I'm scared. Can I stay here?'

I said he could and then he asked, 'Can I go over to the window and look out?'

I said, 'Yes, but please be quiet now, because I'm trying to study.' So Hans stood by that window maybe an hour or an hour-and-a-half

Jewish men being marched to Dachau, 10 November 1938. Sign reads 'Out with Jews'

when suddenly he became very excited. He said, 'Look! Come here.' What we saw were men being marched down the street, four in a row, accompanied by SS men who were hitting them with whips and urging them to walk faster, faster. We didn't know the men, but we assumed that they were Jewish.

After talking about it, we decided to call home. I called my mother and a strange voice answered the phone and said, 'The phone is no longer in service.' I called my father at his place of business, and my aunt, and each time the strange voice answered. Hans called his mother and some other people and got the same message. So we decided to go home. We were afraid, though. You don't just leave school in the middle of the day without permission, yet there was no one there. So we took the back roads and went home.

As I approached my house, it looked quite different from how it had that morning. We had green shutters and they were always open in the daytime, but now they were closed.

I went to the door and it was locked – I hadn't even known you could lock it. I rang the doorbell, but no one answered. I stood in front of the building for a few minutes when I saw a man coming towards me. I knew he was one of the village's worst Nazis. Any other time, if I found myself on the same side of the street as he, I would

SS units marching in formation at Nuremberg

have crossed to the other side because I was afraid of him. But, in my dismay, I went over to him and asked, 'Do you know where my mother is?'

His response – it's language that I would never use – was, 'I don't know where the goddamn bitch is, but if I find her and she's still alive, I'm going to kill her.' With that, I just took off as fast as I could to my aunt's house.

On my way I passed the Jewish hardware store. The two display windows were broken. There were people milling around, laughing and joking. Some of them were reaching in through the broken windows and taking out merchandise. I didn't understand that, either.

As I approached my aunt's house, I could see my mother and my aunt looking out the window. My mother opened the door, and she looked kind of grotesque. She was quite a bit taller and thinner than my aunt, but she wore one of my aunt's dresses. She told me that about ten minutes after I left for school, some Nazis came to the house and arrested my father. He was still in his pyjamas and they didn't even give him a chance to get dressed or put a coat on this very cold morning. As he was being walked out of the door, he said to my mother, 'Try to find Hedy. Try to stay together.'

A couple of the Nazis stayed behind, and they broke the windows, broke some furniture and some dishes. When they left, my mother closed the shutters, locked the door, ran down the street to my aunt's house, not realizing she was still wearing her nightgown. That's why my aunt had given her one of her dresses to wear.

I joined my mother and aunt at the window, hoping to see the men who had been arrested earlier come out of the village hall where they had been taken. It wasn't long after that we saw a group of men from the village hall being marched past my aunt's house. It was exactly the same thing I'd seen earlier that morning at school, except in this group were my father and my uncle and a lot of other Jewish men from Kippenheim that I knew.

The feeling was just indescribable: fear, anger, frustration, wanting to do something and not knowing what to do. I don't know whether I made any sounds or not. I don't remember. But I know my mother called out to my father, 'We have Hedy. We're together.' Whether he saw us or heard, we did not know. We watched them until they went around the bend in the road, and then they were out of sight.

We closed the windows and just sat there in numb silence for a few minutes when we heard loud banging on the door downstairs. When my uncle was arrested earlier, nobody did any damage to the building. But knowing what had happened at our house, we thought, now they're coming here to do the same thing.

My aunt, my mother and I ran up into the attic, and we were hiding in an old abandoned wardrobe up there. I didn't know then, and I certainly don't know today, how long we were in that wardrobe, but I do remember feeling as though I had spent my entire life there. I also remember whispering to my mother, 'I want to get out of here – and not just out of this wardrobe – I want to get out of Germany.'

Afterwards I was so afraid and so traumatized by what had happened, that I did not let my mother or my aunt out of my sight. We couldn't get the windows replaced in our building, so we stayed at my aunt's house. We moved an extra bed into my aunt's bedroom so we could all three sleep in the same room. And if one of us had to go to the bathroom, I absolutely insisted that all three of us go together.

For two weeks there was no information about the men, then within a day or two, everyone received a pre-printed postcard from Dachau. Once we found out where they had been taken, my mother decided to visit the Nazi Gestapo office, which was in Karlsruhe. I begged her, 'Please, don't go, because if you go and they keep you, I won't have a father and I won't have a mother.' But she explained to me that it was important for her to go because maybe she could do something to bring about the speedier return of my father and the other men.

She left early every morning by train, came back late at night by train, but with no information whatsoever, until the Monday of the fourth week after the men were arrested. On that day, she was told that my father would come home that week, but if he was not back by Friday, he wouldn't ever come back because he would no longer be alive.

On that very same day, the first few men arrived back, and we heard about it and we visited them. However, my mother didn't allow me to remain in the room when conversation took place because she said I was still too young. I was fourteen at the time. But one thing made a deep impression on me: every man that came back had his hair completely shaved off. I had never seen anyone look like that before.

On Tuesday morning we went back to our house because that's where my father would naturally come. But he didn't come back on Tuesday, or Wednesday, or on Thursday. On Friday morning, I think my mother temporarily lost some of her sanity. She absolutely refused to get out of bed. She said, 'My husband is dead. He's not coming home any more. There's no sense my getting up. I don't want to live any more.'

My aunt and I both tried to convince her how important it was to get up and go back to our house. But it was to no avail. Shortly afterwards, we heard a knock on the door downstairs, and for the first time in four weeks, I did something on my own: I went to the window and looked out and I thought I saw my father. I went downstairs and I opened the door, and, indeed, it was my father.

Although when he was arrested he was still in his pyjamas, now he was fully clothed. He even wore a hat. When I opened the door, he removed his hat. I said, 'Oh, my God! They shaved your hair.' I'd seen all the other men with their shaved heads, but this was my father. I thought he was different. He was so ashamed when I said this that he not only put his hat back on, but he pulled it practically all the way down to his chin, so that his whole face was shadowed.

It took quite a while before my mother realized that the man standing next to her bed was her husband, my father. But once she came round, she urged my father to take his clothes off, wash, and put on some clean clothes. But he didn't want to do it. He explained, 'When I was in Dachau, I was beaten and my body is sore and swollen, and the clothes they gave me fit real tight, and to take them off is going to hurt even more.'

So my mother got a pair of scissors, and cut open the sleeves of his jacket and sort of peeled him out of it. They both went to the bathroom to remove his clothes, so I didn't see his body and I don't know how badly it really looked.

URSULA ROSENFELD

On the morning of 9 November, there was a strange atmosphere. I had had a strange dream in the night that my father was being arrested. Our meal that evening, that was the last meal I ever remember having with my father. I looked at him, and I thought, well, I hadn't really seen his features properly. You know how you look at somebody intensely. And something told me, I must imprint that image of him on my mind.

In the morning there was a strange, eerie silence everywhere. I got ready to go to school, and when I came into the class, nobody said a word. I sat down and we started our first lesson. Suddenly there was a flicker of light on the window, and then we smelled smoke.

Now our school happened to be just opposite on the street where the synagogue was. It wasn't what you would imagine a synagogue to be. It was just an ordinary small house. The top storey was the prayer room, and at the bottom were two rooms. In one of them lived a Jewish family and the other was a schoolroom where we had religious lessons once or twice a week. When we saw the flames

Ursula Rosenfeld's father, Leopold Simon, late 1930s

flickering in the window, of course, everybody rushed out to watch. I was more or less dragged out with the stream of children. Everybody went to the playground, and I saw, in horror, that the synagogue was alight. The streets were lined with people, and they were all shouting, and jeering, and clapping. I don't know where the family was. I heard later on that the father had been arrested, and the mother had fled with her three children to my grandmother's house.

There was a doll in the street, and children's toys, and the few sticks of furniture, and their clothes – everything had been thrown out of the window. Then two men – I don't think they were uniformed – came out with a Torah and they were dancing around and shouting.

Suddenly somebody said, 'Oh, there's a Jew – let's throw her on the fire as well!' I don't know how I got home. I still don't know today how I got home, but I did eventually manage to get there. And when I did, my mother was absolutely shocked. My father had been arrested.

Later on I remember seeing some Jewish man being dragged through the street, but I didn't connect it at the time. I think I was in a state of shock as well. Of course, we learned later that they had rounded up all the Jewish men into the local marketplace, ill-treated them, and then shut them up in the local prison. The next day, I don't know when exactly, they transported them to Buchenwald concentration camp.

Bonfire of synagogue furnishings, Mosbach, Germany, 9 November 1938

My father was quite an outspoken person, and because he'd known all the people in that area, when they came to Buchenwald and they took away all the men's braces and shoelaces, he protested and said, 'You can't treat these old people like this.' So they made an example of him and they beat him to death in front of everybody in order to instil terror and obedience.

We heard a few days later that he had died of a heart attack, but this was the story the Nazis told all the families of the people they killed. We learned the true story later from people who were released from Buchenwald. The Nazis offered us my father's ashes in return for money. Eventually the urn came, and we buried it in the Jewish cemetery. But, of course, whether it was his ashes one never knows.

This document of identity is issued with the approval of His Majesty's Government in the United Kingdom to young persons to be admitted to the United Kingdom for educational purposes under the care of the Inter-Aid Committee for children.

THIS DOCUMENT REQUIRES NO VISA.

PERSONAL PARTICULARS.

Name *GORBOLZKI ABRASCHA*

Sex *m*   Date of Birth *31·1·22*

Place *Bergedorf*

Full Names and Address of Parents *GORBOLZKI*
Hamburg. 27 Westerstr.

Alexander Gordon's Kindertransport identity card

Chapter Three

A LIGHT IN THE DARKNESS

'If England was willing to take all these children, it proved that there was still humanity left somewhere.'

NORBERT WOLLHEIM

NORBERT WOLLHEIM

One evening my youth leader said, 'Call Otto Hirsch. There's a job to be done.' So I went and saw him. Mr Hirsch was the head of the central organization of Jews in Germany. Like many others, he had been taken into a concentration camp on 9 November and had just been released.

He said, 'Listen, I have a request. We have been informed that the British government, the House of Commons, has discussed the destiny of Jews in Germany after all this publicity, and they are disgusted. Even though Chamberlain's policy of appeasement is still prevailing, they've come to the conclusion they should accept children for a certain time. We've started working on it, but the organization isn't what I wanted it to be. Could you help us?'

I said, 'I have no experience in this area.' He said, 'You're young. You know organizations.' I said, 'But I want to leave Germany like the others. I'm working on that because I see there's no future for me, and I feel a responsibility for my family.' He said, 'OK, we will take care of you after this is over', meaning after the work has been done. He made this commitment, but he could never fulfil it, because during the war he was taken away to Mauthausen where he was brutally murdered.

He told me, 'We have an office for the operations. See what you can do.' When I went there, I must say, I almost fainted when I saw the disorder. There was a big conference room in the office and a big table covered with heaps of cards and a desk which was covered with papers, and the telephone was constantly ringing. I understood then why he had asked me to help. The staff were mostly social workers and although they were doing their very best, they had no experience in technical matters like the transports.

In the youth movement we had been educated to try to help where we could. That was one of our major beliefs. It's not enough what you do for yourself. You have to try also to do something for people who are less lucky than you are or need your help and support. So I started to work.

The first thing I did was to try to organize the cards into alphabetical and geographical order. These were the permits which gave the young people a licence to enter England. Then we had to put together the transports. Lists had to be submitted to England and lists submitted to the Gestapo. Then you had to organize the people from places outside Berlin to come to Berlin and assemble on a certain day, at a certain time. There was also a lot of technical work at the last moment. Children got sick, or parents said, 'No, we can't afford to let our children go', and the lists had to be changed; we had to be in constant contact with London.

Now, to make a telephone call to London at this time could take three or four hours, and communications were very often during the night. This wasn't a nine-to-five job. We worked deep into the night. The office was in West Berlin and I lived in East Berlin and I often came home in the middle of the night. But it was work that had to be done. If England was willing to take all these children, it proved that there was still humanity left somewhere.

NICHOLAS WINTON
Rescue Organizer, London, England

When Hitler came to power in 1933, I was twenty-four and working on the London stock exchange. From my youth I'd always been very politically conscious. My friends and I were all pretty well left-wing and we used to have meetings and discuss things. We regarded Hitler as a terrific menace, but one was obviously influenced by the general feeling in England, particularly among the politicians. The people who thought that Hitler's aggression would continue were firmly

convinced that it would be directed against
Russia rather than us. That's what Hitler
not only said, but I think, at that time,
really believed. Certainly in the early
stages, I don't think he ever thought he
would be involved in war against England.

When Hitler marched into the Sudetenland, that, I suppose, was the big test. I
don't know that everybody in England was
told what the real implications were – that
the annexation deprived Czechoslovakia
of all its defences. Czechoslovakia without
the defences of the Sudetenland was defen-
celess.

Then, of course, we had Chamberlain,
who came back from Munich with the now
famous, or should I say 'notorious', piece

of paper, and said 'I believe it is peace for our time.' One does Nicholas
tend to believe what one wants to believe, and everybody wanted to Winton
believe that we weren't going to be involved in a war; although, in
retrospect, the Germans marching into the Sudetenland should really
have shown us that things weren't quite what we thought them to be.
My own political awareness of Hitler only crystallized when I got to
Prague in December 1938 and saw things for myself.

I had a great friend, Martin Blake, who was a master at Westmin-
ister School. We took the boys to winter sports every Christmas, not
only to do a good deed, but it gave us a free holiday. One day he rang
me up and said, 'I'm off to Prague. I'm at the station and haven't even
got time to tell you why I'm going. But ring up everybody and do as
I've done, which is cancel our trip to Switzerland with the boys and
meet me at the Hotel Sroubek in Prague.' He and I were very much
akin to each other politically, so I knew if he'd almost summoned me,
it was worth going.

When I got to Prague, I found that the lady who had summoned
Martin was Doreen Wariner, who was the representative of the
British Committee for Refugees from Czechoslovakia. She was there
entirely to try and get out of the country all those grown-ups who
would be in danger if Hitler arrived in Prague: writers, communists,

Jews, those people who were on Hitler's blacklist. In Prague their position seemed much more vulnerable and dangerous than it ever appeared in England.

A lot of the people who'd fled the Sudetenland when Hitler marched in were living with friends or relatives they knew in Prague, but a large number of them were in camps. Just after Christmas, we went around the camps to see what was going on. We toured these camps in the dead of winter and snow. It was all rather cold and pathetic.

Czechoslovakians from the Sudetenland in refugee camp

I remember I'd met a gentleman on my way out to Prague. He told me he was out there to deal in motorbikes. I said, 'Well, you won't deal in any motorbikes at this time. If your business is as unlucrative as I think it's going to be, come and join me.' After a couple of days he did. He said, 'You're quite right, you can't do business here.' I took him around the camps with me. On one occasion he wasn't there any more and I went back to the Nissen hut where we'd just been and I found this hardboiled businessman on one of the beds sobbing his eyes out.

When you see conditions like that, it seemed to Martin and to me, and obviously the other people from the British Committee, that the situation was very, very highly explosive. Quite rightly, in retrospect, we had the feeling that the position was much more urgent than anybody in London thought. When one wrote back to London about it, the general opinion was, 'You're too near, you can't see properly.

You want a proper perspective from afar to judge what's happening.' But it seemed obvious to us that the Germans weren't doing in Czechoslovakia what they were doing unless they were going to march in.

The British Committee could only do what their brief said, which was to bring out the adults who were in danger. And Doreen Wariner said to me, 'I don't know what we're going to do about the children. I doubt if we'd ever be able to get them in if we tried.' And almost spontaneously I said, 'Well, when I get back to England, if I find that the Home Office will allow them in, we'll try and get some of them into England.' So it all started in a casual way.

FRANZI GROSZMANN
Mother of Lore Segal, Vienna, Austria

My husband was much cleverer than I. He saw there was a possibility to save Lore's life, and he decided to send her to England on the Kindertransport. I knew that I ought to want to send her away, but I couldn't imagine giving permission for her to go. My husband said, 'She must go.' He didn't listen to me. He just arranged everything for her, and I had to give in.

I saw in the end that he was right. But the hurt is unbelievable. That cannot be described.

I don't know how one does that. How does one send one's child away, not knowing whether she will get across the border of Germany? One didn't know anything about what would happen.

LORE SEGAL

At one point my father came to the house of the friend where I was staying and said, 'Mommy and I cannot leave, but you're going to leave.'

I said, 'What do you mean, I'm going to leave?'

'You're going to England,' he said.

'When?'

'Thursday,' he said.

He took me to the main synagogue in Vienna. It had been gutted on Kristallnacht. There, in the burned-out shell of the hall and in a queue that snaked up the stairs and around the women's gallery, were hundreds of children and their parents. My father and I waited for several hours until I heard my name called. Now, my mother's cousin, Uncle Otto, had a girlfriend who worked for the Wiener Jüdische Kultur Gemeinde, the Jewish organization, and I had the guilt-making good fortune of being called out of that queue and processed ahead of other children.

I remember walking past the parents and children, and they were watching me and my father walk by. I can't say this is a stone on my heart, but I think about it once in a while. Is there someone who did not get on the Kindertransport because I did?

My transport was the first to leave from Vienna. It left on 10 December 1938. I remember that last evening. All the cousins and aunts came to say goodbye. There was one aunt, the mother of twins, who was extremely angry with my parents for getting me on to this transport when she had not managed to get her twins aboard. I remember my father kept trying to explain that we had to be grateful for the cousin's girlfriend who had managed to get me on. But there was grief and panic and fury in that room.

Then came the moment when my father took me between his knees and said, 'Now when you get to England, you have to talk to all the English people you meet, and you have to ask them to get your mother and me out, and your grandparents.' And because this aunt was there, who was so unhappy and so angry, he added, 'and Aunt So-and-So's twins.'

Lore Segal, age 9, Vienna

Before long I had a list of people whom I, at ten years old, had promised to save from Hitler.

ALEXANDER GORDON

After Kristallnacht, I went back to Hamburg, to the orphanage. They directed me to a hostel, on the other side of Hamburg, which was willing to put me up for a while.

When you're young, you brush all these things off. You just accept them as a fact of life. The Nazis don't like us. They're making life difficult for the Jews, and for me personally. That's just the way it is. I never thought much about 'what am I going to do tomorrow?'

I was at the hostel for one or two days and I went to the Gemeinde, the organization that looked after Jewish interests in Hamburg. A wonderful woman I knew there, Nurse Tekla, said to me, 'Abrascha, what are you doing here? Where's your mother?' I said, 'My mother has been deported.' She said, 'You know, there's something happening now, I think you should get on to it.' It was the Kindertransport. She said, 'You better register immediately because you're all by yourself, what are you going to do?' So I said, 'OK, I'll go to England' – just like matter of fact, as if it was nothing.

In the meantime, I heard from my mother. She was in Zbaszyn, the 'No Man's Land' between Germany and Poland, and she wrote to say she didn't have any clothes. I went to the apartment, but it was sealed up. I couldn't do a thing. So I went to the police station, where they made me sit for two days. Eventually, a policeman had pity on me and took me to the apartment and unsealed it.

My mother used to get a few dollars regularly from her brother in America, and I found twenty-five dollars that she had hidden. There was a very strict law in Germany at the time forbidding anyone to possess foreign currency. If you had any, you had to go to the bank immediately. The policeman looked at the dollars and thought he was going to be a hero because he had found somebody who had committed a crime. But I knew my mother always kept the required receipts, from her American relatives, which I finally found, and the policeman was very disappointed.

He had wasted all his time and he said, 'Come on, let's go.' He took me right to the bank and changed the money into German currency. And that was the end of that.

Before I left the apartment I grabbed a suitcase, filled it with clothing, and sent it to my mother. The only reply I got was, naturally, I sent all the wrong things.

A few weeks later, on 14 December, I reported to the railroad station at six o'clock in the morning, for the Kindertransport.

CHARLOTTE LEVY

After Berthold had come back from prison, we tried our utmost to find a way out of Germany. We had applications running for Sweden – Berthold's first choice – England, Australia, the United States. Sweden refused us first, and none of our other applications was granted.

We had, of course, thought before of sending Hans out, but now there was no doubt any more. Yet how could we achieve that? I sent cables to everybody I knew abroad, and one of them called me back. This was a first cousin of my father's in London and she said she would try what she could to help us. She spoke to her daughter, Win, who was married to Bernard Schlesinger. Win talked to her five children about us, and the Schlesingers made a commitment to take my son if he could get out. They also agreed to take the baby. I did not want to send my baby away because what would happen to her? But the hope that we could send Hans away was just a light in the darkness. So we applied for an exit visa for England for him.

The degree of despair to which you can be driven is best revealed by this reversal of one's normal feelings and principles. To feel happiness about what? About being able to send one's little boy of nine away to a foreign country whose language he does not speak, to people one does not know oneself, not sure if one will ever see him again? It was an extraordinary decision to send our young child away and let the Schlesingers, whom we had never met, take care of him, have the responsibility for his upbringing, his education and all the financial part that went with this. Yet to have Hans stay on in Germany would have been a catastrophe. What can you say to your little boy sobbing his heart out as his father has been taken away, whose school has been burned down, his teachers arrested and who asks you, 'Why does God let them do that?' And what will you do with him, a lively child, who has no more school, no place outside where he is allowed to play, no friends left, a dying father, a mother who is busy to capacity with her husband and a baby? All this had made him very difficult. A new life was essential for him.

We prepared for his leaving. As we could not pay anything to the Schlesingers, as a token of our willingness to do our part, we equipped Hans for many years to come with all the clothes we thought he might

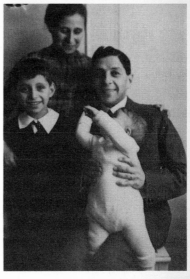

need, in three mounting sizes – coats, sweaters, suits, pyjamas, underwear, shoes, socks, etc. I packed a very large trunk with all of this. Ironically, he could wear none of those clothes as boys' fashions were so different in England and what he needed most were outfits for boarding school, which we would not have been able to get in Germany. But these clothes came in good stead later on for bombed-out British children.

Charlotte, Berthold, Hans and Elisabeth Levy, Germany, 1938

It was very, very difficult to get things ready. While I was sorting out Hans's things, I found a little diary. From the next room, my husband called, 'What is it you have there?' I told him, and he said, 'Better read it.'

I did and I was shaken. Hans had to take two trams when he went to school and he had jotted down what happened to him on the tramway. The jeerings were as anti-Semitic and filthy as you can imagine. Enough to make a mother wish her son far away. And he had never mentioned a word to us of these humiliations.

I put the book in my desk drawer. When I felt lonely for him later, a look would suffice to make me glad he wasn't here.

ROBERT SUGAR

It was my mother who put me on the list for the Kindertransport. She was working near Bloomsbury House in London and arranged it from there. I got on one of the earlier transports, the 10th of January 1939. Word came that I would be in a transport, and my father took me to the Jewish central organization in Vienna, and I received my papers there.

There was a kid in my grandmother's building, a Hitler Youth, and I said, before I go to England, I'm going to beat this kid up. He never did anything to me, but he seemed to me hostile. And, I thought, really some action is necessary, some act of retribution or vengeance before I leave for England.

Now, I don't want to give the impression I was a great fighter or a great hero. This was just a *thought* – a thought I should do this. Then I thought, well Omama – that's what I called my grandmother – is going to stay in the building, and although I'll be safe in England, she'll still be in danger here, so I won't do it.

Over the years I've mulled this over, rehashed it. Some people might say how wonderful, how clever to think of my grandmother like that. But it really wasn't. It was just an indication of what a hostage situation we were in, that even kids eight years old didn't have to be told. It was the situation of European Jewry, total consciousness that each one of us is hostage, that the action of each puts others in danger, which I think was learned *in utero*. Nobody taught me that, but it was almost self-evident, a sign of our slavery.

The strange thing about this period in Vienna is that it is clearly remembered, but it is before I was born, in England, before I became real, what I am now. These things transpired. They happened. But I have no connection to them.

I can't reach back to them. I can reach back to London, January the 12th. I can't reach back to Vienna, January the 10th. It's a different life. I guess I don't want to fully remember it because it's so painful.

JACK HELLMAN

My bar mitzvah was a month after Kristallnacht. It was held in an attic, with either young boys who were below the age of sixteen or old men who were beyond the age of sixty-five. My father was not there. He was still in concentration camp, and it was just my mother. I felt terrible. It's still painful, since a bar mitzvah's a fairly big thing in a religious household. There was no celebration afterwards, there was nothing. You read your part from the Torah, you did your *haftorah*,* and you were finished. We were lucky that a *minyan* showed up altogether.

I felt that the sooner we could get out of Germany, the better off we would be. My parents were certainly not in a position to do any moving. My sister had emigrated to the United States in the early part of 1938. We had a quota number and somebody who guaranteed that we would not become a burden to the American government, but the numbers the United States accepted were so small that it would have taken until 1943 or 1944 before any of my family would have gotten there.

The house mother of my school wrote to Baron James de Roths-child. Would he take 26 of her boys, her husband, herself and her two daughters? He wrote back in January that he would. On 16 March we went with the Kindertransport to England.

Jack Hellman (*seated on window ledge, at right*) at Philanthropin School in Frankfurt

BERTHA LEVERTON

It was by chance that our family learned of the Kindertransport. My sister Inge came home and said a friend had told her a secret, that she was going to England. My mother said, 'Silly child, what are you

* The portion of the *Prophets* read after the Torah on Sabbath, festivals and fast days.

talking about?' But my father took more notice and started asking questions. And Inge said that her friend was going to England, and she wasn't supposed to tell anybody.

My father went around quickly to the friend's parents. They weren't very happy to tell him about it. They were told to keep it quiet. After my father found out, he went to the Jewish welfare department and said he wanted a place for his children on the Kindertransport. My father was very insistent. He said, 'If you don't give me a place, I'm going to tell all my friends about it.' Finally, they gave him two places for my brother and myself. My sister Inge was younger, though, and they said they couldn't possibly take more than two children from one family. We were very, very lucky – there were only twenty children from Munich on that transport, as far as I can remember.

I was fifteen, going on sixteen, and my brother Theo was twelve. We thought of England as a land of lords and ladies because of the king and queen, and the two little princesses appealed to us very much. A year or two before we saw pictures in newspapers of the coronation with their ermine clothes and their crowns on their heads. And we really thought in England that's how people got dressed – perhaps not every day, but sometimes on Sundays. So that was our expectation of England.

It was a land of freedom, a land of hope and glory. Our parents painted a picture of adventure, how lucky we were to go to England. We really felt that.

We were allowed to take one suitcase, which we had to carry ourselves. Somebody came to the house to inspect the contents of the suitcase, to make sure we weren't taking any valuables; then the suitcase was officially sealed. Apart from the suitcase, we were allowed one rucksack, and into that we packed our most treasured possessions.

I was an avid reader, I had a very big collection of books, and what grieved me more than anything was to leave my books behind. So I burned them. It was wintertime. We had an old-fashioned oven that you fed with coal, and I fed my books into it, one by one.

LORRAINE ALLARD

Kristallnacht made people like my father realize that things weren't going to change and he would have to take the chance of leaving Germany, whatever happened. Everything one could think of was tried for immigration. My sister was in South Africa. She applied for my parents to come out there. It didn't happen. Even if you had permission for America, you had to have a waiting number. For England you needed guarantees.

My father was the pessimist in all this. My mother was the optimist. She kept him going. I remember seeing my father cry when they had tried to go somewhere and they were turned down. I was only thirteen on Kristallnacht, and I think they tried to keep quite a lot of what was happening hidden from me, to protect me as much as possible.

Of course, the Jewish school was closed down after Kristallnacht. So that was another thing: what to do with the youngsters? How to occupy them? Again, my mother, with her enthusiasm, knew a non-Jewish tailor in Nuremberg. Somehow she managed to get him to take me as a trainee. I travelled on the tram every day and had a few months' time with him. Most of the time I was sweeping the floors, but he did try to teach me how to use a sewing machine and how to cut out patterns.

During most of this time I was very frightened, and yet I think I've inherited the optimism of my mother. I tried not to let the bad side get me down. I tried to bury my head in the sand. I was frightened, but I was still with my parents.

On 14 April 1939, my parents had a letter to say that I had a place in England with guardians, and I must be ready by 18 April. We had four days to pack and go. And they were just so busy, getting ready, things I was going to take – what I needed, what I didn't need – that I don't think they or I had time to think about what was happening.

I remember, also, that we had to have uniformed people there while the suitcase was packed and sealed, so that if we'd had the Crown Jewels, they weren't included in our baggage. I couldn't take anything of value. I had a stamp collection which had belonged to my grand-father and I wanted to bring it, but I wasn't allowed. What I mainly brought is clothing, one photo album which my mother had made for

Umzugsgut des Auswanderers: *Herbert Friedmann XX. Klosterneuburgerstr 61* 130
(Name) — (letzte inl.Anschrift)

Lfd. Nr.	Stück	Art	Zeitpunkt der Anschaffung	Wert der nach 1.1.38 erworbenen. Gegenstände	Bemerkungen
1	1	Ganze Anzüge od.Kleider			
2		Schürzen			
3	2	Pullover			
4		Weste			
5	3	Hosen			
6		Jacken			
7	2	Nachthemden			
8		Pyjamas			
9	4	Taghemden			
10		Hemdhosen			
11	6	Unterhosen			
12		Strümpfe			
13	6	Socken			
14	18	Taschentücher			
15	1	Mantel			
16	1	Mütze			
17		Regenmantel			
18	2	Schuhe			
19	2	Hausschuhe			
20	1	*Arbeitsmantel* .			
21	1	*Füllfeder*			
22	1	*Bleistift*			

Kindertransport packing list

me as a child – she really didn't want to part with that, but she let me bring it – a scarf of my mother's which she loved. She also said, 'No, I'll bring it when we get together again', but I brought it. I think they scraped together four new towels for me, in case I needed them.

With the optimism in me neither I, nor possibly they, thought this was a permanent parting. It was more of a temporary 'I'm going to England until they get out' attitude. I was told this was the best thing that could happen. I was so lucky because everybody around me was trying to find places for their children. And suddenly, out of the blue, I had a chance to come to England. Apart from that, my father always thought that England was just the top of any country because he had lived there. In those days it was England with all the colonies. How lucky can I be?

HEDY EPSTEIN

The opportunity presented itself for me to leave on the Kindertransport on 18 May 1939. Exactly how that happened, I don't really know. But my parents tried to make it very exciting for me. They said I'll be able to go back to school, that I will learn another language, I will live in London, I will be able to travel on the subway. They painted a wonderful, beautiful picture, and added, again and again, 'And we'll follow soon.'

However, a few days or so before I was to leave, I accused my parents of trying to get rid of me. I said, 'I'm really a gypsy child, and you're now trying to get rid of me. You adopted me, and now you no longer want me.' Though I was glad to 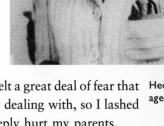 get out of Germany, at the same time I also felt a great deal of fear that I wasn't totally capable of talking about or dealing with, so I lashed out at them. I must have really deeply, deeply hurt my parents.

Hedy Epstein, age 14

Another thing I remember is that I wanted desperately to take my stamp collection with me, but the Nazis didn't give permission for that, because it was an object of value that could be sold. Now, in order to prevent possible customs problems at the border, my parents arranged for an official to come to the house and observe while my suitcase was being packed. The official put thin wires around the suitcase and put a seal on it, so that if the seal or the wires were broken, it would indicate that somebody had added something to the suitcase.

I was determined to take my stamp collection with me anyway, and a few days before I left, without my parents' knowledge, under the covers of my bed, with a flashlight, I took every single stamp out of my albums. The suitcase was already packed and sealed and on the next floor in a room that my grandfather sometimes used when he came to stay with us. I tiptoed up the stairs, hoping my parents wouldn't hear me, and I opened the suitcase. There was a little bit of leeway in the wire that the customs official had put around it, and I pushed every single stamp inside.

Just before we left, I wrote a note to my father and put it in the very back of his middle desk drawer, saying my stamps are my pictures. Before I left on the train, I said to my father, 'When you get home, look in your middle desk drawer, there's something for you.' Then, in my very first letter from England, I wrote, 'My pictures arrived safely.'

URSULA ROSENFELD

In hindsight, I think my sister Hella and I owe our survival to my father's death because they selected children who had problems, who'd lost parents, or whose parents could no longer look after them, to go on the Kindertransport.

After Kristallnacht, Jews weren't allowed to attend German schools any more. We received a curt note from the school director saying that they did not wish my appearance again. My mother found there was a Jewish orphanage in Hamburg and sent both my sister and me there fairly soon afterwards, at the end of November. I was thirteen and Hella was fourteen. And that was really the last time we lived at home. It was almost already a time of parting.

Ursula
Rosenfeld
(*left*) with
sister Hella

We were supposed to go to school in Hamburg – there was still a Jewish school – but with people emigrating, everything was rapidly disintegrating. One day there would be a class teacher, the next day she would be gone. So after the age of thirteen, my schooling virtually ceased.

I don't know whether my mother heard about the Kindertransport, or the orphanage wrote to her about it and they recommended it, but she obviously endorsed it. Quite a number of children from the orphanage signed up. Some went to Sweden, some went to Holland. We were lucky, we went to England.

I remember our mother got all our things ready. She had prepared all our clothes, lovingly embroidered our names in every piece of clothing, even every handkerchief, every sock. It's quite sad that we didn't really know what she was doing because she was still living in Quackenbrück with my grandmother, who was blind at the time, and whom she couldn't leave.

On the one hand, we looked forward to going to England with a certain amount of excitement. On the other hand, we were terrified of leaving my mother. We knew we had to get out of this, and we hoped that we would be able to find a domestic post for her, and she would be able to follow us.

EVA HAYMAN

I believe my mother found out about the transports from her brother Gustav, who lived in Prague. He had two boys that he and his wife very much wanted to send out of Czechoslovakia. They told Auntie Berta, my mother's unmarried sister, who told Mother. My aunt and my mother went in this long queue to present pictures and information about my sister and me and to say we would like to go to England. Mother came home and said that she had enrolled us, and about a fortnight later my parents were told that I can go. A week or two after that, they received something to say that my sister, too, was accepted. That must have been very hard for my parents – to send away both their daughters.

Both Mother and Father said that it was for their sake that they were sending us, because they would be more at peace. If nothing happened, we could come back. If things got worse, we would only be a handicap, and this way they would know that we were somewhere safe. That was the way they presented it to us. I think, in a way, it was a relief that both of us were going. I can't remember how I felt about Vera going too; probably pleased because I wasn't going to be alone, although then we didn't know whether we would be together or not.

We had about a fortnight before we left, and into that fortnight, both Mother and Father were trying to give the instructions, the guidance, that they had hoped to have their whole life to give. As I was the older sister, my father took me aside and said, 'Now Vera will be your responsibility.' He didn't give me instructions. He said, 'I know that you will look after her. I know that you will do your best. I know that you will be brave, that I can be proud of you.'

He put a heavy burden on a fourteen-year-old's shoulders. I didn't see it like that at that time, but when I read my diaries nearly sixty years later, I see I took his words very seriously. I was always trying to act so that my parents would be proud of me. Yet I didn't know, really, what they wanted. I was far stricter with myself than I think they would have been with me.

It was on one of our walks that my father taught me the facts of life. He also said that if I am in England for any length of time, he would be very happy if I could just love my parents. He didn't say, 'Do not fall in love', but he did say to think very hard about it, certainly before

I gave more than a kiss to anybody, that I should think, is he worth it? It was another burden, really. I don't think he had any idea how long we would be in England.

Before we left, my father gave both my sister and me a diary, saying to write into it not only what we do, but what we think, so that he could see the way we grew up when we met again. Actually, for about a year before we left, I'd started writing a diary at home, not knowing what would happen. Into this diary I wrote how I felt when the Germans came and when we had them at school, and in the streets, and everywhere. I wrote how angry I felt.

I also had a great need somehow to put into the diary my love for my parents, which I didn't know how to put into words, but I wrote in the diary how much I loved them, how much I admired them, how I knew how dreadful this sending away would be for them, and how brave I thought they were for doing it. I wrote lots of good things about them, which I would have liked to say to them, but did not. I packed this diary in the bottom of my case, intending to take it with me.

My father asked if he could read my old diary. I told him it was at the bottom of my case. He worried that I might get into trouble if the Germans opened the case and read anything; so I had to unpack everything and take it out. But I gave my parents permission to read it. After they did, I had the most fantastic letter from my father and mother because they could read what I was like and also read about my love for them. I was always pleased that I had written the diary and that they had the chance to read it.

VERA GISSING

We didn't have much time to prepare for our departure. We only had about three weeks. Our mother bought loads of material and had the local dressmaker working hard so she would send us both to England with a decent wardrobe. All the clothes were made to fit. There was no allowance for growth. It was my parents' way of coping with the forlorn thought that our departure was only a temporary one.

The day before our departure my father gave me a leatherbound book, full of empty pages. He said, 'Use it as a diary. Write in it when you're homesick, or when you've been naughty, or when something wonderful's happened, so when you come back to us we can all sit around the table and read the diary together.'

The night before we left, my mother carried me in her arms to an open window. She said, 'Let the stars of the night and the sun of the day be the messengers of our thoughts and of our love. In that way, we shall always remain close.'

In all the excitement of those three weeks, I was more interested in what I should take with me, things such as my doll, my Czech flag, my favourite books, that I didn't really realize until the night before departure what a big step I was taking. It was only then, as I was lying in my bed, thinking of the words that my mother had said, and of the diary that my father had given me, that I realized I might be going away from them for a long, long time.

Lore Segal's identification number

Chapter Four

LAST GOODBYES

'I watched their faces, and tears were streaming down their cheeks. And I knew then: these people really love me. This is why they're sending me away.'

HEDY EPSTEIN

NORBERT WOLLHEIM

We had approximately twenty transports which left Berlin. It was my duty to see them all off. On the day the transports left, we assembled the people at the railway station. I had to rent a special room where everyone could gather. Then came the parents, and the brothers and sisters, and the kids with their knapsacks. There was laughing, there were tears, but finally, there came the time to say to the parents, 'Listen, you cannot go to the platform. The police will not allow it. You have to say goodbye here.'

So I ascended a chair, addressed the people. Where I took the courage to do that, I don't know, but I told the parents, 'Now it's your last goodbye. The guides will take over and they will accompany the children to the platform. Please don't come to the platform because it only causes trouble for us.'

The children went with the hope that the parents will follow, or that one day they could come back and they would see them again. I did not realize, and I could never realize, that only a year-and-a-half later, from the same railway station, trains would go in the other direction to Hitler's slaughterhouses.

LORE SEGAL

The children leaving on the transport were supposed to assemble in a field behind the railroad station. I remember holding my parents'

Fürsorge-Zentrale
der isr.Kultusgemeinde Wien   Wien, 8/12.1938
Abteilung Jugendfürsorge
I.Seitenstetteng. 2

K i n d e r t r a n s p o r t
nach England bezw.Holland.

1.) Die Abreise der Kinder erfolgt S a m s t a g , den 10.Dezember

1938 um 23.10 Uhr vom Bahnhof Hütteldorf-Hacking.

Es wird nochmals darauf aufmerksam gemacht, dass das Gepäck
nichts enthalten darf als Gebrauchsgegenstände des Kindes und
dass jedes Zuwiderhandeln zur Folge hätte, dass das Kind nicht
mitgenommen werden könnte. Das Gepäck bleibt   in Verwahrung
des Zollamtes bis zum Abgang des Zuges.

Bei diesem Anlass wird auch darauf aufmerksam gemacht, dass den
Kindern auf die Reise keinerlei Schmuck oder Wertgegenstand mit-
gegeben werden darf, ebenso ist das Mitnehmen von Musikinstru-
menten und Fotoapparaten untersagt. Geld ist den Kindern gleich-
falls nicht mitzugeben.

Der das Gepäck abliefernde Angehörige des Kindes erhält eine
Nummer, die das Kind sichtbar bei der Abreise zu tragen hat.

2.) Die Kinder werden S a m s t a g , den 10.Dez.l.J. von blos
e i n e m Familienangehörigen zum Platze vor der Reichsbahn-
station Hütteldorf-Hacking (gegenüber Hotel Schneller) gebracht
und zwar die Kinder, welche die

Nummern 1-300 haben, um 21.Uhr, die Kinder mit den
Nummern von 301 aufwärts um 22 Uhr.

Die Begleitpersonen haben sich vor der Station von den Kindern
zu verabschieden; das Betreten des Bahnhofgebäudes sowie des
Bahnsteiges durch Begleitpersonen ist behördlicherseits ausnahm-
los untersagt.

3.) Jedes Kind hat einen unzerbrechlichen Becher und Waschutensilien,
ferner an Proviant ein Gabelfrühstück, ein Mittagessen, ein Nacht-
mahl auf die Reise mitzunehmen.

4.) Sollte ein Kind in der Zwischenzeit von der stattgehabten ärzt-
lichen Untersuchung bis S a m s t a g erkranken, so ist dies
s o f o r t der Jugendfürsorge, beziehungsweise der Reiseleitung
bekanntzugeben.

Durch den Arzt der Kultusgemeinde wird sodann nach erfolgter
Untersuchung des Kindes festgestellt werden, ob dasselbe mitgenommen werden kann oder nicht.

Fürsorge-Zentrale
der isr.Kultusgemeinde Wien
Abt.Jugendfürsorge

Kindertransport instructions sent to parents prior to departure hands as we walked across the bridge that spanned the Danube. And they were talking to each other over my head. My father said, 'I think tomorrow I'll try the Dutch consulate.' My mother said something like, 'I think I heard that people are going to Shanghai. Or what about Switzerland?' I remember this angry feeling that they were already discussing a tomorrow in which I no longer had a part because I was going to be away.

When we got to the collection point, there were already a lot of children milling about. It was dark. There were flashlights, and there were young people from the Jewish Organization with sticks or posts on which they had placards. Each child was given a number. My number, and I still have it, was 152. Each child wore a number around its neck, and the same number was attached to our suitcases.

We stood, in our groups of fifty, I think it was. My mother kept up a conversation with me, as if this was an ordinary and interesting thing that was happening. I remember that she wore a pony fur with a fox collar. I remember her face inside the fox collar. Although her speech was as if everything was ordinary, her face was hot; it was red and hot.

There was one other thing I remember. In the tram, on the way to the railroad station, there had been another little girl with her parents sitting across the aisle. You could tell they were going to the same place, because she also had a rucksack and a little suitcase. And she was howling. She was crying and crying and crying. I said to my mother, 'I'm not crying like that little girl.' My mother said, 'Oh, you're being very brave. You're being just wonderful.'

I wanted to think that I was being brave, but even then I had my doubts. Many times since I've wondered whether not crying was such a good idea. The number I was playing on myself was to say, 'This is terrific, I'm going to England. What a lark! How exciting!' thereby cutting myself off from the disaster of leaving my parents – that was sent underground. When you cut yourself off from your real feelings and focus on what is to the right or the left of it, it's not a good idea. I've compared this survivor's trick with other children in like circumstances, and this is one of the things that many of us do when we can't stand what it is that's happening to us. It's my sense that it took me a couple of decades before I reconnected with my genuine experience of many things.

At some point we were arranged into columns of four, our rucksacks were put on our backs, and our suitcases into our hands. Except my suitcase was too heavy for me. So my mother took it from me and she walked beside me, until one of the helpers came and told me, 'No, you have to carry it.' It was dragging along the ground, and the children at the back were saying, 'Go, already. Go on!'

What's interesting to me is that I remember the events of crossing the bridge, going on the tram, of assembling in the field, in intense detail. But I've often marvelled that I cannot remember myself walking across the platform. I remember looking to my right and suddenly noticing that my parents were no longer there, but after that is a blank.

The next thing I remember is that I was inside the train, and my Uncle Otto's girlfriend, who had facilitated my being accepted on this transport, was looking in the window. I stood on my head for her and wiggled my toes, something I was very proud of being able to do. I remember her face looking in the window. Then the platform was cleared and we were settled down, but it seemed to me it took a long time for the train to get going.

FRANZI GROSZMANN

When we took Lore to the train station, it was already very late, must have been eleven or twelve o'clock at night. I had her suitcase, and she was next to me, and my husband was next to me.

There were many, many children there, and they came and hung this number on her. The children in front of her were all crowded together saying, 'Don't push! Don't push!' And suddenly somebody came and said, 'Now, everybody go take your suitcase.' In no time, the suitcase was gone, the child was gone, the other children were gone – just emptiness. Then we turned around and went home. I did not talk. It was awful.

People have asked me, 'What did you feel?' Nothing. This was such a shock. When we came home, we didn't talk to each other. My parents, my husband and I, we did not talk, we didn't look at each other.

BERTHA LEVERTON

When we left Munich, our parents were not allowed to accompany us to the actual platform because there had been instances of parents weeping and fainting at the platform. So we had to say goodbye in an anteroom, and the scenes were pretty horrendous.

It wasn't an easy thing to part with little children. Today I look at my great-grandchildren and I wonder how the parents could manage to part with little children. I don't think I will ever understand the sacrifice that parents made to let their children go.

Now, we were the big children. We had a background. We knew where we came from. But how do you get a little one – a five-, a six-, a seven-year-old – on to a train? Every parent promised their child, we will soon come and follow. How otherwise did the parents get the little children on to the trains?

'Give us a few weeks, when either things will blow over and you'll come back again, or we'll come and join you.' That was a promise every parent made to their child.

INGE SADAN

When my sister and brother left, everything was terribly sad. It was winter, it was dark, it was bitterly cold; and everything was done in a hurry.

My parents were not allowed to go to the station. Everybody had to meet at the community offices. I remember that very well. They were in a dark room – it was all dark and sinister.

All the other parents were crying, and I was so afraid. I didn't want my mother to cry because she was a very strong person, and I thought, if she cries, then terrible things will happen.

So I kept on looking at her, and I said, 'Don't cry. Don't cry. You won't cry?' And she didn't. She said, 'No, why should I cry? They're going to England. They'll start a new life, and everything will be fine.' And she comforted me.

Then some official must have said, 'It's time to go', and all the children filed down the stairs with their rucksacks and little suitcases, and off they went to the station.

Kinder, July 1939

I left with my parents and we went home. I remember it was just deathly. Nobody to fight with. No big sister to look after me. Also my parents weren't working. It was very eerie. I hated it.

Eventually my father found work in the Jewish hospital, in the laundry there, and he worked terribly hard in the basement. I remember it was awful conditions, but he was only too happy to be able to do something.

At the same time, I had the strange feeling that, for the first time in my life, I had my mother to myself. She wasn't working and I had her full-time. A few weeks later school started again, half a day, in a makeshift building. I would come home from school and my mother was there and lunch was on the table. It was very comforting and I got used to that situation.

JACK HELLMAN

Most of us didn't give a thought to leaving our parents. My father had returned from Buchenwald the first week of January 1939. He came back a broken man. My parents were terribly upset about my leaving, but we waved goodbye at the station and there were no tears. There were some people with an only child who wouldn't let their boy go along. They figured the family would come out together, which, of course, never happened. None of the boys who stayed behind got out. Absolutely none.

CHARLOTTE LEVY

Hans was so happy to be going to England. He knew that he was going to a family where there were twins his own age and all the good things: that they were in the country, that they had dogs, etc. The night before he left he sang in his bed. Baby Elisabeth woke up and chimed in.

On the previous day, Berthold was very sick and the surgeon came to the house. We were so fortunate that this man was so decent; no other doctor would see us any more. I knew my husband had just a very short time to live, and I did not know whether I should tell Hans the truth about his father's condition. I must say, thanks to my sister Martha, I didn't do it. She said to me, 'Let him go with a light heart. Don't let him go with a heavy heart.' England would be a difficult change anyway, so I didn't tell him anything about it. When Hans took leave from his father early in the morning of 15 March, it was a terrible thing to know the two wouldn't see each other again.

I had been asked to take a number of children to meet the transport in Westphalia. There I had to board the train, go along to the next station in order to deliver the children and their papers to those in charge. It was quite an experience to see these many children – every age from tiny babies on up – with only a few grown-ups to accompany them.

I have never been good at saying goodbye. But it couldn't be helped. Hans had to leave and I was happy to be able to take him that far. When I got off the train, I bought a paper. The headline, in big letters, was something like, 'German troops jubilantly greeted in Czechoslovakia'. As terrible as this new invasion was, I was happy about it, because I knew the Nazis would be in high spirits and they would not molest the children at the border.

Berthold died peacefully five and a half weeks later, on 23 April. I was alone with him. He, who had changed so much during his illness, looked himself again in death. I wrote to Hans there in the candlelight. He had lost what had been a marvellous father.

ROBERT SUGAR

By the time I went to the train station, I was already pretty numb. I had moved from our apartment to my father's rented room, then to my grandmother's, and then to my aunt and uncle's. By then I was living in a strange land, so when I went to the train it was nothing special.

The adults stood outside. At our train, there were people on the platform. It was at night, a very dark, cold night. Others noticed people weeping or milling about. I noticed nothing.

My father had a cigarette pack, those flat European packs in which you can write on the back. He wrote something like 'Tell Mutti . . .' some not very memorable greeting. My uncle, a joker, gave me the

Kinder preparing to leave Berlin-Charlottenburg Station, May 1939

advice that if I should spit out of the window, it shouldn't be against the wind. Then the train left.

I was the youngest in the compartment. Being the youngest in anything goes with you all your life. I mean, I've stayed the youngest even though I'm fairly old by now. The older boys put me up on those rope luggage racks to sleep. I had a feeling of warmth come over me, rocking in the bosom of Abraham. I was enclosed by the people of Israel. Unlike my alienation in my family, I felt we were all together. This is really how I felt.

ALEXANDER GORDON

I reported to the train at six o'clock in the morning with one suitcase, ten marks, and very skimpy clothing.

The station was crowded with children of all ages, from four to seventeen, and their parents. I think there must have been three hundred of us. I got on the train, went into one of the compartments and looked out the window. The people were behind gates and the parents were telling the small children to get on to the train. The children didn't want to leave. The parents said, 'We'll see you in England in a few weeks', and there was crying and it was bedlam.

I was sitting all by myself. I had no parents – nobody. I was one of the oldest, and there was nobody whose shoulder I could cry on. All I knew was, I was going away. I was going to England. Whatever would happen, would happen.

LORY CAHN

I was quite huffed-up about the Kindertransport, but after I applied and was accepted, my father wouldn't let go of me. When I was born, I was so tiny I was wrapped in cotton for four weeks. From that I got the nickname Pupe or Pupela. And my father, every day he took me and hugged and kissed me and said, 'Pupela, I don't want you to go – but I want you to go because it'll be good for you.'

The day came and we went. My mother and dad went with me inside the train and put my suitcase up. My seat was right at the window – the German trains had great big windows, and a leather strap, like a belt, to position the window to whatever height you wanted it. My father pulled that all the way down so I could be leaning out of the window.

They hugged me and kissed me inside, and then they went outside. We stood there for quite a while. And I could see my father's face getting whiter and whiter, and I thought, I only hope nothing is going to happen to my father because he looked so terribly, terribly pale. And my poor mother was getting worse and worse. And I couldn't wait for the train to go because I didn't want to remember that.

The guy came, and he waved the signal. When the train started to go, my father said, 'Pupela, let me hold your hands.' And I held out my hands, and I said, 'I have to let go. I have to let go.'

'No, no, no, no. I don't want you to go. I don't want you to go.'

My father couldn't walk very fast because he walked with a cane, and we went already a little bit, and a little bit more, and he took me by my hands and he pulled me out of the window. And I fell – I could have fallen in between the platform and the train. I didn't, but I got hurt and I was bleeding.

I was devastated. Absolutely devastated. And my father was in seventh heaven that he had his little Pupela, his little girl back.

After we got home, my father said, 'Maybe I shouldn't have done that, but we just lost your brother. How can I possibly live without you? You're my sunshine and my everything, and I don't want to ever be separated from you.'

URSULA ROSENFELD

In July 1939, our mother came up to Hamburg to see Hella and me off on the Kindertransport. The parting was terrible. That's the one thing I've never forgotten in all my life.

Mother had been so controlled. She'd always been a sort of solid support for us. And suddenly, at the station, she showed her feelings. It was terrifying, really terrifying. I was quite shocked. We saw this face which showed all the hurt and agony she'd been through.

It was a long time before we were able to collect ourselves. I didn't want to believe it then, that that would be the last time we would see each other. But I suppose somehow there was an intuition that this was a final parting.

I can still see my father that last mealtime, but I would have liked to have had a happier image of my mother. That's the only image, this contorted face, full of agony. It's very sad.

We didn't take any photographs with us. We were so confident, and my mother was confident, we would see each other again. So I haven't got a photograph of my mother, except a passport photograph, which we managed to get from the photographer after the war. He still had the plates.

Ursula Rosenfeld's mother, Erna Simon

EVA HAYMAN

Mother had new clothes made for both of us to take to England. I brought with me a long blue cape, which we wore over bathing costumes going to the beach. That I remember well because I still have it.

Otherwise, around my neck, because we were baptized, hoping that would be of some help, I had a little cross, and I had a little elephant, and I had sort of – it wasn't a Jewish star but a little angel. I put them all together because I thought the Almighty can choose which religion he would like me to belong to. Those are the things that I remember.

Before we left we went to Prague, to my grandparents, for a final meal, which I don't think anybody ate. I always remember seeing my grandfather and my grandmother in the window, waving goodbye to us, although my grandmother was blind. I thought so highly of my grandfather. I used to be a shy little girl, and he sat me on his knees, and I remember him saying once, 'Oh, don't be shy, Evicka, people are far more stupid than you credit them with.' Whether that was a compliment or not, I don't know, but remembering his words sometimes helped.

I remember arriving at the station in Prague and it being full of children and parents – little children, big children, parents crying, some having brave faces. To me, it was all unreal. I didn't believe that this was happening to us. I just wanted to go back in time. Of course, Mother and Father kept saying it won't be for long – as much for their own consolation as for ours.

I knew that if I burst into tears, they would too, and so would Vera. So I tried not to cry. I remember standing by the window of the train, waving goodbye, and just trying very hard to believe that we really will come back, that it won't be for long. But when the train moved and they disappeared from sight, both Vera and I cried in each other's arms. That's when I said to my sister, 'Don't be afraid, you will always have me.' I was making a promise to myself that I would look after her, as well as a promise to her that I would be there for her.

VERA GISSING

When we left our grandparents' house for the train station, my Aunt Berta squeezed herself between my sister and me. She was always very composed and matter-of-fact, and very critical of me, the little ragamuffin of the family. But on the way to the station, she turned to me and said, 'You will write often, won't you? You know your letters will be your parents' only joy and will be read by all of us.' And I suddenly realized that she was shaking.

Then we were at the station: the platform full of concerned parents, Gestapo men everywhere, the last words of advice from our parents, the last words of love. As the train started shunting out of the station, for the first time I noticed fear on our parents' faces. At that moment they could not mask it any longer.

Until then my older sister was someone I loved, but didn't like very much, because she was the elegant one, she was the serious one, she was the clever one, and she was awfully bossy. Moreover, she always got all the new clothes and new bicycles, and I got her cast-offs. But as she stood next to me, she put her arm around me, as if sensing my feelings, and she said, 'You'll always have me. I know I'll be a poor substitute for our parents, but I'll do my best.'

From that moment on, my sister became the most important, reachable person on my new horizon. From a bossy sister, she became the best sister in the world.

HEDY EPSTEIN

When my parents put me on the train in Frankfurt, they were still smiling. On some level I think I understood they weren't really smiling, but I wanted to believe that. I know there were some last-minute instructions that I was given, but I don't really remember what they were.

As the train started to pull out of the station, my parents ran alongside the train on the platform, and I remember, sort of in my head, I heard that refrain, 'You're leaving. You're leaving.' I watched their faces, and tears were streaming down their cheeks. And I knew then: these people really love me. This is why they're sending me away. Many years later I realized that by sending me away, my parents gave me the gift of life a second time.

I had some writing paper with me, and I immediately started to write to my parents. I apologized for what I had said to them, that they were trying to get rid of me. When the train stopped in Cologne, I asked someone on the platform to put it in an envelope and put a stamp on it and mail it to my parents.

I don't remember much about the trip, or who was in the compartment with me. I don't remember getting off the train in Holland or getting on the boat. I must have had an awful lot of feelings and anxieties that I've just blocked out.

I do remember one thing. My parents had taught me some English before I left. One of the things I had learned is the bathroom is called either 'WC' or 'water closet'. At some point, after I was on the boat to England, I needed to go to the bathroom, and so I looked for either 'WC' or 'water closet'. I looked on both sides of the boat – it wasn't such a big boat – and I didn't see it.

With my very best English, I asked one of the people who worked on the boat, 'Where's the WC? Where's the water closet?' He shook his head. I thought, I can't wait until England. We got on the boat around six o'clock in the evening, and we were not going to get to England until six the next morning. Well, around midnight, I crept up on the deck, and I created a waterfall up there.

The next morning I found the bathroom, and it wasn't 'WC' or 'water closet'.

NORBERT WOLLHEIM

I accompanied the first transport. It was important for me because I had to learn what could be done in order to improve it. In the beginning it was made clear to us that the escorts could only take the youngsters to the border; there was no chance to take them to England. Luckily, this changed very soon thereafter because we were able to convince the authorities that it was in German interest to take the children all the way to London. They agreed, under one condition, that all these escorts were to return to Berlin or else the transports would come to an end.

The first transport is still vivid in my memory because when we reached the border at Bentheim, the customs officers were not the ordinary people trained in this but SS guards whom the Nazis wanted to let do something. They got on the coaches and they behaved like animals – actually, to say that is an insult to the animal world. They did not attack the children, but they tore into the luggage. Even if you had some toothpaste, they tried to open it, looking for jewels and for foreign currency and things like that. It was awful. They couldn't find a thing, but there was no possibility to interfere because these were very nasty and vicious SS people. It took them so long that they had to separate the coaches with the Jewish children so that the rest of the train could reach the ferry-port in time.

When the train arrived in Holland without the children, the ladies of the Dutch Committee waiting there couldn't understand it. One of the ladies, a very courageous woman, Truus Wijsmuller-Meijer, the wife of a prominent banker in Holland, came to Bentheim to see what had happened. She lashed out at these SS people and said, 'What's going on?' They said, 'We are doing our duty.' She said, 'You're not doing your duty, you are behaving very badly.'

They said to her, 'Lady, we have the feeling you don't like us too much.' She said, 'Yes, you're absolutely right. Personally, you might be all right, but as a group you're impossible.' I'll never forget this.

Interestingly enough, after her intervention, they stopped their vandalism. An express train which had left Berlin a few hours later arrived, the two coaches were attached to it, and the children arrived in time to make the ferry to England.

ALEXANDER GORDON

When we got to the border in northern Germany, suddenly the train stopped. Our carriage was uncoupled and pulled into a side yard. Before we knew it, the border Gestapo came on to the train and said, 'Everybody out. Take all your luggage with you.' And they took us to a hall where the luggage would be examined.

While they searched the train in case somebody was hiding something, in the hall they took their time unpacking everything on to tables, looking for new things. The children had new clothes and they didn't like that. They gave the children a tough time. The children kept crying and crying. I didn't have much to unpack.

They put us back on the train and suddenly, we were in Holland. Everyone was cheering, 'Those damn Nazis, they should drop dead!' and 'Now we are free!'

And then the train went on to the Hook of Holland. We got on to the boat, which took us to Harwich, which was not a very pleasant trip because the English Channel, whew!, is one of the worst places in wintertime to cross. We had small children, and people got seasick, and oh, oh, it was some how-do-you-do.

URSULA ROSENFELD

I remember crossing the frontier in Bentheim. Not only were the frontier guards on the Dutch side very nice, they had a contingent of ladies who brought us cocoa and Dutch zwieback, which is a sort of a dried bread which they eat. It was like manna from heaven. It was wonderful.

You suddenly felt as though you had been clad in a cloak of lead or iron, and it had been taken from you. It was a wonderful feeling of freedom. We all started to smile. I don't think any of us had smiled for a long time. It was wonderful.

I can't remember anything about the boat journey. I only remember in the morning, standing on the deck, and it was quite cold. And somebody brought us a slice of white bread. Now, white bread in Germany was a luxury – today it's the other way around. It was this typical English white bread, which most English people toast. But I thought it was wonderful. It was like cake.

And every child was given a bar of Cadbury's chocolate, which Cadbury had donated. I hadn't had chocolate for years, but I don't think I ate it. I couldn't have eaten it, it was such a precious thing to have. It was wonderful.

LORE SEGAL

In the morning when I woke up, I remember looking out the train window and seeing rivers and woods and fields and cows. Somebody had said that we had already left Austria and that we were in Germany, and I thought we can't be in Germany because these are just meadows and cows. I don't know what I thought Germany would be, but I thought it would have to be in some way dangerous, inimical. And there was just this normal landscape outside.

The drama came shortly before the end of the day when the light was already greying. The train stopped at the last station before entering Holland. This is clearly imaginary, but my impression was that as the uniformed Nazis boarded, the train sank – the same feeling you have when somebody sits down on your bed and you feel as if the bed lowers. Our helper came in and said, 'Don't worry, they are just checking one child from each carriage.'

The big girls were frightened and scared us. They said, 'Don't move.' You know what happens when you sit and you don't move. If you tense yourself enough, you begin to tremble. I remember sitting there vibrating.

I kept my head down, but I saw the two uniforms in the door. I didn't see their faces, I saw their uniforms, and their buttons, which were very bright. They pointed to one of the girls and took her away. She came back maybe ten minutes later. We stared at her, but she never told us what had happened.

The Nazis got off, and again there was this sense of relief, of settling back to the normal level. Then the train went on, and almost immediately we were across the border, out of Germany and into Holland. Then it was fascinating.

The older kids, who understood politically what was happening in a way that I did not, spilled over into our compartment. Where there had only been girls, there were now a lot of boys. There was howling, yelling, shouting, singing. It was the best party I've ever been at, although I didn't understand what it was that was happening. I was holding a big girl around the waist, and she was holding me, and they knew the songs they were singing. They were very probably Zionist songs, but I sang 'la-la, la-la' because it was so much fun.

I must have gone back to sleep, because the next thing I remember is the train having arrived at its destination. Somebody lifted me down from the train and put me on firm ground. They put the rucksack on my back and the suitcase in my hand. Then I remember finding myself inside a boat, and somebody leading me to my cabin. There was a wonderful white bed with white sheets.

A big black steward brought me something in a cup. I said, 'Coffee?' and he said, 'Tea', which was strange to me because in Vienna you didn't put milk in tea. I remember not wanting him to go away, so I asked him in whatever English I had if I was going to throw up. He said, no, what you do is put your head down and close your eyes, and you don't open them until we're at the other side. I remember him being very large and very nice. I can imagine him now looking at this child in the bed. He was very dear.

I did exactly what he said, except first I cleaned my teeth to please my absent mother. I also remember folding my clothes in a way I'd *never* folded my clothes at home.

Kinder on train at Dutch border

The next morning we arrived in Harwich and the British press came on board and took pictures of all the children. For the life of me, I would have liked to have a picture taken of me, but they wouldn't notice me. I tried looking as if I was asleep. I tried looking as if I was sad. I tried hopping up and down. I couldn't get anybody to take any notice.

EVA HAYMAN

I have only a vague memory of getting on to the ferry in Holland, but I have a very vivid memory of waking up and seeing the sea for the first time, with the sunrise on it, and thinking how beautiful it was.

I can't remember if I woke Vera up or if she woke herself, and we looked at the sun on the water, and we wished our parents could see it. It was only the English Channel, but it seemed a long, long way from home in 1939. It was a mixture of elation, because we saw something so beautiful as the sea. Yet within me was this fear, which never left me for those six years, fear for those we left at home.

Kinder arriving at Harwich, England, 2 December 1938

Chapter Five

INTO THE ARMS OF STRANGERS

*'People wonder how anyone whose life was saved
could qualify how he was saved. He should just be
happy to be saved and take anything. But real life isn't
like that, particularly when you're eight years old.'*

ROBERT SUGAR

NORBERT WOLLHEIM

It was my task to select the escorts for the transports. It was a difficult responsibility. Anybody who had a chance to go to England wanted to take it. Friends and relatives would urge them to stay and say you're stupid to go back. So we needed escorts of a special calibre and I was very, very careful in selecting them.

A couple of times I travelled to England to find out what could be done to make things better. The first transport I accompanied all the way to London was in February 1939. I had relatives there and they pressed me to stay. I said, 'I can't do it. It's impossible because that would stop all the work for these children. How can I take that responsibility?' They couldn't understand. It wasn't easy to return, but after the first time, it became almost routine.

On one of those occasions when I was the transport leader, we came to Harwich and I heard my name. The customs official said, 'Mr Wollheim, there is a problem.'

'What is it?'

He said, 'This young man brought a violin, which is very, very expensive. This is not an ordinary violin and it's not allowed in.' Since children couldn't bring more than ten marks with them, parents sometimes sent them with valuable objects like cameras or musical instruments that they could sell later. The Chamber of Commerce in England had brought this to the attention of the government as unfair

Kind plays violin on the train

competition because the children would sell the goods for whatever they could get for them.

I said, 'Well, don't forget, these young people take music lessons and obviously he liked music very much so he took his violin along.' This didn't sit well with the official.

So I gambled. I said to the boy, 'Are you able to play something?' He said, 'Sure.' I asked the officer if he would like to see if the boy knows music. The boy started and he was playing 'God Save the King'.

All of a sudden everything around us became very quiet. The customs official had to stop work because, after all, this was the national anthem. And that boy, he couldn't be stopped. He played all three stanzas. When he was finished, I asked the fellow, 'Are you now convinced, sir, that he likes music?' And he said, 'Yes!' so the boy got his violin into England.

On another transport where I was leader we had a different problem. We were under very strict regulations to see to it that only children up to the age of seventeen came into England. We were going through the papers on the ferry, preparing them for immigration authorities, and one of my escorts, a friend of mine from the youth movement, said, 'Norbert, we have a problem here.' He showed me the card. 'This boy is eighteen years old.' I looked at the card and it was true. I said, 'For goodness' sake, after all our work in Berlin, how did this happen?'

Well, it was too late to find an answer. The question now was: what are we going to do? I called the escorts together. We went into a huddle. There were two opinions. One was that we should throw ourselves at the mercy of the immigration officers. The other, which I shared, was we should say there was a mistake made by the German police.

We asked the fellow to come down from his bunk. When I saw him, my heart sank because his head was shaven, which meant he had been released from a concentration camp. He came from Dachau, and to send him back to Germany would mean death for him. Obviously he realized that something was wrong, and he was shaking like a leaf. So I said, 'We cannot let it go. We have to get him through.' The majority then joined me and said, 'All right, we will try to say it was a mistake of the German police.' So we told the fellow that, when he was asked, he should say he was born a year later.

We landed in Harwich, all dead tired, and went through the usual process. All of a sudden I heard, 'Mr Wollheim, kindly see the supervisor.' I knew immediately what was going on. The supervisor said, 'Sir, there must have been a mistake. I can't admit this gentleman because he's over eighteen, and that's beyond the age specified under the rules and regulations.'

I pretended to be absolutely flabbergasted. I assured him, 'That can't be. There must be a mistake.'

'Who could have made the mistake?'

'It was most probably the German police.'

But he said, 'The German police are well known for their accuracy.'

Kind arriving at Harwich, England, December 1938

I told him, 'Sir, not any more because now the Nazis have put in many of their own people just to give them work, and it's no longer the same. Let this young fellow tell you for himself.'

The boy came and stuttered when he was born. The admitting immigration officer looked at him, saw his shaven head and that he

Kinder in arrival hall at Harwich, England, 2 December 1938

was shaking. He looked at me, he looked at the boy, he looked at the paper. There was a long moment of silence in which a decision had to be made about the life of a human being. He said to me, 'Sir, could you guarantee that this is a mistake of the German police?' I said, 'Definitely.'

Now he knew that I was lying, and I knew that he knew that I was lying. But he was also overcome by seeing this boy, this unhappy, lost soul, and he knew that if he didn't admit him to the United Kingdom, something terrible might happen to him. So he took a stand and stamped 'Admit' on the papers. And he saved that boy's life.

I went four or five times to England and was supposed to go again on the transport that left Germany at the end of August 1939. By then the political situation was becoming very serious. My wife and I both realized that war could come any day, so I put somebody else, who wasn't married, in charge of the transport. If war would come, we would be cut off from the outside world and I didn't dare to leave my parents and my family alone. My wife was pregnant then and, a few months later, in November we had our child, a boy. So in August I found someone else to take my place and escort the children to England.

LORRAINE ALLARD

On the journey to England what I remember very clearly is that everybody I spoke to on that train knew where they were going. They were going to Auntie Joan, or Uncle So-and-so, or this family they'd met, or this family they'd heard of. I had no idea where I was going. Not a thought. Nobody had told me. My parents didn't know either.

Then came the arrival at Liverpool Street Station, at 6 a.m., still dark, and that was a bit of a disaster. Everybody on our trip was being picked up, and I wasn't. I remember sitting in an enormous arrival hall. It was so big that I couldn't identify anyone entering it at the other end. I just sat there, waiting. Nobody came to me. Nobody talked to me. I think I must have sat an hour. It may have been longer, I don't know.

Then came two people who were my guardians, and they introduced themselves. They explained that they lived in Lincoln. They didn't speak one word of German, and I didn't speak one word of English. If they said 'Lincoln', that could have been anywhere. Never heard of the place. They took me under their arms, so to speak, and we got on the train to Lincoln. That was it.

My foster-parents, who saved my life, which I've never forgotten, were completely different from my family. They had an extremely unhappy marriage. I came across shouting and arguing and throwing things at each other, which were all foreign to me. They were kind to me. They were as kind as they were to their son. But affection didn't exist in the house.

My mother sent me off saying, 'Whoever's going to be good enough to take you in and give you a home, you must treat as temporary mother.' When we arrived back from Liverpool Street, and we all went to bed in the evening, I went up to put my arms around my foster mother and she pushed me away.

The words were, 'That's sissy.' She may have said something else. She may have said, 'We don't do this. That's sissy.' But the words 'that's sissy' have never left me.

A few years later I found out why they had taken me in. Their seventeen-year-old son was in love with a non-Jewish girl. The whole idea at that point was to bring a Jewish girl over from Germany whom he could perhaps fall in love with and marry. When we found this out, it was an absolute giggle to him and to me because we had really developed a lovely relationship like brother and sister. He used to walk around and say, 'This is my sister. This is my sister.'

In the end his girlfriend became Jewish and they did get married. I actually helped them. I used to cover up for them when they were out together. But the basic idea of why they brought me over at the age of fourteen is a bit horrifying.

MARIAM COHEN
Kurt Fuchel's Foster-Mother, Norwich, England

There was a meeting in Norwich of a few Jewish congregants, and other non-Jewish people. They said, 'Any offers to take children?' And my husband and I said yes. Then some photographs were handed around, and I remember there were some boy twins. Oh, my heart ached, but we couldn't afford it in those days. We didn't know what was going to happen. So that's when we took Kurt.

Mariam and Percy Cohen, Norwich, England

I mean it was a reaching-out. You wanted to do something. My sister took a little girl, Erika, and my mother took a little girl, Lizbeth. We didn't choose really. We just took as they were handed out.

I remember motoring to Harwich to pick up Kurt. We got up at dawn – a bitterly cold morning. My sister and her husband came with us. We saw the ship coming in, and then we saw these poor little things straggling off the gangplank. They had been sick, and were dirty, and they smelled of ship and seasickness. And we brought them home.

STOKE NEWINGTON TOWN HALL

(Church Street, Stoke Newington),

MONDAY, DECEMBER 12th, 8 p.m.

•

REPRESENTATIVE SPEAKERS

TO BE SILENT MEANS TO ACQUIESCE

SAVE THE CHILDREN

Advertisement from the *Jewish Chronicle*, December 1938

My sister's little girl, Erika, never really recovered. She cried for three nights, 'Mutti, Mutti, Mutti', and they had her in the middle of their bed, the two of them, but they couldn't comfort her.

Kurt came in, though, and he didn't cry, not at all – not at all – I couldn't understand it. I just put my arm around him and had him on my knee. When we got home, my maid, Selena, was there and she said to me, 'Can't we change it?' He was filthy, and smelled of sick and everything. Anyhow, we gave him a bath, and threw his clothes out. We outfitted him in grey flannels, and shoes and school socks. And he began to settle in.

Kurt was very, very good. He liked the sweet things, and my son John liked the savoury. I remember bathing them every night. My John was very fair-skinned with blond hair, and Kurt was olive-skinned with black hair, black eyes. The two in the bath together, they were so different. But they got on very well together. I noticed, though, every night when it was dark, Kurt would come down the stairs and he'd check that the door was locked. That is one thing I remember vividly.

Another time I remember his parents sent a big suitcase with some of his toys – this must be before they left Vienna. My husband took it up into the bedroom and then Kurt went in and shut the door, and my John was left outside. And my husband said to Kurt, 'Now don't you ever do that again. You're sharing everything because we share with you.' From that day on, he was never, never any trouble at all. A loved and happy member of our family.

KURT FUCHEL

The family that took me in were the Cohens. Mr Cohen, whom I called Uncle Percy, had been a violinist and band leader until his marriage, but now, with his brothers and a sister, ran a small factory which made women's coats. His wife, Aunt Mariam to me, was a housewife who also did some volunteer work.

Percy and Mariam picked me up at the boat at Harwich, and they took me back home. I remember walking into their house. At the entrance stood the maid, who I would learn later actually ran the household, and halfway up the stairs sat John, this little boy of five, looking at his new brother.

Kurt Fuchel (*left*) and John Cohen, Norwich, England

I guess I was scared, but after I came in, I was taken upstairs. My grubby clothes after three days of travel were torn off me – burned, I learned later – and I was scrubbed from head to toe, and dressed in English clothes. Then the family got together for a chicken dinner, and that I remember. That's a language I could understand. And I started to feel more at ease.

I learned English by being sent to a German man, rather old, who lived a few houses down on the same street. He was tall and thin, with thick glasses, and looked very threatening. Maybe I thought he was a Nazi – I was terrified of him. In fact, I was so terrified that I learned English very quickly so I wouldn't have to see him again. Six weeks later, I wrote to my parents in English: 'I no longer speak German.' I never have, and I've never been able to re-learn it. I much regret it now, but that's what happened.

After lessons with this German man, I went to a small, private school – in the American sense. It was by no means a great educational institution, but John and I went there, and it was probably just right for me at the time. The teachers were very nice to me. They understood my situation. I started to fit in.

Initially, of course, I cried for my parents, and Mariam took me on her knee and consoled me. Afterwards, when I understood a bit more, I don't think I gave them very much thought, except that I was able to write to them, for the first two years actually, because they had gotten out of Austria through Italy and into the South of France. During that time, we could correspond. I remember Percy standing over me once and saying, 'You will not go out and play until you've written to your parents.' I had to be made to sit down and write, otherwise I wouldn't have.

URSULA ROSENFELD

We arrived at Liverpool Street Station and were taken across the street to a gymnasium in the basement. We sat on benches there and waited for the people to come who were going to take a child into their home. Gradually the hall became emptier. Finally, there were about five children left, including Hella and me, and we thought nobody wants us.

Then there was a frantic effort to find the five of us accommodations. Eventually they found us a hostel near Kensington where we could spend the night. The following morning they asked us to go to the Refugee Committee in Bloomsbury. I thought I could speak English. I'd had English at school for two years, and I always liked the language. But I suddenly realized I couldn't speak, I couldn't understand. They explained to us the underground and its intricacies and wrote down exactly where we had to go. We had to change at Leicester Square, and I said, 'Is this Lei-ces-ter Square?' pronouncing it phonetically. Of course, people didn't know what you were talking about. But we got there.

The Refugee Committee at Bloomsbury House was utter chaos. It was manned by a number of voluntary bodies, who hadn't got properly co-ordinated. We waited there all day before they finally decided to send us to stay with a widow near Brighton, in Sussex. We were just given our ticket; the journey we had to negotiate on our own. Meanwhile, we realized that our luggage had got lost, but they assured us, 'Don't worry, we will send it on.' And three months later it did come.

Perhaps my mother had had an instinct that something like this might happen, because when we were at the railway station in Hamburg, she had tucked a swimsuit in each of our rucksacks. For the next three months, these swimsuits were our lifesavers. We had no money to buy clothes, and every Saturday we would don our swimsuits and wash our underwear and our blouse, and wait for them to dry so that we could put them on again. I know today this doesn't seem very hygienic – to wash your clothes once a week – but it was better than nothing.

When we got to Brighton, a station official came up and said there'd been a lady waiting there for several hours. She said, if two children come, would he put them in a taxi, which he did. Eventually we arrived at the woman's house. She opened the door and her face fell. I was fourteen by that time, and Hella was fifteen, and we were as tall as we are now. Here she'd expected two small children, and there were these quite big girls.

She said, 'Well, I'm sorry, but I've only got one bed.' It was a single bed, and it wasn't particularly wide either. She had thought she could put one child at one end, and the other child at the other. Now, my sister is a rather restless sleeper, so for the first two months or so we had rather disturbed nights, not that it mattered much because when we arrived it was still warm, and quite often one of us could sleep on the floor.

The woman who took us in was the widow of a colonial official who had drowned in Egypt. She had one son, but unfortunately he'd died of TB, so she was on her own and lived on a small pension. I think she wanted to take some children in and hoped the money from the Refugee Committee would add to her pension.

She was very nice to us, really, but she had a very small appetite. Although she was only in her late fifties, at the time I thought she was very old. She didn't really understand that teenagers needed to eat more than she did. Besides, she always told us that the Refugee Committee didn't pay her enough for us.

I think they were allowing us sixpence a week pocket money, but we were so embarrassed that she didn't get enough money for us, we said, 'Oh, we don't want it', which made it, of course, difficult for us even to buy postage stamps to write home. The ten German marks we were allowed to take with us from Germany converted into twenty shillings, which did not go very far.

That was August 1939. It was still a month before war broke out. And I wanted to write to my mother nearly every day. I did write to her, but we weren't always able to post the letters, because we couldn't afford the stamps. Of course, once war broke out in the beginning of September, that was the end of the mail.

VERA GISSING

At Liverpool Street Station, we were ushered into a great big hall, full of benches, and there we sat with labels around our necks, waiting for our foster-parents or, for the lucky ones, relatives to claim us. Name after name was called. Then my sister disappeared through the side door, but came back and pushed a piece of paper into my hand and said, 'Look, Vera, this is my address. Send me yours the minute you arrive at your destination.'

Slowly the hall was emptied. Eventually it was only me left sitting in that great empty hall. I was filled with incredible panic. You can imagine: I had no address, no knowledge of English. I was so frightened what would become of me. Perhaps the family had changed their mind. Perhaps they didn't want me.

It was a tremendous relief when the leader of the transport came to me and said, 'Don't worry, your foster-family can't come for you for a couple of days, but we'll look after you.'

Kind in England

I was then taken to a very posh house, which even had a lift and a butler. I believe it belonged to some high church dignitary, bishop or an archbishop, but I've never been able to find out who it was.

The people in this house had twin daughters, I was told, and the companion of the twin daughters happened to be Czech, although she spoke extremely bad Czech. I was horrified, and with the cheek of an eleven-year-old, I asked her, 'How is it that you have forgotten your Czech?' because she'd only been in England a year. She said, 'You wait, my dear, when you've been here a year, you will probably have forgotten every word.'

This filled me with horror, because I thought, how could I go back home to my family and not be able to speak to them in my language? It was that experience which made me determined that I would read my books from 'A' to 'Z', and 'Z' to 'A', and write avidly in my diary, and talk to my doll and, through the sun and the stars, to my parents in my own language. I vowed I would not forget a single word.

Two days after my arrival, I was taken to a house in Bloomsbury. I was left in an empty room, where there was no furniture, just a chair. I stood by the chair, shaking at the knees, wondering who it would be that would open that door and come to claim me. It was an incredible feeling of curiosity and dread at the same time.

Then the door opened, and there stood this little lady, barely taller than myself. Her hat sat all askew on her head, and her mackintosh was buttoned up all wrong. She peered at me from behind a big pair of glasses. Suddenly, her face broke into the most wonderful smile, and she ran to me and hugged me, and spoke to me words I did not understand then, but they were, 'You shall be loved.' And those were the most important words any child in a foreign land, away from her family, could hear. And loved I was.

It was much later, when I was grown up really, and interested in the background of the transports, that I asked my foster-father, Daddy Rainford – they asked me to call them 'Mummy Rainford' and 'Daddy Rainford' – why they had chosen me to be in their family. He answered, 'I knew I could not save the world. I knew I could not stop the war from starting. But I knew I could save one human life. And as Chamberlain broke his pledge to Czechoslovakia, and as Jews were in the greatest danger, I decided it must be a Czech Jewish child.'

They gave their daughter, Dorothy, who was two years older than I, the job of choosing which little girl she would like for a sister. They were given a postcard with several photos and details of children and

Dorothy chose me because she liked my sad smile. I looked sad then, though I was a very happy child.

Some people may think it awful that siblings were split apart, that I ended up with a family in Lancashire, whereas Eva was in a boarding school in Bournemouth. Much later I asked Nicholas Winton why he didn't find a family for us both. He said, 'Had I waited for a family to take you both, you probably wouldn't be here today.' It was a tremendous undertaking for a family to agree to take a child as their own for an unknown period of time – to finance that child from their own pocket, and educate that child. To take two children would have been double that undertaking. There were very few people who were willing to do that.

I was very grateful to be in a loving family like the Rainfords, but when I arrived in England, I really felt as if I was being watched. I felt as if I was a representative, not just of my family, but almost of my nation because I was so patriotic, and because hardly anything was known about Czechoslovakia in England in those days. So I tried very hard to be on my best behaviour.

The fact that my father gave me the diary also made me want to write in it things that he would be proud of. I tried very, very hard to be sensible, like my sister: I could never stop being a tomboy, and I could never become a serious young eleven-year-old. But I did do my best to be a little girl my parents would approve of.

In fact, just a couple of weeks before the war, I suddenly felt that a letter was needed to show, particularly my father, who didn't have much faith in my behaviour, that he could rely on me. I can't remember exactly what I wrote, but it was obvious the words were something he hankered for, because he said he was so proud of me, he danced mother around the kitchen.

In the end, he said in a letter which I've got to this day, 'I could not believe that my little tomboyish Veruska could write such a serious and such a much-needed letter because it was written by a very sensible girl.'

EVA HAYMAN

I hated leaving Vera at the station, not knowing what would happen to her, but I was told by whoever looked after us not to worry, she'd be all right, that her guardian would come for her.

I knew that I was going to a school near Bournemouth in Dorset. The person who came for me was a German teacher, and I could speak German and communicate with her. I didn't speak any English at this time. I thought I could say a few words until I tried.

There was a film with Deanna Durbin that I had seen once about a British boarding school, and in the back of my mind I thought that this one will be the same. In some ways it was very similar. The people who owned the school owned three different ones. There was a posh one, mine was the middle one, and there was another one in Hastings. It was the headmistress of the school who guaranteed to look after me. The owners gave me free education and board.

When I arrived at the school, there were all these girls in their uniforms, very polite and very nice, very kind. I couldn't understand a word they said. I was given my bed, and the curtains could be drawn, to give me some privacy. I remember the first thing I did was put a picture of my parents on the side table so that I could say goodnight to them.

The first three months before war broke out, we could still write home, so I could share my experiences with my parents, and receive their very frequent letters. So I didn't feel quite so isolated. Before we left Čelákovice, my mother had said to me, if a time came when they couldn't write any more, they would send their love by the moon and the stars. After the war started, when they couldn't write any more, every time I saw the moon and the stars, I thought of them.

HEDY EPSTEIN

We were taken into this huge hall at Liverpool Street Station and told they would call our names alphabetically. Since my name at that time started with a 'W', I thought, well, that's going to take a long time. I sat on my suitcase, and I must have fallen asleep at some point. When I woke up there was hardly anybody left. I started to cry because, I thought, nobody's here to pick me up, what am I going to do now?

Somebody saw that I was crying and came over and asked who I was. They said, 'Well, we've been looking for you.' And there was somebody waiting for me, a Mrs Mayer. She had such a sweet, kind face, which gave me some confidence. But she started talking to me in

English, almost non-stop. I had no idea what she was saying. I understood, though, that I was to follow her.

We went into the underground. I had never even seen an escalator before. Here I had my suitcase and all kinds of other things that I was carrying with me. How can I get on the escalator with them?

Mrs Mayer just went ahead and down the escalator. It was a huge, steep escalator, and, from down below, she was motioning me to come. But what do I do with my luggage? I can't hold my luggage and hold on to the sides of the escalator at the same time.

Other people came, and I motioned them to get on. Finally, I put my suitcases and all my things on the escalator and saw them disappear somewhere into the underworld. Then I just took a huge jump and got on to the escalator and held on to both sides. My knees were shaking, but I made it. Mrs Mayer was waiting for me down there and she had my luggage.

A roaring red train arrived, we got on the train, travelled for ever, I thought, and got out at the last station, which was Edgware. Then we took a taxi to the place where I was going to be living, which was with the Rose family. Mrs Rose showed me to my room, which I was going to be sharing with one of their daughters. They had three daughters: one was about nineteen at the time, one was about my age, and the other was two or three years younger.

I immediately started to unpack my suitcase, and I had to shake out everything because there were stamps everywhere. Soon afterwards, the two younger children arrived home from school, and I remember their laughing and giggling as they watched me because there were stamps all over that room.

The Rose family spoke some Yiddish, which is a little bit like German, so it helped to communicate with them at the beginning. They said that because I had been starving in Germany – which really wasn't true at all – I needed to slowly increase my daily diet. They understood that now that I was in England I would see lots of food and I would want to eat everything, but it wasn't healthy for me.

My diet consisted of a piece of toast and butter, and a cup of tea for breakfast; two more pieces of toast and butter, and a cup of tea for lunch; and two more pieces of toast and butter, and a cup of tea for dinner. On Sundays Mr Rose used to get up before everyone else and he'd serve a cup of tea and a cookie to everyone in bed. So, on Sunday morning, I got an extra cup of tea and a cookie.

I have no idea why they did this, but they certainly ate and, when they were eating, I was sent out of the house, into the backyard. I never told my parents that I was starving because I felt I would only worry them, and there was nothing they could do about it. I wanted to protect them from that. I never told anyone else either.

I recall one Sunday the Roses were going away somewhere, and I was not going with them. They had had this wonderful Sunday dinner at noon. It smelled so good. When they had gone, I went into the pantry and there was some left-over roast beef and all kinds of other things. I cut off a piece of roast beef and a piece of bread, and I bit into it. Oh, that was good.

Then the door opened and they came back. They'd forgotten something. I had a piece of meat in one hand, and a piece of bread in the other. They told me how terrible I was, that I was a thief, and if my parents knew this, they would be very upset. They took away what I had in my hand. What I had in my mouth, I was allowed to swallow. Then they left again, and warned me not to touch anything. I did go back in the pantry and I just looked, and I sniffed the aroma of whatever was there, but I didn't take anything else. I was afraid that they might actually let my parents know.

After I was there about eight weeks, Mrs Mayer called one day around four-thirty in the afternoon, and asked me how things were. Other people had asked me how I was, and I'd said, 'I'm fine.' But when Mrs Mayer asked me, for the first time I was honest and said, 'I'm hungry.'

She said, 'Well, what time is supper?'

I said, 'It's not going to make any difference.'

She said, 'What do you mean?'

I was afraid to answer her because what if Mrs Rose heard, but she must have suspected something was wrong, because she said, 'Why don't you come and have lunch with us on Saturday, and then we can talk.'

I said, 'I can't come.'

'Why not?'

I knew that I would have to use the underground to get there, and I said, 'I don't have any money.'

She said, 'Don't you get an allowance?' I didn't understand what that was, so I couldn't really answer her. She said, 'Let me talk to Mrs Rose.' Then I was really afraid: what if she tells Mrs Rose what I just said to her?

After she had talked to Mrs Rose, I was put back on the phone and told that Mrs Rose would give me directions and car fare to Mrs Mayer's home and tell me how to get there. That Saturday, when I got to Mrs Mayer's home, I ate non-stop, everything that was put in front of me. Mrs Mayer said, 'You know you can eat as much as you want to, but I'm really afraid you're going to be sick.'

I said, 'Well, I have to eat ahead, because tomorrow, and the next day, and the day after, I'm going to get toast and tea again.'

After that she told me she would try to find another family for me. I stayed two more weeks with the Rose family and then for a few days at Mrs Mayer's home before she found another family for me, which was also in Edgware, which meant I could continue at the same school. This was the Simmons family. They were also Jewish and had two children, David, who was thirteen, and Janice, who was six.

When I moved I had to tell my parents why, because until then I had told them everything was fine. But if everything was fine, why would I be moving someplace else? So I had to tell them the truth.

That created a real problem for my parents and for me, because there was a lack of trust then: could my parents really trust me to tell them the truth? Even though I wrote again and again and said, 'Everything is fine now and it really is', my mother still worried that maybe there was some other problem that I wasn't talking about. It took quite a while, I think, before they firmly believed that everything was really all right with the Simmons family.

ROBERT SUGAR

I arrived at the London station, and my mother just picked me up and took me where she was working. Of course, you're supposed to register. People are still looking for me there. She just took me.

Then I stayed in this very cold – oh, God! – this cold, fancy house in England where they were exploiting the European maids. If you've ever been the child of a maid, you know that maids are not supposed to have children. They're not welcome. You can't stay there.

So I had to go somewhere else. We searched around London and I came to this really poor house, which was wealthier than we were in Vienna, but the smells were different, and the people were different. They were Sephardic Jews, and everything was just different. I began to cry, 'Mutti, I don't want to stay here.' In Vienna, I didn't cry.

Then – I don't know how these decisions were made – but it was decided I would be sent to Belfast, to the Jewish refugee hostel. On the journey I made up my mind not to throw up because on the first ferry ride from Holland to England, I got seasick. My great hero was Captain Cook. I wanted to go to sea, and the first night I said: here goes another dream. I can't even be a sailor. So on the trip to Belfast, I made up my mind, I'm not going to throw up, even though it was a pretty rough sea.

We came to the hostel in Belfast. When you see your life has been saved, and you're brought into a hostel which is clean, and there's food there, and there are other children there, how could you not be happy in that place? But to me it smelled of orphanage, which, of course, in due course it became. And orphanages, those things frighten every child out of its wits. I mean, Charles Dickens, to be in a workhouse, to be in an orphanage.

People wonder how anyone whose life was saved could qualify how he was saved. He should just be happy to be saved and take anything. But real life isn't like that, particularly when you're eight years old.

My very good friend Gert has an older sister, and she wrote an unpublished diary. She wrote things which as boys we wouldn't even permit ourselves to think. She was three or four years older than we were and sickly a lot when she was young. She wrote in her diary, 'I would give a kingdom for a kind word.' We were not able to articulate this, that we were treated in such an unkind way.

The Belfast committee people who had established the hostel, and who rightfully congratulated themselves about it, came to visit us like sponsors, like patrons, like we were not real kids to them. I felt that we were among strangers.

There was a religious angle to this too. One of the first nights we were there the chief rabbi of Belfast invited us to his house. He was a very dignified man, very handsome, with a top hat, the way a chief rabbi of any place should be. We hoped there would be something there for us. We were hungry – not starving, but hungry. Perhaps there'll be cake there! Perhaps there'll be something special, kindness perhaps.

And there was a cold room, with cold fruit on the table, and the rabbi told us that it was our fault that Hitler came to Vienna, because there was a synagogue there with an organ in it. We understood what he meant, that we were assimilationists, and not really Orthodox Jews. That was really a slap. It was our fault!

I was in an unusual position at the orphanage. I was not only the youngest, I was also the only one there with a mother. I don't think I rubbed it in, but it was something special I had. I was not sharing the fate of everyone.

My mother came to visit me. I was looking forward to her visit, but she was a different mother from the one I knew. She was nice to my friend Harry. He was from Vienna, too, a few years older than I, but very streetwise. He had taken me under his wing at the hostel, like an older brother. My mother took us out, had our photos taken at a famous Belfast photo studio. After a while, though, I began to feel uncomfortable that I had a mother. I wanted her to be everyone's mother. I didn't want to be special. But that's not the sort of mother she was.

It came time for her to leave, and all the things which had gone on before just welled up in me and I wept . . . like you see in the movies. My heart was breaking. I felt abandoned. She was leaving and I couldn't do anything about it.

Robert Sugar's parents, Greta and Sandor Sugar

She came back once again and this time she tried to get a job in Belfast as a domestic in one of the Jewish families there. It didn't last. She felt exploited. I think she was. These domestics were always under the control of the government and people could threaten them and say, 'If you don't do this, we won't sign for your work permit.' I don't know the exact details, but she left again.

This time I remember feeling a sort of relief. I just couldn't live in two worlds any more. To visit your mother in some fancy house and not be allowed out of the kitchen. At that point I wanted to be with the other kids.

The first time she left something broke in me, I guess. The second time – it's difficult to reconstruct completely how you felt after sixty years – but it was more a feeling of giving in, or relief, or both together. Anyway, life got a bit easier afterwards.

Then in the beginning of the summer, liberation came: they decided to send all the kids to a farm in the country. This Belfast community was cold as hell to the kids, but very far-seeing. They had leased a farm for twenty years where refugees could be self-sufficient.

Robert Sugar (*bottom left*) at refugee settlement farm, Millisle, County Down, Northern Ireland, June 1939

A whole group of us went to this farm. I was nine years old by then. Now what nine-year-old doesn't want to live in a tent, in a camp bed, as opposed to a hostel in the middle of a city? So I loved it. The younger you were, the more you loved it. The older kids were immediately put to work, real hard farm labour. The younger kids were put to work pretty soon, too, weeding these long rows of cabbages and scallions, which the Zionist *chalutzim** had planted. We didn't work the whole day, or every day of the week – I mean it was bearable – but at night I would go to sleep and I'd see these rows of carrots and beetroots dancing before my eyes. So this is an ambivalent memory now.

Even though I've showed off to my kids about it, what a tough kid I was, how I was out in the fields at the age of nine, when I read these stories of child labourers in India, working from morning to night, this is really what I identify with. If I would have thought of some adult running after my son when he was nine, yelling 'You crooked dog' if he missed a few weeds, I would have killed that guy. So there is a difference between my memory of this and how I feel about it now, like prisoners who are very proud that they survived, but nevertheless don't want to relive the experience.

JACK HELLMAN

We arrived in England and were taken to the de Rothschild estate. My first impression of Waddesdon Manor was it was like a dream, like a castle I'd seen in pictures. It was so humongous, I couldn't possibly reconcile the idea of just two people living in it. The Cedars was the servants' house. Twenty-six of us lived in the Cedars, three or four to a room.

The Cedars, Jack Hellman's home at Waddesdon Manor

* Zionist agricultural pioneers.

The first day that we got to the Cedars, the first thing we did was throw a soccer ball on the lawn and kick it around. The local boys came to see what was all of a sudden being brought into their little village. When it was time for dinner, they said, 'We'll see you tomorrow.' I was so excited. I was absolutely so exuberant. I ran into my house mother and told her, 'Somebody who's not Jewish wants to see us tomorrow.' I mean, we were absolutely just flabbergasted.

ALEXANDER GORDON

We arrived in Harwich and were taken to a holiday camp at Lowestoft that had no heat. It was raining, freezing cold, and we were in these little huts.

I was with all boys who were my age. After sitting there a couple of days, a notice came: they are looking for fifty Orthodox volunteers to go to Leeds. Everything comes back to religion. I said, 'Anything – let's get out of here because it's winter.' It was cold, and we were freezing.

Fifty of us, including me and my friend Jacob Hammer, from Hamburg, went to Leeds. There I got my first impression of English people and my surroundings, because up until then we didn't have any contact with anybody outside the Kindertransport.

They made a big fuss when we arrived, because we were the only children from Germany to come to Leeds. The press was there taking pictures. They organized a hostel, but it wasn't ready, so they commandeered a whole hotel for us. They organized a swimming party. They took us to movies – Paul Robeson gave a performance at one of the first shows. We were taken to get new shoes and a suit. It was wonderful.

The good thing about life is you remember all the good things that happen to you, but you forget the bad things, and you have to make an effort to really remember them. Our life was like being in limbo. We didn't do anything. We were just sitting there, wondering, 'What is the future? What are we going to do?'

After a while, Jacob came to me and said, 'They're looking for two boys to go to London. You want to come with me?' I said, 'Yes, anything – just let's get out.' I didn't want to stay in a hostel. I'd been in an orphanage for nine years; I had enough of this living in crowds of kids.

We came to the committee of the Kindertransport in London. They didn't expect us, so they put us up at the YMCA. The first morning I came down for breakfast and they served us something. I said, 'What kind of fish is this?' The server looked at me and said, 'What's the matter? You don't recognize bacon?' That was the first time I had bacon in my life.

We were sent to a house in Stamford Hill, north London. There was no personal contact with any people, except going to the synagogue. And suddenly, I met my old English teacher. His English was terrible! I spoke better English than he did.

LORE SEGAL

We were taken into a huge glass and iron hall and told to find our suitcases. I suppose it didn't occur to me that all I had to do was find number 152. Seeing the rows and rows of suitcases, it seemed an improbability that I would ever happen upon mine, so I sat down on the nearest suitcase and this was another time I howled. I thought I was howling about my distress at not knowing how to find my suitcase, but, of course, it was about other things. Finally a grown-up took me by the hand and led me to my luggage.

That was a full day of waiting. You waited to be processed. You waited to find the suitcase. You waited for the buses to come. They were big double-decker buses and took us to Dovercourt Camp, a summer holiday camp that had little streets of huts. The children were assigned to these different huts, four little ones and one older one to each cottage as I remember.

The memorable part of this camp experience was that that night the temperature dropped radically. It was one of the coldest winters in history. The water froze in our sink so that we couldn't wash and couldn't clean our teeth. In the morning we went for breakfast to this big hall made out of glass, and the snow seeped in between the panes, which was very exciting.

They served us curious food – kippers. I mean, what little Austrian-Jewish child had ever heard of kippers? Here was this salty shoe

Refugee children arriving in London

leather on our plates, and it had snow on it. It was pretty interesting. Meanwhile they were putting in stoves in various parts of the hall to warm it up somehow.

They did try and keep us busy. I remember they brought in a strongman who demonstrated wiggling his stomach muscles and showing the width of his biceps. And the mayor came and addressed us without any of us, of course, understanding what he said.

While we were sitting around the stoves, always with our coats on and with our little gloves on, there would come groups of people to choose children to take away with them. I remember sitting there, writing a letter to my parents, and one of these ladies in a fur coat bent down to me and asked me if I would like to come to Liverpool. I said, 'Yes, I would like to come to Liverpool.'

She said to the other woman with her, 'Oh, she speaks English.' By 'speaking English', I could understand, 'Would you like to come to Liverpool?' and could say yes. Then they said to me, 'Are you Orthodox?' and I said yes. They wrote that down. It was understood that I was going to go to Liverpool the next day. When the ladies had gone, I wrote in my letter to my parents, 'By the way, what is "Orthodox"?'

The next day there were twenty little girls assembled in the great eating hall earlier than the other children because there were cars waiting for us. We were taken to a train – twenty little girls going to be distributed to foster families in Liverpool.

When we got to Liverpool, they took us to a big house, where we sat at long tables and ate a very curious thing – what the Americans call Jello and the English jelly. I had never seen such a thing before in my life; some was green, and some was red, and it wiggled. While I was eating it, I felt people standing behind me. One of them was one of the ladies who had brought us over from the camp, the other was a huge fur coat. And over the fur coat were these big glasses. And around the glasses was a lot of hair.

I now marvel that my English was up to understanding what she said, but I certainly heard her saying, 'We want one around ten years old – old enough to do for herself, but not too old to learn nice ways.' I did not want to go home with this prickly fur coat, and I looked up and said, 'I'm not ten. I'm half past ten.' And the woman said, 'That's OK.'

The first night in the new house was curious. Everybody had come to see the new child. It was a big Victorian house, and all the lights were on, and I was taken inside and sat down in front of one of these strange square holes in the wall with a fire in it. That was another thing I'd never seen before, because in my Vienna childhood we had tile stoves.

Somebody brought me hot soup, which I said I didn't want. Eventually they took me up one flight of stairs and then another. They wanted me to have a bath and I was embarrassed. I didn't want to get undressed in front of these strangers, so they let me go to bed without a bath.

The next morning I woke up and I was alone. All the activity of the night before was gone, and there was this silent house. I didn't know what I was supposed to do or if I was allowed to go down. I got myself dressed and walked down the first flight of stairs, and there were so many rooms and doors. I pushed one door open, and there was a bedroom. There was nobody inside.

I walked down the next flight of stairs, and I could hear voices behind the frosted-glass door. The book I've written about my experiences as a refugee child is called *Other People's Houses*, and it seems to me one of the experiences of living in other people's houses is that you're never quite sure you're allowed to walk into a room without having some excuse. So I stood and looked through the frosted glass. Of course, my shadow limned itself on the glass, and a voice inside said, 'So come in.'

I opened the door, and there was this elderly woman sitting at the kitchen table. I think it took me a month before I could figure out that this woman at the table was the same one who had worn the prickly fur coat.

The family that had taken me in were called Cohen. The elderly husband was a manufacturer or salesman of furniture. He was one of those small, quiet men, oppressed by being married to the prickly fur coat, and having six daughters. He reminded me of my grandfather, who had also been a little man oppressed by the activity and energy of his family. Mr Cohen was very sweet and he and I made a quiet bond.

That first day, as I was sitting on a low stool in front of the fire, I noticed that he was watching me. He curled his finger for me to come to him, and I got up and stood beside him. He put his hand in his pocket, opened his purse, and he gave me what I think was a sixpence. Then he put his finger to his lips and winked at me to signify secrecy.

I spent my first day trying to blanket myself in grief. I sat on the stool facing the fire, wishing that I could cry but not wanting to cry. I remember that very clearly: trying to call up tears, but only to the edge of weeping. If you could fill your head up with tears and arrest them there, you didn't have to notice what was going on around you.

I now look back on the Cohens, who were my first foster-family, and I have to tell you that after three months, they had had enough of me and suggested that I be taken care of elsewhere.

FRANZI GROSZMANN

I was extremely grateful for anybody who would take Lore in and be good to her. But when she wrote 'a nice Orthodox family', I was upset. She had no idea of religion at all. We were Jews, but we were not religious Jews. We never talked about religion.

Later I got a letter from this foster-mother in which she said, 'Lore is a miserable child.' I didn't know the word miserable and I looked it up in the dictionary. The dictionary said it meant a terrible, an awful thing. Can you imagine how I felt? I didn't know that in English miserable also meant sad, unhappy.

BERTHA LEVERTON

We went to sleep on the ferry and the next morning we woke up and we were in England. Off the boat and on to a double-decker bus. Everybody made a beeline for upstairs. Then we were afraid that there were so many of us upstairs that the bus might turn over. We'd never seen a double-decker bus before.

It wasn't a very long ride before we arrived in Dovercourt. They made us feel very welcome there. People used to come from neighbouring houses to teach us English and to entertain us. In the evenings we had concerts.

Every Saturday and Sunday, they had what we called the 'cattle market'. We were told to put on our best clothes, and we'd sit around

Kinder,
Dovercourt
Holiday
Camp,
December
1938

the tables and visitors used to come. We felt a bit like monkeys in the zoo. We were being stared at and evaluated and people were chosen and taken away from the tables and interviewed. Prospective host families would interview you to see if you were suitable to be taken into their families.

We were grateful, but probably we weren't as grateful as we should have been or could have been because we felt a bit like second-class citizens, which we, of course, were. Most people in England expected refugees to look like refugees. I think it was a minus for us that we didn't look bedraggled, ragged, in old and torn clothes. We didn't look pathetic. But when you pack a suitcase, your parents don't pack your ordinary, everyday clothes. How much does a suitcase hold? So, you came with your best clothes, and 99 per cent of us were well dressed.

Most families wanted little blue-eyed and blonde girls from about three to seven. Little boys were accepted as well. The older children found it a bit more difficult to find foster-parents. They hastily established hostels to take a big influx of the children who weren't chosen quickly because we had to be chosen fast, in and out. Every week another transport would arrive from Germany, so the children had to be sent out to make room for the new ones.

There weren't enough Jewish people coming forward to take us in. A lot of us had to go to non-Jewish homes. I never thought it could happen to me. My brother had been chosen first to be the playmate of a little boy in Coventry. Then they asked me if I'd like to go to a family in Coventry. I jumped at the chance. I wanted to be near my little brother. It never dawned on me to ask, 'Are they Jewish or not?' People who are not brought up in Orthodox families don't realize the trauma for a child to be taken completely out of its Jewish environment and having to adjust to a Christian home.

It was very, very difficult. On the one hand, you couldn't speak a word, you couldn't express yourself. On the other hand, you also realized that those people took you in out of the kindness of their heart, and how dare you say you would rather be in a Jewish home when there wasn't a Jewish home for you to go to? It was quite a dilemma for older children like myself.

There were several reasons why a family would choose to take somebody in. I was a strong, healthy young girl – I had my sixteenth birthday in Dovercourt camp – and the family who took me chose me as a maid. Only I didn't know I was supposed to be a maid. That was a shock. I hadn't ever thought of becoming a servant. I drew the line, though, I point-blank refused to wear a uniform. I think they took me to show off in front of the neighbours because they were only working-class people.

Since I was above school-leaving age, I never went to school in

Bertha Leverton, age 21

England. To this day, I find it a great disadvantage. The people I came to not only didn't encourage me to pursue a secondary education like night school, they actively discouraged me. The way I learned English was from the radio and the one woman's magazine in the house. For me, an avid reader, it was absolutely traumatic to find a house without a book. Can you imagine it? Nothing to read, nothing to learn English from. Some children came to families who were more cultured than theirs; with others it was the opposite – the luck of the draw.

For me the culture shock was very great. Also the fact that my clothes were better than the wife's. She took great exception to that. She took the clothes and all. So there I was, without English to express myself, feeling guilty for not feeling as grateful as I should have been, and not liking very much where I found myself.

I suppose they were shocked as well that I didn't want to do the work that they expected me to do. Instead of a maid they had a rebellious teenager who didn't want to scrub the front steps when people were walking by. So they suffered too.

NICHOLAS WINTON

The breakdown of the children we brought over to England is that about 90 to 92 per cent of them were Jewish. The others were children of parents who were either on Hitler's blacklist or were communists or writers. At the time everybody said, 'Isn't it wonderful what you've done for the Jews? You saved all these Jewish people.' When it was first said to me, it came almost as a revelation because I didn't do it particularly for that reason. I don't think I had any feelings at that time for religion at all. I was there to save children. I wasn't there particularly to save the Jews.

Nicholas Winton with *Kind*, Prague, Czecho-slovakia, 11 January 1939

My parents were Jewish but completely non-religious. I had no connection with the Jewish community in England because I was baptized and brought up as a Christian. Through what I can only say is my ignorance about all these things, I got myself into a lot of trouble with the Orthodox Jews. They were very upset that I had dared to put a Jewish child into a Christian family. There was one organization over here, the Barbican Mission, which took quite a few children. I had no clue at the time that that particular organization was there for converting Jews to Christianity. All they did was come to me and say, 'We'll take so many children.' I said, 'Marvellous.'

The Jews were very upset and a lot of them marched into my office and told me that I couldn't go on doing this. I remember saying, 'You prefer a dead Jew to a living Jew converted to a Christian?' I thought the most important thing was to save the children rather than save the religion. Anybody who would fulfil the conditions laid down by the Home Office to bring a child over and save its life was OK by me.

The conditions set by the Home Office were that we had to produce somebody who'd guarantee £50 against each child's re-emigration, about £1,000 today. It was quite a lot of money. Then I had to find a family who'd take each individual child. It certainly wasn't easy, but it wasn't that difficult. I mean, it's easier to get somebody to take a child than to take a grown-up. Children and animals are the two easiest things for which to get sympathy and raise money.

After visiting the Home Office, I alerted them in Prague that it would be feasible. And I got them to have all the children who were due to come out photographed, which helped in getting them selected. Trevor Chadwick ran the office in Prague. He arranged for the transport of the children from there, while we arranged for their reception at Liverpool Street Station.

The British Committee for Refugees from Czechoslovakia couldn't fund me at all. I was entirely on my own. Once I was 'in business', if I can put it that way, in order to talk to people, to advertise, I had to call myself something official. So I had paper printed, which was the same as the official refugee committee's, and just put 'Children's Section' underneath. I appointed myself Honorary Secretary and was in business.

I tried to get America involved and wrote to a lot of the senators and got a lot of answers saying how concerned they were and all the various reasons why they couldn't do anything. It was a pity because, in retrospect, we could have brought out many more. We brought out about 600, but we had lists of about 6,000 children.

ADMISSION OF
GERMAN REFUGEE CHILDREN

JOINT HEARINGS

BEFORE A

SUBCOMMITTEE OF THE
COMMITTEE ON IMMIGRATION
UNITED STATES SENATE

AND A

SUBCOMMITTEE OF THE COMMITTEE ON
IMMIGRATION AND NATURALIZATION
HOUSE OF REPRESENTATIVES

SEVENTY-SIXTH CONGRESS

FIRST SESSION

ON

S. J. Res. 64 and H. J. Res. 168

JOINT RESOLUTIONS TO AUTHORIZE THE ADMISSION INTO
THE UNITED STATES OF A LIMITED NUMBER
OF GERMAN REFUGEE CHILDREN

APRIL 20, 21, 22, AND 24, 1939

Printed for the use of the Committees on Immigration

UNITED STATES
GOVERNMENT PRINTING OFFICE
145754
WASHINGTON : 1939

Joint Resolution to admit refugee children into the United States

The children who came over from Germany and Austria came over in bulk and went to camps like Dovercourt. If the Czech transports could have worked in the same way, we would have very likely filled the camps in a fortnight. But my brief from the Home Office was quite different. I wasn't allowed to bring anybody in until I had a family and guarantors that would look after them, and it wasn't always easy to get people to make that very big commitment because some of the children were very, very young.

The Home Office was true to their word completely. If I filled in a form and said, 'I've got the fifty pounds and I've got a family that has promised to look after a child until they're seventeen', there was no problem at all. I didn't have any request for a permit refused.

The children whom we brought over were placed, I think, in the main satisfactorily. One can never claim 100 per cent. There were certainly some who weren't; there were some who were misused and used as servants if they were of the right age. There were those cases where the guarantor broke down and we had to find another home for the child. I wouldn't claim that it was 100 per cent successful, but I would claim that everybody who came over was alive at the end of the war.

Postcard from Lorraine Allard's parents, 1944

Chapter Six

A THOUSAND KISSES

Excerpts of letters to Lorraine Allard in Lincoln
from her parents in Fürth, Bavaria, Germany
21 April 1939–4 September 1939

'I keep running to the mailbox. Every line from
you overwhelms me. Every day I thank God that
you are in such good hands . . . But please show
your gratefulness.'

YOUR MUM.

Fürth, 21 April 1939

My dearest Lo,

We were very happy to get both your cards. It went very fast as your card from London arrived today already. It was good that you entertained each other so well on the way so that you overcame the separation pain. The fact that both your foster-parents came to the railway station is touching and promises that you got into good hands. We are glad that you won't be in London. You'll be in better care in a smaller town. I checked out the geographic location of Lincoln and found it NW of Washbusen. I suspect that it is about the same size as Fürth. I saw that it is a very ancient town with remarkable edifices. You'll have the occasion to get an introduction to genuine English history.

Anyway, I do wish you all the luck in your new homeland and the best of everything. After all, you know how much we love you and how much the luck and future of our child means to us. Stay well mannered and tidy and always keep in mind that your foster-parents make a sacrifice caring for you. So in return try to show particularly good behaviour and obey them as well as being diligent in school. Whatever you learn, you are learning it for yourself and your future.

Keep your head up high and get over the separation of your parents who always think of you and don't give up the hope that fate will reunite us. The way the situation lies we have to consider ourselves fortunate that you are settled, which is one worry less on our part.

Give my best compliments to your foster-parents and receive all my love and kisses,

Your Dad.

Fürth, 24 April 1939

My dear Lorie,

I wrote you a card yesterday so that you had news from us immediately after receiving your letter. I cannot describe the joy you are giving us with your detailed lines. We are so happy that you hit it off so greatly, staying with such wonderful people. We are much at ease knowing that you are in such good care even if our little rascal is missing here. We hope too that you'll have a lucky future and that's how we find our consolation. I just have to endure the fact that I get hugged for two from now on.

I am sorry that you felt cold on the boat – that's because you wore socks. In the meantime you will have slept and rested up and slowly but surely you're getting used to all the differences of everyday life. The kindness of your host-parents will help in the adjusting. I am glad for many reasons that you didn't get to stay in London. Anyway, you couldn't have found a better home.

Meanwhile, you have to strive to please your foster-parents by good behaviour which is the way of showing them your gratitude. Stay modest and always remember that, after all, total strangers accepted you out of sheer compassion, human love.

From Dad.

Fürth, 27 April 1939

My sweet one,

I keep running to the mailbox. Every line from you overwhelms me. Every day I thank God that you are in such good hands. I'm really happy for you. But please show your gratefulness. Write to me always in great detail. It's understandable that you are homesick, so am I! However, I console myself with the fact that this is your luck. Stay well.

I hug you,

Your Mum.

Fürth, 1 May 1939

My dearest Lo,

Yesterday we had a lovely day. Plenty of mail! From you, Liese,* Mrs Schreiber,† Aunt Erna and Aunt Ida. Who could ask for anything more? We were especially happy with your detailed and nice letter. So it will find a rapid answer.

Your English will surely improve in no time. You'll have to admit that your parents were right when they preached that you should study and how important it is to learn the language. I recommend that you do quite a lot of English reading, as speaking it alone isn't everything. The spelling of the language is as important and so different from the pronunciation. I want to correct right now some words in your letter! I *spiek* is written SPEAK. *Grepefruit* is GRAPE-FRUIT and *Porige* is PORRIDGE. *Leeg* is spelled Leeds. Since Mrs Schreiber has no maid, I'd like to know who is doing the housework and the cooking? Mrs Schreiber wrote that she does not let you do any work, you are too young. But I am in favour of you making yourself useful. Then she writes, perhaps later I may train her in my workroom or as a saleslady in the shop. I would rather favour the idea that you learn more about dressmaking than selling. That opens bigger opportunities for the future. I will write to Mrs Schreiber in this regard. I got a kick out of your drawing. Now I know my way around your house quite well. I do feel that the way to the toilet is quite far. But don't let this discourage you and use it with diligence and regularly.

Your loving Dad.

My sweetie, my heaven,

If only you knew how happy we are with your letters. They are so

---

* Lorraine's sister in South Africa.
† Lorraine's foster-mother in Lincoln.

darling, clever and written in such detail and so naturally that we read them over again and again aloud laughing together. Dad who misses you *very much* comes alive whenever one of your signs of life arrives. You are having a wonderful life and I am thrilled for you, you are so well off. You are my sunny darling little being and we'll see each other again when you'll have become smart and efficient.

Mum.

Fürth, 4 May 1939

My dear Laura, previously named 'Lo',

We were especially happy with Mr Schreiber's letter. He writes that he looks after our little one as though she was his own. You couldn't ask for more. What's more, I found it very interesting that you were sent there on a trial for just a few weeks after which they'd have to decide whether or not to keep you for three years. Well the decision came promptly and they are keeping our little one. This is one worry that has been removed from us. I cannot insist enough on asking you to show these wonderful people your constant appreciation and grate-fulness, by showing first class behaviour, making yourself useful, and getting good grades in school. Keep thinking about the fact that they accepted you out of the sheer goodness in their hearts. So be sure to do the best of schoolwork, which by the way is in your own interest. Be happy to have hit it off so well, and in your good fortune keep your parents in mind as they are still awaiting news from South Africa.

Your Dad.

My sweet Lo,

Do people like your clothes or is there a different fashion over there? How about the school uniform? Write to us about your school schedule and continue the witty, darling, detailed letters! Soon you'll find a special friend. Today, Thursday evening, is Dad's night off – especially lonesome, but I am satisfied as long as I know you are well and happy. Very much loved are you and kissed profoundly by

Your dear Mummy.

Fürth, 9 May 1939

My sweet darling Lorle,

Don't let the Schreibers drive you crazy and tell them that you promised us a minimum of one letter and one card a week. Otherwise we are really *not* happy.

It doesn't appear to be a perfect household where you can learn. It would be nice if my Lo could cook so as to make a warm meal at lunchtime. Who's doing the washing, the dishes, the ironing? Doesn't anyone come to straighten out the place? I don't understand, such rich people! Please don't start the habit of getting *sloppy*. It would be to your disadvantage. It's not the end of the world if everything is not 'tip-top' my dear little Princess. There you can see a difference. The main thing is that they are *good* to *you* and that they are kindhearted. Their English writing leaves something to be desired. Please *tear up* this letter *immediately*.

We have no news from Liese and Dad is often in a bad mood about it. You are my sweet courageous girl. You must be homesick but you never mention it. Do you miss all the good little kisses? I certainly do! I only think of my sweetie but I'm reasonable and quiet and keep telling myself it's your good luck and our dear God will reunite us. It is lovely that the teachers are so nice to you. The weather here is not nice and I still have a lot of work. It is Monday evening and Dad went out. That's when I miss my little imp the most. With which of the family members do you get along the best?

Eat a lot of fruit and stay well. Who prepares breakfast for school? Bye my golden one. Write again soon to

Your loving Mum.

Fürth, 21 May 1939

Lo, my dearest, my heaven,

Your letter of yesterday was again so sweet and written with so much love that tears came running down your mummy's face! Your writing is so natural, it makes me imagine that you are standing before me. I am happy and satisfied as long as you are. I can understand that everyone over there loves you. You needn't worry about us. It's a big consolation for us that in case of emergency we can come to your place. Dad can feel encouraged and doesn't have to view

Lorraine Allard, age 15, Lincoln, England

a black future since we have such a darling and smart girl – ah! There I go again, bawling. That's because I love you such a great big lot. God willing, one day we'll be together again. I am always with you in spirit, am hugging and kissing you a thousand times,

Your Mum.

Fürth, 31 May 1939

My dear Lo,

I have to let you know that we had a telegram from Liese yesterday informing us that our application to South Africa was refused. Naturally, this was a terrible disappointment for me. I'll tell Mum after she returns home. If the suggestion of Mr Schreiber is meant seriously, there'll be no other alternative than you try to get her over there. As soon as possible I'll send you the necessary documents. What will become of me, I don't know yet, the main thing is that Mum will be in a secure place. Continue to stay well and accept much love and a kiss from

Your loving Dad.

Fürth, 4 June 1939

My sweet Lo!

Liese's cancellation aggravated me terribly. Dad imagines that I'd leave without him. I'd love to accept the job at the Schreibers' but I wouldn't leave him alone here, you'll understand that. My golden one is so efficient that she'll get him a 'permit'. When or if a few good people would help together it could work out in time. Dad could be very useful too. I thank the good Lord that he helped me. He will continue to do that. So long, sweetie.

Many kisses from

Your Mum.

Fürth, 6 June 1939

My darling sweet Lorle!

You have no idea how happy I was with your lovely lines, your heartwarming activities in favour of 'Old Ones' – (us!). The result would be great but right now I'm waiting for the letter from Liese to see if there still are possibilities to get to South Africa. In her telegram she said 'working on re-acceptance, staying hopeful'. Now I want to see what those possibilities are. All our friends drift away and so does the general cosiness. I was very interested in your report about London. Your English still has a lot of mistakes and I'll return the corrected letter one of these days. But it doesn't matter, soon you'll learn it. Even Mrs Schreiber's English is not so perfect altogether!!! You seem to go dancing quite a lot and you were proud with the soldier from the King's guard (not *gard*) as if he had been a general. Well, they only accept the tallest men.

There were 3,300 members in the Jewish community in Fürth seventeen years ago. February 1939 there were 849 and today we are 720, including us (unfortunately).

Well, continue corresponding about the papers . . . So for today Adios and lots of hugs and a great big smacker from

Your loving Dad.

Fürth, 10 June 1939

My sweet Lorle,

Yesterday I wrote to Cape Town: 'Lore's letters come to us like sunshine.' *That's exactly how it is!* You are giving us so much pleasure with your loving care proving to us your great love. You are having God's reward by being well and hopefully remaining so always. We hear with much pleasure that you are doing well in school and that you are making yourself so useful at home. It's our future that gives us *big worries* because for the time being we cannot go to Liese. So we have to depend on the ability of our dear Lo. We yearn to get away from here, that's our fondest wish. Now, I see how important it was for you to leave here. I'm afraid that we are too old to qualify for a couple's job. If the Schreibers would hire me for their housework and someone else could be found for Dad, that'd be a great opportunity for us to come to England. Are you able to get informed sufficiently? How about addressing the Jewish community over there? Or maybe in Leeds where there are so many Jews. I could take a simple room with Dad and the relationship between you and the Schreibers would be unchanged. I hear from many friends that there are homes who care for the elderly but that's too expensive. Here we have nothing to look forward to because Dad regards everything as hopeless.

The Karps are leaving soon for London. Their container is gone already. Soon we'll be the only ones left here. It'll be a difficult task for you to bring us over there! But I have the feeling that you'll manage it in time. We want to wait patiently. If it only works out over there we could run an ad in the Jewish paper. Dad'll make fun of my ideas because I mix up all the subjects in this letter. But my sweetie understands me!

Give regards to the Schreibers and stay good and healthy. Get lots of hugs in spirit and lots of kisses from

Your very much loving Mum.

KISSES!

My sweet Lo,

Your lines from the 7th gave me great joy. I was really touched! It is excellent how you take care of your elders and how eagerly you take pains in your endeavours. How wonderful it would be if you're successful! If, however, it doesn't turn out well then please don't worry either as you know in your heart that you did your duty to the utmost.

Liese wrote very sadly. She had certainly counted on the approval and now she is helpless. Naturally she'll continue and try to apply again but I have no great hopes, in fact, I feel more secure in your endeavours, because even if it is so hard, I know you won't give up.

I am so happy that you are doing well and being praised in school. Continue that way. You know well for whom you are doing it. For yourself. It is absolutely normal that you give a hand around the house, that's the least you can do to show thanks to those good people.

Dad.

Fürth, 28 June 1939

My dearest Lorle,

Your old Dad too is always so happy to read your letters. And happiness is something we really need a lot of. But I am sad today because now even the old war women from Spiegel Str. are leaving. Since you wrote that there are so many Jews in Leeds, even relatives of the Schreibers, do you suppose that we could find refuge there? Then the Schreibers wouldn't need to fear that we'd monopolize you.

As I hear, the demands of the guarantee-givers are increasing constantly. This shrinks the chances of getting over there. It's a pity and the fate of the emigrants is not pretty. If you couldn't get into secondary school, that would be very regrettable for me. First of all, you'd never learn proper English, i.e. spelling and grammar, and secondly, I am not sure if a technical school certificate will be regarded as valid education. Secondary school education is of importance for your whole life. Naturally you have to do whatever the Schreibers wish. However, they said in the beginning that they'd send you to secondary school. My suggestion is that you read as many English books as possible in your free time so that you learn English perfectly. It's nice that so many Germans appear in Lincoln, but it is not to your advantage as far as speaking English goes.

It is lovely in the garden. The fruit trees are full, more than usual. Also there are lots of berries: straw, goose, rasp, and currants. It is our most fervent desire not to see them ripen all together. Dare we hope to be gone by that time?

Now I don't know any more to report for today and remain with all my love and a great big smacker,

Your loving Dad.

Fürth, 11 July 1939

My beloved goldchild,

Now you have really transported your Mum into deep suspense, writing: 'The house is just around the corner from the people who want to hire you, maybe!' Who are these people and in what capacity would we serve them? Are they Aryans, rich? I don't dare to hope because it involves a lot of money. Would this become a reality, HOW HAPPY we'd be! It'll probably take a long time until you'll get an answer from London. Just keep up your energy, you might achieve something yet!

Stay well my little gold and in spirit receive my squeezy hugs from

Your loving Mommele.

My dear Lo,

You really made your Mommele very curious. You can imagine the reactions and the sleeplessness! On top of that it got cold today so that we couldn't go into the garden. And if we can't go into the garden, we are only half a person! The answer from South Africa is missing too and now we are waiting for the permits from England. I'm mentioning all that to show you all our concerns. We are expecting mail from Liese. We have no idea if she re-applied for us. We heard that out of 400 applications only 12 were accepted, so our possibilities are shrinking!

I too am anxiously looking forward to your next news and the result of your endeavour. Anyway I love you madly, so long my dear one. Stay well. Find a nice house.

Regards to the Schreibers and for you lots of hugs and a big fat smacker from

Your loving Dad.

Fürth, 12 August 1939

My sweet Lo,

Our main occupation is waiting for mail from you. Obviously you can't find out if the Schreibers will give the guarantee. I'd do housecleaning! but *soon*. This week twenty-six people left from here. Do you *really* believe that it'll work out? With whom can you discuss this? Please write a bit more about this so that we fully understand it.

For you kisses,

Your Mum.

Fürth, 19 August 1939

Dearest Lo,

Finally we had a letter from you today – we were really yearning for it. However, it was not too comprehensive, not detailing how things are coming along. We are not so sure whether this Mrs Dove is the right person. Actually this would be our second question. The number one, the most important one still being the guarantee and that's why we are waiting anxiously for your news. Also I hope Liese's confirmation will arrive soon, and that Mr Schreiber will seriously pursue this matter upon his return. We don't give up on the hope that if Liese continues to try hard eventually one of the two cases will materialize. Lately your cards and letters have been quite vague, the reason being obviously that you are not alone when you are writing.

I hope that your next letter will be written in more detail and not in such a hurry.

Many dear hugs and that many kisses from

Your much loving Dad.

Postcard, 22 August 1939

Dearest Lo,

Today we received your card of the day before yesterday. It seems that 'BUSY' is your normal condition now. As a result your reports are ever so short. But to make up for it the heels on your shoes are getting higher and higher. I consider this unhealthy and even dangerous for such a young person. You can damage your feet for the rest of your life, so drop that nonsense and if a customer wants to buy a gown, it will be sold as well by a saleslady with normal heels.

Lots of love and kisses,

Your loving Dad.

My sweet one!

When will it happen? Please answer the last questions. AND, no more high heels! It is very unhealthy.

Many dear good kisses from

Your Mum.

Fürth, 4 September 1939

My dearest Lo!

After a long wait your lines of the 30th came today and we are happy about your well-being. We too are in good health, only you can imagine how the excitement of the outbreak of war is wearing on our nervous system! The separation of our dear ones is twice as difficult and we have to hope that we'll all be able to surmount these hard times and that some good fate will some day lead us to be together. Just stay well and tranquil and remember that we are in God's hands, all of us. The direct contact with our children now is paralyzed and I'm trying today writing through a neutral country, so I am directing this to Aunt Nelly in Holland, asking her to send it to you as a first attempt.

All your troubles were in vain but we have to keep hoping, maybe later on there will be a possibility to join you or Liese.

Keep your head up high and for you the best of hugs and a very fast smacker from

Your loving Dad.

Lore Segal and her mother, Franzi Groszmann, Guildford, England, 1942

Chapter Seven

ON THE SHOULDERS OF CHILDREN

*'I think I had a sense that when I was lying in
bed I was wasting time, that while I was playing,
for instance, or while I was laughing, that might
be the moment in which I could have and should
have been doing something about this demand on
me that I should bring my parents out.'*

LORE SEGAL

LORRAINE ALLARD

When I arrived in England, I knew how desperate people were in
Germany. And although my English was not very good, I set myself a
task to try and find homes for people. I found a home for my then
boyfriend – the boy who used to walk me home with a bike from
school. The boy went to the milkman, and he survived. I found a
home for my best girlfriend, and I found a home as a domestic for a
cousin through people my guardians knew.

But my biggest problem was to try and get my parents out. That
was more difficult because, again, it was either finding them a job –
bearing in mind my father's age – or getting this hundred-pound
guarantee, which was just nowhere to be seen.

I couldn't ask my guardians directly because I felt they had already
saved my life. What more could they do? It might even interfere with
my affection for them. Would I leave them if they said no? I couldn't
ask.

So I proceeded to find large houses and knock at the door to find
out whether I could get them a job – my mother as cook, bottle-
washer, my father as gardener – anything just to get them out.
Sometimes I knocked at the door and I burst into tears, sometimes
I knocked at the door and with my very poor English tried to explain
what it was all about, who I was, what I wanted, what I needed, help!

And I did find someone. It was just like an unbelievable dream come true. Everything was being done to get the papers for my parents to come out, and war started. And that was the end of that.

BERTHA LEVERTON

I realized that the family who had taken me in were the only people I could rely on – if I worked hard enough – to provide a visa for my little sister, Inge. She was a beautiful little girl. They had no children. I showed them her photograph, they seemed to like her very much, and they gave permission for her to come and agreed to take her in.

I was very happy that night. I did all the scrubbing and the polishing, and I did everything even better than they wanted. I realized one thing, though, that Uncle Billy – I had to call them Aunt and Uncle – Uncle Billy hated red hair so much that if anybody in the street had red hair, he would spit in anger. I said once to Aunty, 'Why Uncle Billy no like red hair?' She explained to me: Uncle Billy was paying maintenance for a red-haired child, not his, by his first wife.

Say no more. Inge was a bright redhead. The question of hair colour never arose because I had brown hair and the photograph I showed them of Inge was black and white, like all photographs in those days. One day Uncle Billy said to me, quite idly, 'And what colour hair does your sister have?' I said, 'Like mine.' No more was said.

Six months later Inge arrived on the train, her hair aflame, Titian red. Uncle Billy was furious, absolutely raging. I won't repeat the language he used. I learned a lot of English language a polite child shouldn't have learned. He turned around and he called me a 'so-and-so liar'. I said to him, 'Because Inge has red hair, I leave her at home in Germany?' I said, 'Now you send her away. Don't mind. Thank you for asking her here.'

In the end he calmed down and he did accept her into the house. In retrospect, though, I realize that really and truly, had I told them she was a redhead, they would have *never* given permission for her to enter.

At first they treated Inge a lot differently than they treated me – they treated her like a little princess. They took her out to all their friends, showing her off, and they had the notion of adopting her after Uncle Billy got over the red hair episode.

That drove a wedge between us. In the beginning they succeeded because I was working at home like Cinderella, and she was taken out and shown off everywhere. But it didn't last for long. Blood is thicker than water, and nothing could drive a real wedge between us. In the end, they treated her no better than they treated me.

The main thing was that Inge and Theo and I were together. Theo came to join us because even though the family that took him in liked him very much, the boy of the family became jealous and didn't want him around any more. Uncle Billy never had a son, he liked Theo, and he was quite happy to offer him a home.

Of course, they got paid as well, not a fortune, but Theo then went out to work when he was fourteen and I also went to work in the cotton mill. But we were all together and, for me, that was the biggest thing.

INGE SADAN

My sister wrote fantastic letters from England – everything was all wonderful – she was having a marvellous time, and so was my brother, and she would very much like me to come. I was very keen to join them.

By then everything was getting very, very tense in Germany. We had to leave our home and my parents moved into the Jewish hospital to live, but children weren't allowed there. I was farmed out to a widow whose husband had been Jewish, but she wasn't, so it was OK to go there. Every day I used to go to the hospital to visit my parents and the patients. I had a really good time in the hospital; as a little girl I was spoiled by all the patients. Then, suddenly, in July, my parents said it was my turn to go and within a week I was off to England.

I went very happily. It was exciting to go abroad, to go on a train, to go on a boat, to see the sea, and to see my brother and sister again. The parting was different than it had been in January, because in July parents and children were allowed to go to the station together, as long as we weren't too obvious. There were about ten children in my

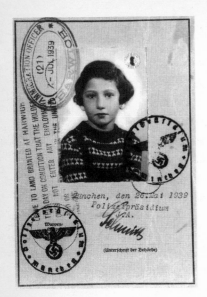

Inge Sadan's German passport, 1939

group and the parents met a little before midnight and we went to the platform. Midnight is rather a dramatic time to depart from a place, but it was summer and it was holiday season as well.

My mother didn't cry the first time, and she didn't cry this time either. My father, who was maybe softer than my mother, didn't cry either. He blessed me as he used to on Friday evenings and he gave me his *kiddush** cup. He wanted me to have it and to save it.

The train left, I saw my parents wave, and I immediately wrote a card to them that I would do everything in my power to get them to England. Well, at nine, you don't have much power, but the card got there. The whole hospital, of course, read it and thought it was very typical of me.

When my brother and sister wrote home, they told fantastic stories. My brother had a dog specially for himself. I got to England and, actually, there was a dog and a cat. The dog bit me, so I didn't think much of that.

Life in Coventry was a shock, I must say. First, everybody spoke English, which I didn't approve of. I thought everybody should learn German. It took me about three weeks to find out I was on the wrong track, and it was up to me to learn English.

School was a disaster at first. Germans are terribly exact. If they say 'one' or 'two', it is one or two. In England, the teacher said, 'One or two children are making an awful noise.' Now it was the whole class that was making the awful noise, and I thought, that's wrong. I took them literally. I think that may have been culture shock.

Gradually I got to know the children, I got to know the teachers and the language. I'd say it took about six months before I was already top of the class in English. So it didn't take too long to acclimatize.

The war broke out six weeks after I arrived in England. My sister

---

* *Kiddush* is the prayer recited over a cup of wine to consecrate the Sabbath or festival.

was already sixteen, she read the newspapers, and she knew what was happening in Germany. I told her terrific lies about our parents, that they're living well, they've got enough of everything, and they're coming soon. She wanted to know good things and she believed them and that comforted her.

But even as a nine-year-old child I knew how serious things were in Germany. I knew from my class in school. We started as fifty children. By the time I left, there were twenty, and four of my class, including me, left on the same train so there were sixteen children left. I knew it was bad, but by nature I'm an optimist. You always hope it'll be all right in the end. I still feel that most times.

LORE SEGAL

When I got to Dovercourt Camp, I remembered very promptly that it was my job to save my parents, and my grandparents, and my aunt and the twins. I think I had a sense that when I was lying in bed I was wasting time, that while I was playing, for instance, or while I was laughing, that might be the moment in which I could have and should have been doing something about this demand on me that I should bring my parents out. So whenever I saw an English grown-up, I would say, 'Could you bring my parents out?'

Now, all you have to do is imagine yourself with this little kid looking up at you and saying, 'Get my parents out.' There was always a look of embarrassment – a dislike of the subject. It's almost as if the grown-ups, inside their heads, were saying, 'Get me out of this.'

At Dovercourt I would go back to the hut and, wearing my coat and my gloves because it was very, very cold, I would write letters about the calamities I had so recently escaped and which continued to endanger the very lives of my parents and other relatives. I remember one of the images that I came up with. In the flower bed at the back of the hut there was a single rose still growing, and it had snow on it. I wrote that my parents were like this rose, still alive in a winter of snow and ice, and if somebody didn't save them soon, they would die. It was not a particularly apt metaphor, but I was wonderfully proud of it. I was ten years old and turning into a writer.

Letter from Lore Segal to Relatives in England

Dear Uncle Ernst, Aunt Erna and Inge,

I am writing you today, 14 December. We live in a 'holiday camp' together with the boys. Tomorrow we girls go to our own camp. Our address will be Dovercourt Holiday Camp, Harwich, England. Where I am now it is beautiful. We live in dark brown huts in which no more than four children can sleep. We have two little windows with red curtains. When we, in the hut, put the light on it looks, from outside, as if there were a fire inside. In front of the hut are small green wooden fences. In the morning, when I sit up in bed, I can look through the window and see far out across the ocean. Sometimes the sun has reddened the sky so that it looks as if there were pink silk drawn across it. The juicy green grass, too, adds to the beauty of the region. Just imagine – it is so beautiful here and yet it is not beautiful. I would almost say that it is ugly – because whatever I am doing I must think of my beloved parents. Though it is good to think of one's parents, it is not good when one doesn't know whether they were still able to sleep last night, when one doesn't know if they will have enough money to pay for the emigration ticket, if it is going to take a very long time. – No! then it is truly not good to think about it. Sometimes, when I think about it, I have to keep myself from crying, and not out of homesickness but because of the above-mentioned reasons. That is why I beg you a thousand times to give me news of my parents. I have written to them too late to expect an answer by next week. And I am afraid that they might not get my letter, and beg you to answer me *immediately*. And one more request, and this is the biggest one that I have ever had: in case my parents are not able to emigrate, please, please, try and buy them a visa to Paraguay, or get my poor 1,000,000,000 times beloved parents out of Germany somehow. Please, please write to me even if there is no good news to be told. Many, many, many kisses from your already-ahead-of-anything-that-you-are-going-to-do grateful

Lore

I addressed the letters I wrote at Dovercourt to some cousins already in England because I didn't know whom else to address them to. My father had said, 'Talk to the English people.' What English people? I'm in Dovercourt Camp. Whom am I supposed to say this to?

zusammenkommen darf. Ich habe so ein großes Glück
das ich dem lieben Gott nur danken kann. Mein Glück
ist aber nicht mit Deinem, lieb. Inge, zu vergleichen.
Denn Du darfst mit Deinen Eltern sein. Aber ich
hoffe das der liebe Gott auch mir so ein Glück
schickt. Die Hoffentlich kann ich am 8. März an mei
nen Geburtstag meine Eltern schon küssen. Nun
schließe ich meinen Brief, da ich nichts mehr
zu schreiben habe, mit der Bitt mir gleich zu ant
worten und mit dem innigen Wunsch meine Eltern
bald in die Arme schließen zu können. Es grüßt und
küsst Euch herzlich Eure

Lore

Pappa   Mutti   Lore.

c/o Mrs. Cohen
2, Fairfield Crescent
Liverpool 6.

Lore Segal letter and drawing, 1939

The cousins were moved by the letters, and sent them on to Bloomsbury House, and perhaps to other people. In any case, these letters did, as far as I know, produce activity on my parents' behalf.

In those days England needed servants because there was a decline in the servant class. One way immigrants could get into England was to agree to become what was called 'a married couple', that is to say a cook and a butler. My parents were sent a domestic service visa to come to a couple in Kent. While I was with the Cohens in Liverpool, Mrs Cohen came to school one day. I was called out of class, and she said, 'I have a surprise for you. Your parents are coming.'

I remember feeling that some weight that I hadn't known I had been carrying was lifted off my back. While I was concentrating on this terrific physical relief, Mrs Cohen was watching me with disappointment. She said to the headmaster, into whose study I had been called for this communication, 'You see how funny children are. Here she sits in front of the fireplace and won't talk to anyone, and is miserable. Now I tell her her parents are coming, and she's not even happy.'

So I began to jump up and down in order to fulfil Mrs Cohen's idea of how one is supposed to be happy when one's parents are coming. She took me home and I jumped up and down some more and, I hope, satisfied her.

My parents, it so happened, arrived the day before my eleventh birthday. I don't know what name to give to my feelings. My experience was of intense excitement and intense embarrassment. I remember I saw my mother first. I was standing on top of the stairs, and my mother and father were standing down in the well of the hallway, having just entered by the door. And I did some kind of show-off thing. I took a little time before I ran down to them. What was the expected way to behave when your parents had been saved from Vienna?

My parents were miraculously there for my birthday party. I remember that whenever I looked around, I could see my mother's eyes following me – great, tear-filled eyes. She was sitting and watching me.

My father was a wreck. My father had done the heroic and powerful thing of getting me on to this Kindertransport, and then I think he had largely fallen apart. By the time he came to Liverpool, he did nothing except sit in a chair. He looked appalled.

Three days later, my parents went south to take up their jobs as butler and cook. My mother very rapidly and very easily learned to do what she was in the habit of doing, which is run a household, except that this time it was from the point of view of the cook in the kitchen. My father, who was the one who was supposed to be knowledgeable in English, forgot his English when he came. My mother, who knew very little English, learned it promptly. My father became more and more incapacitated.

I think the middle-class Jewish male in Vienna did not wish to know that there was a kitchen. When my father passed our maid in the hallway, he would look the other direction. And here he was supposed to be the butler. He was neither mentally nor physically agile. And, of course, he was a very sick man. He had been sick in Vienna and he was going to be sick again in England.

I remember looking out of the window once when I was visiting in Kent, and seeing my father, who by then had been relegated to being the gardener, which he knew nothing about. I saw him walking up the path, and I had an understanding that my father probably felt ill most minutes of most hours, and that he was just barely putting one foot in front of the other. It was one of those imaginative understandings that you then put aside because you can't live with it.

FRANZI GROSZMANN

We arrived in England and we came to the house where Lore was. That was her birthday – her eleventh birthday. There was a birthday party, and guests came and we were celebrated in a very English way, which we didn't understand very well.

In any case, we sat there. And poor Lore didn't know, shall she be happy for her birthday or happy with her parents? She was already away four months in different surroundings, and then came her parents, so out of place.

There was a meal and we spent the night there. People came and they collected money and gave it to us, which hurt me very much, that people had to give us money. Terrible.

The next morning, after breakfast, we said goodbye to Lore. She was on the first floor, we were downstairs. She did not come down.

We didn't go up. It was very strange. We had to go. She had to say goodbye.

I don't know whether you can imagine that strangeness between parents and child. That's something I do not like to think about: first leaving in Vienna without really saying goodbye, then in England, this strangeness.

We were picked up and taken to this very beautiful house in Kent, taken to the back door of the house, and sent upstairs to an open place. There were two low beds, no door to the room. The man said there would be a curtain later on.

The beds were unbelievable. When I lay down on one, I said to my husband, 'Can you remember the room our maid had in Vienna?' It was a small room behind the kitchen with just a bed and a cupboard, no table, no chair. We had it a little bit worse in England, and I thought, it serves us right. It was very, very painful. It didn't become better, but we became more used to it.

The lady of the house showed me the house and the kitchen and told me what I would have to do and when I would have to do it. The first morning I asked what kind of breakfast they wanted. She said, 'Well, just make scrambled eggs.' I had no idea what scrambled eggs were. So I asked my husband to look in the dictionary. In the dictionary there are no scrambled eggs.

I also brought tea to the table – there was no tea and it was just water. I'd forgotten to put the tea in. They were nice – they forgave me for all that.

They didn't treat me badly. They treated me like an English maid. But I wasn't an English maid – I couldn't behave like that. I made my own rules in the kitchen to be able to work. And I made it so that I did not have to wear a little cap and a little apron. I got rid of it somehow. Pure cheek, but I did it.

My husband was told what to do, what the butler does. He tried to be a butler, but he couldn't learn it. He was a bookkeeper. He could do all kinds of things, but only in the office, nothing else. It was so terrible when they told him over and over again the same thing: 'You have to come from the left side when you serve.' But again he did it wrong.

So I asked, 'Could I please wait at the table too?' They let me and he did harder work on the floor and so on. But he didn't do that right either, so he started in the garden, and there he couldn't do much wrong. He fed the chickens, and that was halfway possible. He was always very surprised when something he planted in the garden grew. He couldn't imagine he'd plant something and it would really grow. That was very nice.

JACK HELLMAN

My father had a first cousin in London. He had immigrated early, in 1923, and was fairly well-to-do. Every weekend I took the train into London and bombarded him. I said, 'Uncle Stephan, you've got to get my parents out of Germany.' He said, 'I can't do it.' Every weekend I made the pilgrimage to see him and asked again. Finally, after my being so insistent, he said, 'I'll do it if your father has a working permit.'

I went back to the Rothschild estate and knocked on the door. The butler, who was about 10 foot 6, came out and looked at me. 'What do you want?' I said, 'I want to speak to Baron Rothschild.' He said, 'Wait here.'

I waited a couple of minutes, and he said, 'Follow me.' Mr and Mrs de Rothschild were sitting around a fireplace. It was June, but it was a cold June. I said to him, 'Baron Rothschild, it looks to me like war is coming.' He needed me to tell him that!

I said, 'My father's cousin will give him and my mother a visa, providing he has a working permit.' Without hesitation, he said to me, 'Would he work on the chicken farm?' I said, 'He'll do anything.'

Baron James and Dorothy de Rothschild at Waddesdon Manor

He went to a notary, which wasn't terribly far, and made out a working permit for my parents. The next weekend I went back to London, gave it to my father's cousin. And my parents got their permission to come to England.

It didn't go quite that easily, though. On 30 August 1939, my parents were able to leave Germany. But only my mother got across the border. My father, they held. He didn't have a 'J' for 'Jew' on his passport. My mother, of course, wouldn't go alone, so back to Germany they went.

The next day my father emptied out his pockets to a local bureaucrat in the town of Emmerich and said, 'Can you please put a "J" on my passport?' That's how they got out. They arrived in Harwich on 1 September 1939, the day the Germans invaded Poland and the war started.

I got my parents a little flat, which was no bigger than about six foot by eight foot, with an open stairway, which had room for a bed and dresser. It was certainly no way near a bathroom. But, in my lifetime, I don't think I've ever seen my parents more content or more happy than they were in that little flat. My father went to work. He enjoyed his work. Once in a while from London he was able to get a kosher meal so he didn't have to eat fish or noodles all the time. And they were extremely happy there.

HEDY EPSTEIN

As it seemed more likely that war would break out, my parents' desperation increased. I remember a letter from my father. He said they were willing to do anything, any kind of work, live in a village, live in a town, get very little pay, just enough so they could survive, and I should ask Mrs Mayer to go with me to Woburn House or Bloomsbury House in London, the refugee organizations that were helping people get out of Germany.

It took a long, long time before I was able to forgive myself that I didn't push Mrs Mayer hard enough, but I didn't know how then. I was afraid, too. Today I have a whole long life's experience behind me. I would do things differently now, but I just didn't know how at that time.

Theresienstadt

Chapter Eight

WAR AND DEPORTATION

'It was an exciting time to live. We were unaware
of the horror.'

KURT FUCHEL

LORRAINE ALLARD

I can still see myself in the room where I lived with my guardians
when war was announced on the radio. Dreadful! Dreadful! I just felt
the world's come to an end. Terrible. Shattering if I think about it,
because everything was built around the hope of reunion with my
parents and my temporary stay in England. Everything we'd ever
talked about, or written about, and thought about, it had all collapsed. Everything had collapsed.

How was I going to manage without my parents? How were they
going to survive in Germany? I think I cried for, not weeks, not
months, I cried for years.

KURT FUCHEL

I remember very clearly the day war was declared. The adults were all
grouped around the radio, and I was hiding in one of my favourite
places, under the Cohens' grand piano in the living room.

I was very worried because a few days after that, 11 September, was
my eighth birthday, and I wondered if the war was going to affect my
birthday. A serious question for one in my position because it would
indicate how well I was being accepted into my new family.

As a young boy, though, the predominant feeling I had about the
war was that it was exciting. There was no sense of fear. Every night
Percy put on his hard hat and went up to the roof somewhere as an
air-raid warden. When the sirens went off, we all went downstairs

and hid in a coat closet under the staircase, which was reputed to be the safest part of the house. Then we went out in the morning and picked up pieces of shrapnel. Maybe we saw a downed airplane. It was an exciting time to live. We were unaware of the horror.

VERA GISSING

We had two boy cousins, more or less the same age as we were, whose names had been put on the Czech Committee for Refugees' list to come to England. At the time we left, they had not been chosen because most families actually preferred little girls because they felt they were easier to look after.

After we were in England a couple of months, we heard that they were due to come – on 3 September. And we were so pleased that they would be joining us.

It wasn't until years later that I found out that they were already seated on the train, ready to depart, but that was the day war broke out, and the train was not allowed to leave. As far as I know, none of the children on that transport, including our cousins, survived the war. Eventually they went on another train, which took them to the camps.

NICHOLAS WINTON

Our biggest transport was due to leave Czechoslovakia at the beginning of September. We had 250 children due to come out from Prague. We had 250 families, guarantors, destined to arrive at Liverpool Street Station to collect them.

War broke out and the transport was cancelled. If the train had been a day earlier, it would have come through. Not a single one of those children was heard of again, which is an awful feeling, isn't it?

The war started and the job I was doing bringing over children was finished. I was still in my pacifist outlook on life and joined the Red Cross, went with the first ambulance unit to France for about eight months. Then, inevitably, I came back to England. I wasn't a pacifist for any kind of fundamental reason other than I thought that the politicians had mucked up the whole situation, that it could have been avoided. But, as Hamlet says: once you're in it, you're in it. And I joined the Royal Air Force.

CHARLOTTE LEVY

After Berthold's death, the seriousness of life took over and I wanted as soon as possible to leave Germany. In the last months, my life was a race against the coming war. The newspaperwoman started her route with our house at 5 a.m. I heard the click of the mailbox where she put the paper and each day dashed to see if we were still at peace. I remember the inflaming headlines: 'Poles murder German baby'; 'Poles ransack German home.'

As our intended emigration had been based on Berthold's business skills, I had to start everything from scratch after his death. I might have gotten domestic work in England, but it would have meant putting Elisabeth in a nursery and only seeing her on my day off. This was entirely unacceptable. I had lost Berthold, Hans was away from me. I had to keep Elisabeth.

About that time, I learned of the possibility of going to England under 'guarantee'. Bloomsbury House would give one-third of the required money, we had a small sum with a friend in Holland, which would be the second third, and Win Schlesinger's mother gave a written guarantee that in case of need we could stay in her house. That covered the third part. I am glad to say I never had to take advantage of her offer.

On 21 August 1939, my father took Elisabeth and me to the plane. Another hard goodbye. It was my first flight. It seemed symbolic to see the land under me become smaller and smaller and then invisible, the land where I had of late experienced so much humiliation and grief.

When I got to England, I was most anxious to see Hans. The Schlesingers had evacuated themselves to a country house they had bought during the September crisis in 1938, and they did not want to send Hans to London. Before I could go there, however, I had to register at Bloomsbury House. This every immigrant had to do. You can't imagine the scene there. It was jammed with last-minute escapees who had no place to go, and whole families were stuck there with their baggage. It took me three days of waiting at Bloomsbury House before I could be registered.

Finally, on the fourth day, I was able to travel with Elisabeth to Kintbury. Win and Hans were at Kintbury station. It had been five and a half months since we had seen each other. A suntanned, healthy, happy little boy rushed into my arms. He could not marvel enough about his little sister he loved so much.

Bernard and Win made me welcome right away. In Germany we had always heard how stiff, formal and cold the British were. Only in England did I realize how stiff and formal the Germans were. I had never experienced an atmosphere as relaxed as in the Schlesinger house. It was a wonderful reception I had. It was just really like coming home.

After a very nice lunch, Bernard shouldered a bike that needed repair, and he and Win and the five children went down to the village so that I could be alone with Hans in the garden. He immediately emptied his heart; he had some worries and I could put them right. Elisabeth had been put to nap on a mattress where we found her later asleep, her arm around the Schlesingers' big dog, which guarded her.

Later the Schlesingers and I had a talk about Hans, what they felt, and what I felt. It was a wonderful feeling for me that he was in such wholesome surroundings, and with such fine people. Bernard Schlesinger was a well-known paediatrician with an office in Harley Street. The Schlesingers were very well-to-do people who made the best use of their money for others too. They had rescued twelve Jewish children from Germany and set up a hostel for them. Hans was the thirteenth child they saved. Since he was a distant relative, they took him into their own home.

It was an incredible stroke of luck that Hans, who was so shaken by his experiences and the loss of his father, came to live with such understanding, humane people, and in such a stable atmosphere in his formative years. Like most English people I met, the Schlesingers understated what they did. I cannot overstate what they have done for us and the spirit in which they have done it. When war was declared a few days later, and Elisabeth and I had to be immediately shipped off to an unknown destination under the evacuation scheme, I could leave Hans there with a quiet heart.

ALEXANDER GORDON

I got a new job in London, and I was working there until 28 June 1940. It was lunchtime and I was sitting, having a sandwich, when suddenly two men appeared: 'CID.'

'What have I done?'

Enemy aliens taken to internment camp, England, 1940

'Nothing. You are Abrascha Gorbulski, et cetera, et cetera? You are now under arrest.'

'Under arrest. For what?'

'You are an enemy alien, and please come with us.'

I said, 'Wait a minute, if you're taking me, let me go home and get my things.'

I lived forty-five minutes away by car and they wouldn't let me go. They took my friend and he got his stuff, but he didn't have time to grab mine. He brought me a toothbrush and a couple of small things, a towel, but no clothes. I had nothing. I was arrested in my work clothes, which was all I had to wear now.

They took me to an assembly area and then we went by bus to Kempton Park, a racecourse. They gave us a mattress and we slept on the floor. We were starving because they put some food in the kitchen, but nobody knew how to cook.

We were there for several days until they put us on a train to a suburb of Liverpool called Huyton, where there was a big field with tents surrounded by barbed wire. We were sleeping on the floor and starving half the time because there wasn't enough food, and what little there was wasn't good either.

After ten days we were told we were going to be shipped overseas to Canada and they were looking for volunteers. We knew there was a ship of refugee prisoners called the *Arandora Star* that had left England and been sunk. The idea of going to Canada was not exactly something to brighten your day. But I had family in America, so I said, 'I'll go, maybe somehow I can eventually get to America.' They had to meet a quota and they wanted single men, but they found they didn't have enough volunteers. Those who didn't volunteer were forced to go. A lot of married people went too.

On 10 July 1940, we had to go to the ship. Soldiers were standing there with bayonets mounted on their rifles and they pushed us along and said, 'Leave your luggage over there. You'll get it later on', and they pushed us along the deck and before you knew it, we went down the stairs and another stairs – I was on the third deck.

The *Dunera* was originally a troop ship that was supposed to carry 150 people on one deck. We were over three hundred, so we were more or less sitting on top of each other. There were long tables and a bench along the length of the table. 'Where do we sleep?' There were only hammocks. I slept under the table and sometimes, when the ship was reeling, I would slide up and down.

On the second day out of Liverpool, suddenly something hit the ship. The lights went out. We thought, this is the end of it. Everybody gravitated towards the stairway, which went to the deck above. After about two minutes, you couldn't get up there because there were so many on the stairs – we were just choking.

Suddenly the lights went on again. Everybody stopped in their steps, and went back down. You could hear the motor going, so the ship was still going. What actually happened was we were hit by a torpedo. The torpedo didn't explode, but I was under the impression that it hit us sideways. It just bounced off.

Our luck, because we would have been powerless, we would have been finished. There was only one stairway, and we were three hundred people on the lower deck, and two more decks above that, so there were about a thousand people trying to get up to the top.

On the ship, most people worried about their luggage. I didn't have that problem. We saw some of the troops and the crew with nice clothes on, walking around with fountain pens and so on. They had cut the suitcases open and taken the contents for themselves. Eventually they returned the clothes which nobody had any use for. They threw them in a pile and said, 'You sort out whom it belongs to.'

The food they had onboard was for half the number of people they carried. Naturally, the soldiers took the best part for themselves. We got a loaf of bread and it had to be divided into twenty slices. Everybody wanted the crust.

From the moment I was arrested, I was continuously hungry. I'd never been hungry – I never had very good food, but my stomach was always full. All I was thinking about was the next meal and what I was going to do. Everybody talked the same way. 'What are you going to have when you come back to normal life?' Food is number one in the world. It's the only thing you want. Everything else is secondary.

The facilities for toilets were absolutely horrible. They became particularly bad when we hit a very stormy sea. Everybody got seasick. I didn't get seasick directly, but watching other people, I got seasick from that. Everybody was running to the toilets. There were just two rows of seats, fifteen on one side and fifteen on the other. You would line up, and almost as soon as you sat down, the next person would pull you off. 'You get out of here.' It was unbelievable. There was no bath, nothing. The water we washed ourselves in was salt water. We never got fresh water.

Another problem was that the toilets were the only place we had contact with the outside world, because they had portholes. Otherwise, we just stayed below. We couldn't do anything. Eventually they decided to take us up on deck for exercise. On each side there was a machine gun. We were barefoot and we weren't allowed to walk, we had to run. Sometimes they threw a bottle on the deck, hoping that we would step on the broken pieces.

One day I was on deck when somebody jumped overboard and committed suicide. The story we were told was the man had a visa to go to America, and on that day when he committed suicide, the visa expired and he knew that he would never be able to go.

We were travelling, going west for several days – but suddenly our lookout said, 'Something has happened and we are not going west.' We were turning south. We were speculating, 'Where the heck are we going?' There was nothing to be seen on the horizon. All we saw was water, water, water – three days, three weeks, water.

We had no idea where we were going, except it must have been Australia. We were starving. They were treating us like pigs. Being hungry every day, people were lining up in the kitchen to get an empty pot where the jam was, just to scrape it out. The existence from one day to another was worse than the day before. And we were on the ship for almost two months!

What happened on the *Dunera* – years later I'm looking at it – this didn't happen to me, it must have been somebody else because it was horrible, too horrible to describe.

We arrived in Sydney 6 September. Before we knew it, we were off the ship and the first thing I remember is that each one of us got a box of food. That was the best meal I ever had in my life. After starving for two months, I opened it up – there were two thick cheese sandwiches, and a banana, and an apple, and an orange. And they're giving second helpings. It was unbelievable.

We were put on a train going north through Sydney and into the desert. The only thing we saw were thousands of sheep, raising dust. We arrived at a camp called Hay the next day and stayed for eight months. Our stomachs were full, but our eyes told us this was going to be a miserable time. The Australians treated us very nicely and never said one nasty word, but they still didn't grasp that we were Jewish refugees.

They fed us wonderfully, but it was hot and there were tons of flies. We got organized – we had a camp leader, we played football. We were on our own: no soldiers came into the camp. Once a day we had roll-call. There was double barbed wire and there were watchtowers in convenient corners. Exercise consisted of running around the perimeter of the camp. It got to be 120 degrees during the daytime and at night it sometimes got cold.

We moved to another camp named Tatura in Victoria for several months. Food was terrific. We were eating like horses. We got so much food, we buried the surplus in trenches because we were afraid they would find out they gave us too much food and take it away.

We had lawyers in camp and we wrote a memorandum and submitted it to the High Commissioner of the British government in Australia. It was sent to England, questions were asked in Parliament,

"G"

PIONEER CORPS.
HOME OFFICE.
Aliens Department.

The bearer of this document _GODBULSKI. A_

whose signature is appended at the foot, was interned under the Royal Prerogative
and has now been enlisted in the Pioneer Corps.

He has accordingly been released from internment and ordered to report
for duty at _Ilfracombe. No. 3 Co. Pioneers_

on _9.12.41_ He is in possession of Army
Form B.216.

Certified by _Alexander Gordon_
                                              Commandant.
Internment Camp
Date

Signature of bearer _Alexander Godbulski_

S.H.31.   M.P.-41'22401/2,000

Alexander
Gordon's
internment
release for
the Pioneer
Corps, 1941

and reports were submitted recommending alternatives. Those who wanted to go back to England would be sent under one condition – they would join the army. Those who didn't want to go could stay in Australia.

I went back to England because, first of all, I hated the Germans, I hated their guts, and I wanted to be part of the war. Besides, what was I going to do in Australia? Sit there throughout the whole war? God forbid.

And I hated the climate. I can't stand the heat. I grew up in northern Germany, where it would be 80 degrees once every five years. So, sitting in Australia, in a camp, was not my cup of tea.

Alexander
Gordon, age
23, Sergeant,
British Army,
Occupied
Germany

In October 1941, we got on the ship and left for England. Basically we were still prisoners. We were only free once we got into England.

I accepted things the way they came. I was a young kid, England was a strange country. All I know is, there was a war going on. I was on the side of the good people, and Hitler was on the other side, so I hoped that eventually he'd be defeated, even if it would take years.

HEDY EPSTEIN

After the war began, my parents found various ways to correspond with me because you could no longer correspond directly. But my parents never told me of anything that was happening to their lives. Everything was always fine; they told me not to worry about anything.

Then, around November of 1940, I was invited to the home of the former cantor of Kippenheim, and they showed me a newspaper article which indicated that all the Jews from the section of Germany where I came from had been deported to France. My immediate response was, 'But not my parents.'

They said, 'Oh, yes, your parents were deported.'

I said, 'No, not my parents.' I was into heavy, heavy denial. There was a long period where I did not hear anything from my parents, and I said, well, it's wartime, and I found all kinds of reasons and excuses. Then, finally, I received a letter from my parents, dated 20 November 1940. At the top of the letter, my father put his address, and in the body of the letter, he said, 'You will notice from the top of the letter, we have changed our address.' Actually, they had been deported. But still, I think, my parents were trying to protect me.

At first my father and my mother and other family members were all in the same camp in Camp de Gurs, which was in Vichy France. Men and women were separated by barbed wire, but, in the beginning, once a month they were allowed to spend one hour together.

I found out that you could send money to your parents. There was a black market with the farmers in the community there; apparently through the fence they sold things to the prisoners in the camp. So in late 1941 I sold my stamp collection in order to be able to send money to my parents. I didn't tell them I sold my stamp collection. I told them the money came from Mrs Mayer, which really wasn't true.

The last letter I had from my father was dated 9 August 1941. He said, 'Tomorrow I'm going to be deported to an unknown destina-

tion. And it may be a very long time before you hear from me again.'
Then I received a letter from my mother, dated 1 September, in which
she also tells me that my father was deported, and that she's not heard
from him since and doesn't know where he was sent. Then she says,
'Tomorrow I'm going to be deported from here.' And she encouraged
me to be good, and honest, and courageous, and to hold my head high
– and to never give up hope, and this at a time when I think she knew
what might be happening to her.

There was one more communication from her – a postcard dated
4 September 1942, and it's written in real shaky handwriting. And
she's saying that she's travelling to the east, and is saying a very final
goodbye to me.

But for many, many, many years, I would see the postcard in front
of me, and I would see she's saying 'travelling to the east', and yet I
would understand that she's saying she's travelling in an easterly
direction. Then I would say to myself: well, maybe she's going back to
Kippenheim, and maybe that's good. And the final goodbye, I didn't
understand either.

Both my parents had written, 'It may be a long time before you hear
from me again.' How long is a long time? Is it a week? A month? A
year? Ten years? So I just kept on saying to myself, 'A long time just
isn't over yet and I have to wait some more.'

LORY CAHN

My father was always optimistic: nothing is going to happen to us.
We're going to be able to stay in Germany, and we'll see whatever
happens.

We were given a Jewish star to wear, which I didn't like, because we
couldn't go to the movies and we couldn't go to school any more. I
used to meet my girlfriend, who didn't look Jewish at all, to go to
Shirley Temple movies. I didn't look Jewish either and I wasn't afraid,
so I said, 'Come on, they don't know the difference.' We took that
yellow star off and put it in our pockets.

I told my parents I was going to this girlfriend's birthday party –
which I did, but then we went to see another Shirley Temple movie.
My parents were getting unexpected company from one of my

father's cousins, who was a big judge in Italy. My father called my friend's house and said he wanted me home. My friend's mother told him, 'Oh, no, they're not here. They all went to the movies.'

So my father went to the movies with a light, looking for me, and he pulled me out and that's the only time he slapped me. 'How dare you do that? You ought to be ashamed of yourself.' That was the last of my movies.

There was very little one could do at this time. My mother used to go shopping with me but most of the stores had big signs, 'Jews Can't Shop Here'. There were other stores you could go into, but as soon as you walked in, whether you wore a star or not, they always said, '*Heil Hitler*.' We had little choice but to respond. My mother discovered you could say something else which sounded like '*Heil Hitler*': 'Three litre' – in German it's '*Drei Liter*'. So my mother walked with me into the store to buy something, and we would say, '*Drei Liter*.' They didn't think anything of it, even though we had a star on, and they helped us.

My father knew all the judges and all the big lawyers and was always very much informed of what was going to happen. He still had a secretary. One day he heard they're going to use some of the women for forced labour. He thought my mother might be called. But in the end the authorities told me I was old enough and would have to go. It was 1940. I was just about fifteen years old. I started to cry. 'What can I do?'

'Well, we're going to use you to clean the streets.'

'Where?'

'Not in this part of Breslau. You have to go somewhere else.'

We weren't allowed to use the trolley cars any more, which meant I had to walk. My mother said, 'I'm not going to let that child go out.' We had to be there by five-thirty, six o'clock in the morning, which meant I had to get up at four o'clock and walk almost three-quarters of an hour to get to the assembly place.

My mother and father were absolutely devastated. They used to wake me up, and I was scared to death. I was all by myself in the middle of the night on the street. There were people around, but I was a kid, and always with this star on me.

Somehow my father found out that a friend of his, also a lawyer, had another friend who worked there. My father begged him to come and pick me up. And this man, who was my father's age, came every morning and picked me up and walked with me.

Lory Cahn's parents, Else and Louis Grüenberger

After I cleaned the streets, I was put in a uniform factory, cleaning dirty uniforms and seeing what needed to be fixed. I did forced labour for almost two years, till about the end of 1941. By then my father was saying that this judge or that lawyer had come to visit him and had warned that sooner or later they were going to get to us. From that day on, we were just waiting for it to happen. There was nothing we could prepare for because we had no idea what they wanted us to take or what not to take.

My father came down with a very, very high fever and we were hoping they wouldn't come while my father was sick. Sure enough, the SS came and almost broke our door down. (To this day, I don't allow anybody to call me after nine o'clock at night because although I'm not frightened of anything, when that phone rings at night, it always reminds me of when they came and almost broke our door down.)

It was about four-thirty in the morning: 'Get up! Get dressed! Ten marks each. Nothing to take with you, just what you can put on.' Nothing. My mother had us put on two or three different layers, one on top of the other, and they gave us about ten, fifteen minutes to get out.

We walked out of that house, and that was it. They took us into a truck, and they took my father on a stretcher into another truck. We said goodbye to him – we didn't know where they were taking us, and we didn't know what they were going to do with us.

They took us to a synagogue, which had a great, great, big yard, and it was March and it was very cold. We congregated in that yard, and my mother was desperately looking for my father, but he was not to be found anywhere. We had no idea what they'd done with him.

There were hundreds of people and we were there for about two days, day and night, outside. We were scared and freezing. Then they came and said, 'Into the trucks', and they took us to the railroad station. We were loaded into cattle cars. I think that's what broke up my mother. Cattle cars? This is for animals.

While we were being put in, they stood outside with sticks, and if we didn't go fast enough, they started to hit. My mother cried and asked one of these SS guys whether they knew where my father was. He said, 'I don't know where he is. I don't know anything. You get in there.'

We were approximately thirty-five, forty people, men and women. The worst for my mother, who was always a real lady, was that they had a bucket in the middle. I think that part almost started to kill her right there. When my mother saw that she said, 'I wish I'd had something that I could take. I don't want to go on this trip, wherever we're going. How can I go on that bucket?' She wouldn't go on that thing for the whole trip, and we were two days on the go.

They locked that wagon, and it was complete darkness. No way you can see anything. All they did when we stopped was give us some water – we had nothing to eat in there. Nothing. Everybody was in there crying, and scared, and, oh, it was awful. Just absolutely awful.

After two days, they opened up the car: 'Out! Out! Out! Fast, fast, fast!' The light was blinding. My father was standing outside waiting for us. It was unreal. He looked like there was nothing wrong with him, but he couldn't go with us. We didn't know whether we were ever going to see him again.

They put us on trucks, and we went for quite a while, through wooded areas, into a big place through a big gate. Somehow we knew we were in Theresienstadt. As we got out of the truck, they took away our jewelry, including my mother's wedding ring. They asked if people had false teeth and they took them away too.

I was with my mother in Theresienstadt the whole time, with 300 other people. We lived in the same barracks on wooden stilts with straw mattresses. There were three on top of us, three below us. Ninety-nine per cent of the population was from Czechoslovakia; it was crowded and there were very few people from Germany.

After two or three days, we found out my dad was in a regular house, with five or six rooms. Everyone there was older and sickly. We went to see my father almost every day, and I worked in 'The Work Place', where they had all the supplies for fixing buildings or broken objects.

We were surrounded by Czech soldiers, backed up by the SS. I wasn't there too terribly long when I started to complain of very bad headaches. I couldn't get out of bed any more. I was taken to the hospital, where all the doctors were our own people. Within days, they found out I had spinal meningitis.

The doctor told my mother, 'She is the youngest we have ever had in here – I'll try to get some medication for her through the Swiss Red Cross.' I was in the hospital for four months and, miraculously, they were able to get medication for me. By the time I left the hospital, I could walk and move my arm again, but the doctor said I will forever suffer from very bad headaches – which I did until many years ago.

I was in Theresienstadt about a year and a half, and a lot of people were sent away on transports. My mother was scared to death they'd pick me and not take her, and what will happen to my father? We had no idea how they selected you or where they sent you, and you lived with that all the time.

At one point, we were told the Swiss Red Cross was going to come and take some pictures. Theresienstadt was fixed up – a little painting here and there, and they planted flowers in a plot of land in the middle of the camp. Now, I had joined a children's group to keep active. One evening we were singing. They told us to go and sit there and sing while they took pictures. What the Red Cross saw wasn't really what was there. They just saw the outer façade of the whole thing.

Over time Theresienstadt became more and more overcrowded. There was a day and a night shift: we slept during the day and we had to get out so other people could sleep at night. One day they came into our barrack and my name was called to report in the afternoon to the railroad station. I had no idea where that was, so I went with my mother to see my father. I told him they called me and I would have to leave. So again, we said goodbye, and I left.

I went to the railroad station. As they called your name you had to go and see this SS officer. He crossed you off the list, and then you went into the car. I got there, and I repeated my name. He said, 'You're not going.' I didn't dare ask why or what, but that was the end of it. They sent me back. When my mother saw me, she thought she was going to pass out. Then we went to my father, who nearly passed out as well. This went on for about two weeks, maybe longer.

I'd been at the railroad station, I think, four times. I was a complete wreck, but I didn't want to show it to my mother or my father. I had no idea why they called me back, but some said it was because my father was 100 per cent disabled, and apparently, it still meant something.

To say goodbye to your parents one time, a second time, a third time, and a fourth time, and once before when I was in the Kinder-transport, was just absolutely devastating. Every time I said goodbye, I think I tore a little piece out of my mother, and out of my father, and also a big piece out of myself.

The last time it happened, I told my mother, if it comes to pass again, I think I'm going to say, 'I want to go.' She said, 'Well, you wait and see what happens.'

When they called me, I said to the guy, 'Would you terribly mind, but I want to go.'

'Are you sure of that?'

I said, 'Yes.' He crossed my name off, and I went.

Little did I know that we were going to Auschwitz.

I don't know how long we were riding, but then, on the last stretch, we all had this awful, awful smell in our nose – I'll never forget that as long as I live. When we stopped, they opened up the door, and Dr Mengele was standing there with his stick. 'Get out, you goddamn Jews!'

Ever since I had had spinal meningitis, the doctor had recom-mended wearing glasses – not for my eyes, but for the nerves, to take the pressure off. When I left I took them with me so I wouldn't have so many headaches. When they chased us out of the train, I stumbled and the glasses fell off my face. I tried to pick them up and I noticed either the glass was shattered or broken altogether. And a voice inside of me said, 'Don't take them.'

That saved my life. When we got out of the train, anybody who had any kind of deficiency – looking old, walking funny, glasses – was sent to the left. I went to the right. We somehow all knew what it meant: left was gas chamber, right we were allowed to live, at least for the time being.

NORBERT WOLLHEIM

When war broke out we all lived with the expectation that the Nazis might put us into labour camps, but nothing happened at first. I continued to work for a year or so in the Central Jewish Office in Berlin. They shifted me to the department for vocational education. These were very good schools set up to help children acquire vocational skills like carpentry, plumbing, metal work and so on. I had also learned a trade, namely welding. I was not a bad welder, and I would say it helped save my life later in Auschwitz.

Then, in the summer of 1941, after Germany was successful in Poland and in Norway and in France, there started what was called the Final Solution. In December 1942 my parents, of blessed memory, were deported. Later I found out that they were in one of the first transports which went directly from Berlin to Auschwitz and, certainly, they were murdered the moment they arrived. But, at the time, we didn't know about Auschwitz.

In the spring of 1943 the city of Berlin was cleansed of the last Jews. They came in the afternoon and took my family and myself. I was thirty years old. My wife was my age. My son was approximately three and a half years old. We were taken to a collection point, and after a couple of days we were deported to Auschwitz, though we did not know when we got to the train, which consisted of cattle cars, where we were going.

When we left Berlin it was Friday, Sabbath eve. When it became dark, one lady on our transport took two candles out and lit them and said the blessings and the prayers to welcome the Sabbath. Later, I often thought about this. Where did we find this spiritual power, riding in a rolling prison, a death wagon of a hundred people? Ninety per cent of them did not live to see the next evening. But, still it was Friday evening, and they were singing and welcoming the Sabbath in the name of God.

We landed in Auschwitz, and the moment we landed there, we were commanded to leave the trains. Women with children to the left, and men to the right. And that was the last time I saw my wife, my then wife, and child.

Lorraine Allard in the ATS, Oxford Circus, London, 1945

Chapter Nine

SOMEWHERE TO BELONG

'I hurt within me because of my parents. There was a terrible void and a terrible loneliness for love and for warmth.'

LORRAINE ALLARD

KURT FUCHEL

I really tried to please my foster-parents because I loved them and felt very dependent. Mariam was somewhat aloof. It was her manner. She was loving, but she didn't hug and kiss me, whereas my mother was the exact opposite. She used to, not just kiss me once, in fact, she sort of kissed me rat-tat-tat like a machine gun. In contrast, Mariam was distant and nice, and I think that's what I needed because I had trouble really feeling that I belonged there. To have pushed me into it would have, I think, been difficult.

Percy was much more demonstrative than Mariam. He was a volatile, but very affectionate man. I adored him. He was very good with us boys, played ball with us, took us to interesting places.

Suddenly having a brother was, I suppose, a shock, yet nice in the sense that I was not the only child. But I was jealous. I always watched what John got on his plate to see whether it was more than I was getting. And, at times, I used to pester Mariam and say, 'You don't love me as much as John.' Then she said, 'I do so', and would put a piece of chocolate in my mouth.

The one thing I remember really clearly was John getting a bicycle before I did – I think it was Christmas – and I was two and a half years older. I was very angry, and yet, logically, I knew that he had learned to ride before I did.

So what I did was, one afternoon I was visiting some relative who had a bicycle, and I learned to ride that afternoon. I came back absolutely battered and scraped from head to foot, but I now could ride a bicycle. Indeed, not long afterwards, I also got a bike.

To give the Cohens their credit, they treated us equally as far as it was humanly possible. I didn't really realize it for a long time, but they were very fair. The British sense of fairness is what I carry away most of all.

Kurt Fuchel (*left*) and Mariam, Percy and John Cohen, England, 1939

John and I fought at times, but we never told on each other. We were always together in that sense. We'd fight with each other, but neither of us tattled to the grown-ups on anything we did.

I used to help him with his homework and, alas, I used to do it for him, which I'm afraid inhibited him at times and he didn't do well at school. I believe each child in a family carves out a niche for himself, and once that niche is occupied, the other one can't fill it. I took on the niche of the 'good student'. That's how I made my mark. John didn't excel in school, but he excelled in other ways: sports and in sociability.

One of my main worries, after I was more or less established with the Cohens, was that I would be sent away. I know this happened to another boy, somewhat older, who was taken in by some friends of the Cohens. He was arrogant and impossible, and eventually they simply had to send him to some other home. I'd heard of other places where this happened too. So I felt very much on edge.

I knew that there were several other children from Vienna or Germany in the community. One was little Erika, who lived down the block with Mariam's sister and was a crybaby. We knew that she had difficulties. She wet the bed until I don't know when.

Another family we knew, the Goodmans, had an only daughter Joan, who was somewhat older than I. They took in an Austrian girl about the same age. One of my most vivid memories is the two tearing each other's hair out, literally, and screaming and fighting with each other, which terribly frightened me. Eventually, I think the girl found some relatives somewhere and that's where she went.

You would have thought that we exiles would have gotten together, spoken the old language, talked over old times. But we didn't. We kept as far away from each other as we could. I know I, and I suspect the others too, were terrified of having one of us screw up and it branding the rest of us. I knew what happened to ones who misbehaved, or at least, that's how I read their leaving Norwich. For this reason I was a good boy, very compliant; I always tried to do the right thing. I even helped around the house, including helping the maid. Maybe I felt some affinity to her, since she also wasn't family.

There was no doubt a cost to trying to be good all the time and keeping my anger in. Only once did it slip. One day John and I were having breakfast, and there was some silly argument over who got the marmalade first. I threw a knife I had in my hand at him, and it hit him on his nose, near his eye, and terrified the entire family. And me, too.

That was the only time that Percy ever hit me. Everybody was in an uproar. It was a terrible scene and I don't know how it even happened.

They took me to see the headmaster of the school, who talked to me and talked them down, told them what I must be feeling. And things passed. Since then I've been rather afraid of the possibility of letting go to anger. It's never happened since.

The other sign that I had a lot inside me was that I always had some intestinal problems, until I went in the army, and then I had the most terrible food and felt fine.

MARIAM COHEN

Kurt was 'cute'. That was his nickname, 'Cute'. He was very bright, and very popular. He just fitted in. John was only five when Kurt came. He was only a little boy, but they got along like a house on fire. Absolutely.

Just once they had a row. John was teasing him about his love for jam or marmalade, and Kurt threw a knife. That was the only time he was naughty. And John had a little wound near his eye. It wasn't very nice.

Dr Rose, who was our great friend, lived a few doors down, and he came in and he was furious. 'You shouldn't have taken this child in, and da-da-da-da-da-da-da.' But that was the only time when Kurt was terribly upset. It was the only time there was any antipathy. They were great, great friends. Brothers!

VERA GISSING

I was just getting used to the Rainfords and their way of life when, barely two months after my arrival in England, I was evacuated to a little town outside Southport. I was placed in another Methodist family with a lady I called 'Aunty Margery'. At first my foster-sister, Dorothy, was with me, but she was very outspoken and she clashed with Aunty Margery and was soon shipped back to her own home. This was a shame because I was now on my own and faced with another strange family with a very different lifestyle.

Aunty Margery was very kind, but she wanted the whole world to know about it. She was very active in her church, and every Wednesday she had the ladies of the church come to tea. I hated Wednesdays because she would make me stand on a pedestal, and she would say to her ladies, 'This little Czech refugee, if it wasn't for me, she'd stand here naked. If it wasn't for me, she'd go hungry', and so forth.

I hated to be on show, and I thought, how dare she? What about all the beautiful clothes my mother sent? What about all the wonderful dishes my mother cooked? I really felt like a poor little refugee. But I got back at her after all that. They always said prayers before we ate, and one day Aunty Margery said, 'Vera, why don't you say a prayer in Czech?' Without a moment's hesitation, I said in Czech, 'Dear God, please, can't you stop this woman from being so bossy and such a show-off? Amen.' I said this prayer day-in and day-out for the rest of the year that I was there, and it made me feel much better.

When I was living with the Rainfords, they took me to church with them, but they did not try to make me into a Methodist. Aunty Margery made me go to church and Sunday school, and on Sundays I was allowed only to read the Bible, or write letters, or play the piano. I didn't like any of those things except writing letters. But there again, I was one of the family, and I spent my time in church happily singing the hymns, and otherwise thinking of my parents. I felt it wasn't a bad thing to go to church. Surely it didn't matter where I worshipped as long as I believed in God, and as long as I prayed for the safety and the lives of my parents.

I remember that first year in England, just before Christmas, I wrote in my diary, as a prayer to God, that if I was given an armful of the most wonderful gifts, and among them was just a little note which said: 'Czechoslovakia is free. Your parents are safe', that would be the only gift I wanted.

When France fell, the Czech government-in-exile moved to Britain from France, among them the Czech president, Dr Beneš. Now, apart from asking God to keep my parents safe, I always asked Him to look after President Beneš because I had faith he would eventually lead us back to our free country. I wrote him that in a letter I sent him for his first Christmas in England, and he sent me a little visiting card in return.

By then I was living with the Rainfords again. They had moved to Ainsdale, a small seaside town halfway between Liverpool and Southport, and I joined them at the end of the summer term in 1940. Sometime after my Christmas letter to Dr Beneš I heard there was going to be a concert held in a Liverpool theatre and that he would be attending, and I nagged the Rainfords to let me go. Eventually Daddy Rainford took me. During the interval, brazen as I was at the age of twelve and a half, I marched to the box in which President Beneš was sitting with his wife, and presented the visiting card to the two Czech soldiers who were standing on duty. I said, 'Please tell the president that Vera Diamant would like to speak to him.'

They looked at me rather amusedly and then they went into the box. The president not only asked me in, but he remembered my letter. He introduced me to his wife and he quizzed me on my life in England. When he heard that I was well-looked-after and happy, but homesick, not just for my parents but for everything Czech – for the food, the education, the company of other Czechs – he said, 'But you can have all that because we have founded a Czechoslovak school in Britain for just such refugees as you. I'll tell you what, I'll make it my own personal business to get you there within three weeks.' And he did.

The Czech school really changed my life. We were more like an extended family. There were many children there who came on the Kindertransport, who shared my anxiety about what was happening to our parents and my hopes. I spent three and a half years at this school. They were the happiest I had in England. I was very glad that I was with people who understood when I first heard on the radio what was happening to the Jews of Czechoslovakia.

EVA HAYMAN

Isolation came when the letters from home ceased. I was in a very nice and very friendly school, but I was the only stranger. It was accepted that you didn't talk about what hurt you. I couldn't speak Czech with anybody. I didn't want to tell my sister how unhappy I was because I felt she was too young anyhow.

I was very, very lonely. I wrote of that time in my diary: 'I never dreamed that one could be so lonely and go on living with this constant fear for our loved ones. The tears I shed at night do not ease my pain, yet I was told that one feels better after a good cry. All I have is a swollen face and my heart is as heavy as it was before.' My pillow often was very wet in the morning.

But there were good things in the school, too. I had a teacher, Miss Vinall, who took it upon herself to teach me English outside of class. She would walk me around the garden, pointing out things, 'This is a flower, this is something else . . .' After about two months, actually, I could communicate in English. I had to.

There was also a gardener who didn't understand perhaps what I was going through, but he always said to me, 'Don't worry, the war won't last long.' Whether I believed him or not, it was good to hear him say that. And he always gave me a flower.

I must say the waiter was very good, too. He used to remove the food which I didn't like before anybody saw that I left it on the plate. But otherwise, I don't think there was anybody around who could understand fully what I was going through. I bottled it all up. I wouldn't tell anyone because they might feel sorry for me, and that was the last thing I wanted. I didn't want pity.

The greatest relief I had was writing in my diary. I think my father might have been a psychologist before his time telling me to write, to put things down. I don't know if I would have survived if I couldn't have poured out into the diary all my thoughts and feelings, because I did not speak of them.

After a year, during which I got to know the girls and two of the families with whom I spent part of my holidays, the school, unfortunately, had to close because of the bombings. I was sent to a sister school, which was evacuated from Hastings to an estate in Monmouth, Wales. It was a beautiful estate, but unbelievably cold in the winter. We froze to bits. There I had to start all over again and make new friends. In the first school I was homesick and lonely; in this one I was unhappy for the year I spent there.

When the year finished, I took my exams and passed, because I really did very well at school all during those two years. Even in some English classes I came out on top, which surprised me, too. Miss Dunn, the headmistress, who was my sponsor, wanted me to study for one more year and then go to university, but I didn't want to stay at this school any more. I wanted to do something to help finish the war and I proposed nursing.

Eva Hayman

Wartime hospitals were pretty rough, and I had a sheltered life in the boarding school. Miss Dunn thought it would be too difficult for me. She thought maybe I should go to a place near Windsor, which was near where she lived, and learn how to look after children. I stayed there only three months. I found it completely heartbreaking to have to take care of all these orphan children with whom I could so identify.

So I got a place in a hospital, which wasn't difficult because they were so short of nurses, and I wrote to Miss Dunn and said, 'I would like to go. Is that all right?' She came to see me and said, 'Yes, you can go, but I don't think you will be able to stand it.'

The first year, I nearly gave up. I found it very difficult, but remembering her words, I was determined to stand it. The second year was better. Then nursing grew on me, and we were so busy I didn't have time to think of myself anyhow. It was the end of 1941 when I started nursing in Poole, in Dorset. I was there for four years, till the war was finished.

All through that time I was aware of my responsibility for Vera. If she had any problems, she would write and tell me. But I often had great difficulty knowing how to answer in a way which I would have hoped my parents would have answered. I took upon myself a burden which I'm sure they wouldn't have wanted me to take upon myself, to try to act in the way they wanted me to, without really knowing what that was. I always chose the hardest path for myself.

For Vera it was different, even though she was young. She had a very different nature, much more happy-go-lucky, much clearer about what she wanted, while I tried to please my parents, which I have discovered wasn't the best thing.

I remember, sometime in 1944, Vera was going to come to stay with my friend so that we could see a bit more of each other. She had written that she was given a new coat by her English parents. At that time I was tired – I had been on night duty – and I wished the same thing was happening to me. I wrote about it in my diary:

I could see my sister arriving in her new coat and dress. Here was a pretty girl, looking at the world through rose-coloured glasses as I used to once upon a time, full of self-confidence and, like most sixteen-year-olds, assured of her popularity.

I don't want to harm Vera. I love her dearly. But I visualized myself next to her in my ancient coat, with my unruly hair. I saw my tired face next to her bright one, my dark brown eyes forever searching and full of pain, next to her sparkling blue eyes, and something hurt a little.

Suddenly I realized that how we look is largely dependent on our character – bad temper, selfishness and meanness look at the world through our eyes, faith and joy beautify our countenance . . .

Everything depends on us alone. A coat will not alter our nature, but our nature will alter our countenance.

My dearest Vera, stay as you are, a happy child. The day of our reunion with Mother and Father is drawing close, and they will not look at our coats. They will gaze into our eyes, looking for joy and laughter. Both of us are so much theirs, yet my heart is heavy with fear for them.

I remember that feeling, but when Vera arrived in her new coat, I didn't notice the new coat any more than she noticed my old one. We were very happy to be together.

INGE SADAN

At home in Germany we were a very loving family. Europeans and Jews all together are very warm. They hug and kiss – although my brother and I used to get smacked sometimes too when we were naughty. But in England everybody seemed very reserved. There were no hugs and no kisses. Everything was cold.

Uncle Billy and Aunty Vera didn't have children. Aunty Vera really wanted a child and wanted to adopt me after the war started, but, of course, my sister wouldn't allow it. Not having children, they didn't have much idea how to treat us. One of their punishments, for instance, which I found very strange, was if I spilled the tea or something, I would be sent to bed. If I was very naughty, I'd be sent to bed without supper. To me that was a terrible thing because I hated the dark and the curtains were pulled, and I had to go to bed in the middle of the day. Also sometimes they kept me away from school. I loved learning and I was very happy at school. To me, that was a real punishment.

I want to mention my favourite saint, though, a housewife who lived about two hundred yards away. She was on the parents' committee at the school and knew that a few children weren't getting their daily half pint of milk. My aunty, of course, didn't pay the ha'penny it cost.

This woman found out I was a refugee child and insisted that I come to her house every morning, and she'd give me a penny and an apple. I said, 'But, milk's only a ha'penny.' She replied, 'Well, the other half penny, you go spend on ice cream, or chewing gum, or sweets, or anything like that.' I'll never, never forget that, because it was warmth and help and kindness when it was most needed.

I used to go there every morning and take my penny. Her house was across the road, and I was terrified that Aunty Vera would look out the window and see what I was doing, going up someone's garden path. But she never found out.

We lived in a sort of sub-world during that time. If we were angry, we kept it within ourselves. I know I became very sly and very closed and, I'm sorry to say, I learned to lie and to steal. It was a way to survive, especially when food was short. I had to do the shopping and used to keep some of the money and spend it on food.

Once I even invested in a bottle of lemonade in a shop but I couldn't finish the lemonade so I said, 'Can I keep it in the shop?' Every time I went to the village, I would go and they would give me a glass and I would have some of my lemonade. I felt like royalty. The shopkeeper may have thought I was a peculiar little girl, but I had my glass of lemonade, then they closed the bottle. It was a little secret life of my own.

I always felt I should be grateful that we had been saved, and that these people had taken us in, and I should be happier there. But facts are facts and it wasn't a good place to be. Children are somehow resilient, though. Thank God I went to school, and my brother and sister went to work. We had an outside life until we came home, and that helped a lot.

When the bombs started falling, though, it got quite serious. Uncle Billy was not a very courageous man. Every night they would go into the country and take us with them to escape the air raids. One day the people where we were staying said they didn't want the German children. So we didn't go into the countryside any more. We stayed with Aunty Vera's mother, who had a boarding house. Aunty Vera's mother was warm, and she always used to tell Aunty Vera to stop bullying us. We enjoyed staying with her very much.

One day, around six o'clock, before it was even dark, the siren sounded and what was known as the Coventry Blitz started. The whole night long bombs rained down. Coventry was a very hot place to be! We were in one of the boarding houses, and that was bombed. There was a big fire upstairs and everybody rushed out.

Morning after the main German bombing raid on Coventry, England, 15 November 1940

In the morning, when Aunty Vera and Uncle Billy came back and they saw one of the boarding houses without any house, just a spiral of a bedstead, they were very shocked and they thought we'd all been killed. They rushed over to the other house, and there we were, all drinking tea, as alive as anything. That was the only time I saw Aunty Vera cry, I think relief, because I guess she had a heart after all.

BERTHA LEVERTON

I lived with Uncle Billy and Aunty Vera for five years. It was difficult. The memory of those five years can never be erased. Aunty Vera was a semi-invalid, and she resented my youth and my good health. She tormented us in many different ways, little unkindnesses, things which hurt me very much at the time. I had no new clothes while I was there, but my aunt had sent me a beautiful camel coat from America. After two or three years of use, it became so dirty I couldn't wear it any more. It was very light-coloured, and I said, 'Please, may I send it to the cleaners?' And she said, 'No. There's no money for that. You can wash it.'

I'll never forget my beautiful coat, all shrunk and horrible on the line. Of course, I could never wear it again. To me, as a teenager, that was tragic. But Aunty Vera's spitefulness and her torment was *nothing* compared to Uncle Billy's 'trying to be friendly-ness', which I successfully managed to avoid for five years. I didn't let him become friendly.

We lived in Coventry for about two years, but after the Coventry Blitz, Uncle Billy and Auntie Vera decided to evacuate completely to a little village in Yorkshire. There I went to work in a cotton mill. I enjoyed the work, and I became one of their top workers, earning top rates.

Of course, I had to deliver my wage packet at home every week, from which I was paid an eighth of what I'd earned. That didn't help much because it was borrowed back again next day. One of the girls at the mill had a stepmother and also had no money; she showed me how to falsify the wage packet. I did that once or twice, but, honestly, it just wasn't worth the effort, because if I had bought anything, it would have been noticed straight away. So I couldn't spend the money anyway.

All that didn't matter so much, though. When I think back now, I realize how many children who had to live through the hell in Germany would have changed places with me. My ordeal wasn't as great as I thought of it at the time. I felt like Cinderella, which I was, but one can live with it – you learn to live with it.

ROBERT SUGAR

One day I was called into the farm office and asked, I think a bit gleefully, if I knew that my mother was no longer in London. I said no.

'She went back to Vienna,' they told me. I couldn't believe it. Why would she go back to Vienna?

Years later she explained it to me, that she was going back to get my father – who was impassive – and her mother, my grandmother, to move. The three of them would go to Shanghai, which was still an open port.

Before she left England, her friends said to her, 'You're crazy, the war is starting.' She said, 'I can always get back to England.' I wasn't eyewitness to this, but this is what I reconstruct from what she told me later. Of course, I've always felt she just couldn't stand to be a domestic any longer.

So now my mother's no longer in England and war is starting. The news came over the radio from outside our room. I remember going back to my camp bed next to the window in the old farmhouse, and everyone was piling on my bed to listen to the radio. All of a sudden I couldn't stand the closeness of all the bodies there, and I did the unthinkable. I said, 'If you don't get off my bed, I will tell Mr Blumenberg.' In other words, I will break the universal code of childhood: I will tell an adult.

They didn't get off, and I told an adult, and so I was hazed. I became an outcast, and I began to fight. I began to count how many times I lost, how many times I won. I really did make up my mind I would be as tough as nails. Nothing would hurt me. I would have no emotions. And it carried me through for about six or seven years.

I got a scholarship to a grammar school and people were saying to me, partly in jealousy, 'You know there are snobs in these schools, and they're anti-Semites, and you've got to watch yourself. They're going to take it out on you.'

I went to school the first day. I had a school tie, I guess, or a blazer. I mean, I was just entering a new world. The sun was shining. And a fellow came up to me and he said, 'Who are you?' And I just knocked him down.

Later on I found out that it was an all-Protestant school, and this boy was the only Catholic in the school. He had come over in friendliness. But that didn't matter. They told me I had to watch myself and by now I had transformed myself into this person who could just knock down a stranger in the schoolyard. By the time I left school, I was back to what I used to be. I wouldn't have done that any more.

LORE SEGAL

When the school holiday started in Liverpool, my mother got permission for me to visit the house where she and my father were working in Kent. While I was visiting there, the Cohens discovered, I think, how delightful it was not to have this little prickly child in their house and they wrote to my parents saying, 'Wouldn't it be nice for you to have her close to you? In any case, we have a relative who's going to need a lot of attention.'

My mother was appalled, not knowing what to do with me because you can't be a cook and butler in an upper-class English household and have your kid around. So she went to the church committee in the nearby town of Tonbridge, and they found me a new foster family to live with.

This family, too, soon discovered a blind aunt who needed to move in. After that I went to live with the family of a munitions factory worker, and when they moved to Croydon in the stress of the war, they sent me to live with the wife's father, who was a milkman. None of the foster-parents with whom I stayed – and there were five of them – none of them could stand me for long, but I am moved that all of them had the grace to take in a Jewish child.

I am now impressed that they took in this alien child with a foreign language. I have noticed with interest that I have not done the same in the many political situations where there were children who needed taking in. The families who took me were not particularly warm. They did not love me. I did not love them. Nevertheless, they did what most of us don't do, which is to burden the household – the kitchens and the bedroom and the living room – with this little foreigner.

When Mrs Cohen picked me up she had said that she wanted to teach me nice ways. Now, the way that English people hold their knives and forks is not the way Austrian people hold their knives and forks. From this I have deduced something that has interested me. When you say to a child, 'You're holding your fork wrong', you're saying to the child, 'Your mother holds her fork wrong. Your mother taught you bad manners.' I've often thought that when a black American child is told, 'You talk wrong', what's being said is, 'Your parents talk wrong.' The repercussions are terrific when you do that.

On the other hand, we children were probably not particularly lovable. I have an analogy for this. We've all had the experience of finding a bird with a broken wing. You pick up this bird and you hold it in your hand, and you think it's going to sit there quietly, sweetly, with its warm feathers, and be darling. It's not. What it does is immediately to use its muscles. And it's a very uncomfortable thing to hold in your hand because there's this fluttering. What it wants is to get away from you. It may need you to hold it and to nurse it, but what it wants is to get the heck out of there.

I think that's what we were like. Certainly that's what I was like. I was not nice to have around. I refused, for instance, to call my first foster-mother, the prickly fur coat, 'Aunt'. She wanted me to call her Aunt Lena and I couldn't. I didn't know what to call her. I never called her anything, which made being in the same room with her awkward. So, whenever she looked at me, I would find some excuse to get away. And she didn't know how to be loving and warm to this unloving, unwarm child. It was an uncomfortable relationship.

URSULA ROSENFELD

We started going to school in England and it was marvellous. I'd never realized what school really was like, that you could participate. And I did enjoy school. The wonderful part about it: it had a library. When I was at school in Germany, there was no access to books. We had a few books at home, but I'd read all those a long time ago.

In England I waded through that library, right through it, and that's how I learned to speak English, really. Through that I acquired a love of English literature. And the children were so friendly to us. It was lovely, really lovely.

Hella and I found it very difficult taking charity, though. We wanted to be independent as soon as possible. In November Hella turned sixteen, and she found out that she could go to a fever hospital, where she was able to work and get her keep. So she became independent.

I stayed at school for nine months. The headmistress would have liked me to stay on. I can't recall whether the Refugee Committee said there was no money, or whether I wanted to earn my living. It was probably a little bit of both. The Refugee Committee decided that the best thing for me would be to learn a trade. I'd always been quite good at sewing, so they said they would apprentice me to a dressmaker.

Of course, they didn't send me just to an ordinary dressmaker. A lady on the Refugee Committee who was quite rich used to have her dresses made in Mayfair, in a very high-class establishment. She spoke to the proprietor there and they took me in as an apprentice. I was quite shocked – it was my first experience of class differentials.

Even though it was wartime, there was still a court, there were still debutantes, they still had balls and all these wonderful coming-out parties for which rich people ordered lavish gowns. In those days, the cost of a gown was probably as much as what you would pay for a small house. It was incredible.

It was so incongruous, this lavishness compared to the conditions in which we worked. We sewed on wooden benches in the damp basement, where there was no natural light. Upstairs, in the showroom, it was deep carpets, gilt mirrors from wall to ceiling, wonderful furnishings, and an air of luxury. There was a little panel in the wall, with a ladder, not stairs, going down into the basement. There I sewed pearls and sequins on silk material. Hours and hours of doing that. You felt like little gremlins, beavering away in the basement. It gave me an insight into the difference between the people who have and have not.

Fortunately, I didn't stay there very long. By that time, Hella was working in a fever hospital in Oxford, and she wanted me to come to Oxford. She got me a job there at a gown shop helping to do alterations. As an apprentice, you don't earn very much, and I was still dependent on the Refugee Committee for my keep, but at the gown shop I earned a little more and was able to maintain myself fully. I later learned that Hella secretly subsidized my rent from her own meagre earnings.

While I was working in the gown shop, I went to evening classes. I wanted to study to improve my education. I had thought eventually that I might do some further education. At Oxford I was befriended by the wife of an anthropology professor. Their daughters, who were roughly about my age, had been evacuated to the United States, and I think she missed them. She invited me to come to her house once or twice a week, and we read poetry together. It was my first introduction to poetry. And it was wonderful.

In the evenings it was black-out time because of the air raids. For some reason or other, coming back one evening, I had a road traffic accident. I was knocked over by a bus. I was admitted to the Infirmary at the Oxford Hospital. The doctor took one look at me and he said that I was emaciated, and very much underweight for my size and age. He asked a social worker to come and see me.

I was living in a small room then and not looking after myself very well. They decided that working in a dingy room all day dressmaking – hours were much longer then, fifty-two hours a week was the norm – was not healthy for me. They suggested I should go to the nursery attached to the hospital, where they looked after the children of servicemen's wives when the mothers had to go into the hospital for treatment. Working there, I very much enjoyed.

LORRAINE ALLARD

I was the first refugee to arrive in Lincoln, so I was like a novelty to this town. I dressed differently. I wore knee-length socks and people used to turn around to have another look as I passed them. I wore those socks for a few months because I didn't have anything else to wear.

My guardians decided that since I was fourteen, I should go to school. I was placed in the class of my age group. Although I had to leave school in Germany before I was fourteen, I could keep up in arithmetic and in some of the other subjects as well, if I understood what the teachers were saying. But one of my memories is that I had to sit in on Shakespeare. And I certainly didn't know what that was all about.

I remember playing cricket at school, and I didn't know what cricket was. Somebody shouted, 'Run!' so I ran. I was just thrown in at the deep end. I was at the school for four months. That was it. I was really sent there to learn English because my guardians' plan was for me to help in their fashion shops. Later I did win a scholarship to art school, but I went two or three days a week only. The other days and weekends I worked in their shops.

That I didn't have further education was contrary to anything my father had ever talked about. He used to say, 'What you've learned, you've got for the rest of your life.' I had certainly not learned a lot when the school was burned down in Nuremberg. And I didn't have a further education.

By then, of course, the war had started. I just accepted the situation. There wasn't a lot I could do. I had no alternative really. Going to art school was probably a bit of a stop-gap.

While I was in Lincoln, I was never contacted by anyone from Bloomsbury House, or any refugee committee, or anyone who had arranged the place for me in Lincoln. I was completely on my own. I think I just slipped through the net.

In their own way my guardians were kind. And my foster-brother was kind, and his future wife, who was a friend, and actually worked in the shop, they were all very kind to me. It was just that I hurt within me because of my parents. There was a terrible void and a terrible loneliness for love and for warmth.

When I was eighteen, I had to do either work of importance or join the forces. I thought, this is the moment where I can up and go without hurting my guardians. I decided to join the forces because this was a way of not upsetting them. I also felt I was saying thank you to England for saving my life. So in 1943 I joined the ATS (Auxiliary Territorial Service). I applied to become a driver. You had to take lots of ability tests, but I was lucky and I passed. I was even luckier because I was posted to London.

As a soldier, suddenly I was in an environment where I was the same as everybody else – for the first time in my life. In Lincoln I more or less 'existed', because I was waiting for tomorrow and tomorrow and tomorrow. In the army – 277072 was my army number – I felt like everybody else. The people on my left, the people on my right, we were all the same. That was the first time in my life I felt that I could do everything the other people are doing. If I felt lonely and didn't have a home, there were others who didn't have a home. They were separated from their families too, in a different way, but it was a great equalizer for me.

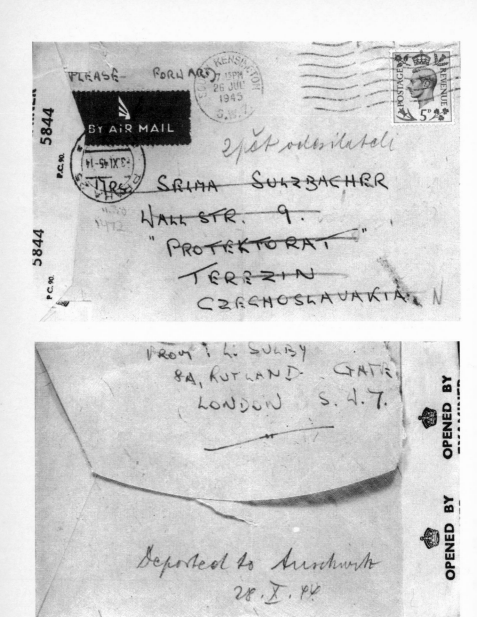

Lorraine Allard's letter to her mother in Theresienstadt

Chapter Ten

NONE TO COMFORT THEM

*'It's that sort of faint feeling in the air of hope,
and that hope suddenly fading.'*

URSULA ROSENFELD

LORRAINE ALLARD

Letters from Lorraine Allard to her parents after VE Day

Dearest Darling Papi,

This, I hope and pray, might reach you, now that this ghastly war is over and will very soon bring me news of your present whereabouts and your well-being.

It's been so terribly long, and sitting here it's been so hard, as we have been so very helpless to make your existence easier. I hope that you have received at least some of the Red Cross parcels.

I want you to know that no stone is being left unturned by any of us to secure your future happiness, and that I am sure we shall be reunited again very soon. For the last two years, I have been in the British Army, which I know you will be very pleased to hear now. I am driving staff-cars and teaching German too.

Keep that chin up and you will see the happy ending at last. I am writing another note, as I have two addresses from you.

10,000,000 kisses from

Your Lore.

Mutschi Dearest Darling,

I am writing to you too, in case Papi's note doesn't reach you both – of all the things you have been through in your life and faced so bravely, this was too much, but now it has been avenged. I have helped by joining the army here. And I know, I feel it, that we shall be reunited again very soon . . . You know that now your troubles at long last are over. I have grown up very much and am now the same size as Liese. We compare measurements through the post!

I am very much hoping to visit the continent in the near future to see you, but it might be a little while yet. After that you are coming here and we are all going to take care of you and make you forget the mere name of Theresienstadt.

Bless you darlings and take good care of yourself.

Very many kisses from

Your Lore.

I remember VE Day very clearly. It was just wonderful, wonderful. We all danced in Piccadilly Circus. And for me, I just thought, well this is it, I'm going to see my parents next week. That's all one thought about.

I went straight back and wrote to both of them – wrote separately, because I had separate addresses, through Red Cross messages, in Theresienstadt. The letters were returned to me, about three, four months later – it took a long time. All it said on the back was: 'Deported to Auschwitz 28. X. 44'. That's how I found out.

It took about a year before they published lists of the people who perished – or, as my husband rightly says, were murdered in Auschwitz and the other camps. All the lists were available. By then I was living and working in the country and I came up to London and looked at the lists at Bloomsbury House. I think I knew because of the returned letters, but there I saw it in print, hanging on the wall, which wasn't the first shock. It was just confirmation.

I was devastated. The world had collapsed. I was about twenty then and everything had changed. I felt just lost. Between the ages of fourteen to twenty, I was waiting and waiting, biding time as opposed to living life, I suppose. I had a number of boyfriends, but I never ever took anyone seriously because everything was postponed until I was with my parents. I would never have thought of a serious relationship until I was with them again. And suddenly I had to accept I was on my own. That was a shock.

How did I cope with it? I thought my parents must have been terribly relieved that I was alive, that they had sent me out. I think this was a comfort, that that must have been their comfort.

Did I need love? Very desperately. I had a boyfriend whose mother thought he ought to marry someone with lots of money, which I didn't have. After being engaged and waiting for him for quite a long time – two and a half years I think – I decided I had waited long enough. I met someone else, who from the moment I met him, decided that I was the right person for him. I wasn't really, or he wasn't for me, but we married within two months. It didn't work out too well.

All those experiences have left a mark on me. I think I would have been greatly helped if there had been someone to do counselling then, which is all around us now. It wasn't then. I am left with a legacy that I am oversensitive with my family and still in desperate need to be loved. My husband will always say, 'But I've told you this is good.' I say, 'I'd like to hear it again.' I'm still very insecure, and I'm an old lady by now.

LORE SEGAL

My father died a week before the end of the European war. I had been used to his falling ill in Vienna, and he had started doing it again in England. His recurring illnesses were probably as heavy a burden, as terrible a part of my childhood, as Hitler, or immigration. I had noticed that he always got ill when I didn't expect it, always had some disaster that I hadn't thought of. So it came to me that what I had to do was to consider as possibilities all disasters, at all moments of the day, because then they wouldn't happen. And that was pretty strenuous.

In 1940, along with other refugees, he was interned as an 'enemy alien' on the Isle of Man. There he had a slight stroke, his first. I think the English took one look at him and saw that he was not going to be a danger to the British Commonwealth, and sent him home at a time when we had no home.

My mother and I were staying in a little room at the head of a very steep staircase when my father rejoined us. There were only two beds in that room. I lay in one and fitfully slept. When I woke up, I would see my parents sitting side by side on the other bed. I remember my father weeping out of despair.

My father then had a series of strokes and became more and more incompetent and less able to take care of himself. His final stroke came just before VE Day. My father's death was certainly a relief to him, to my mother, and to me. I remember having a dreadful dream after his death. I heard his walking stick, and was horrified at the continuation of his suffering, of my mother's being burdened by him, of waiting for the next disaster.

When my father died, I had one burst of weeping and then couldn't manage it again. I remember walking up on the downs on a very stormy day, hoping to generate some feeling. I've always connected my inability to mourn for my father with having cut myself off from my real feelings during that first separation from my parents, and supplanting the word 'grief' with the word 'interesting'. To this day, I tend to say 'Isn't that interesting?' when I mean 'This is intolerable.'

URSULA ROSENFELD

As soon as the war finished, Hella and I went to the Red Cross Committee and asked them to search for Mother. It took some time, but eventually we got a letter from them to say that it was suspected that she had been killed in Minsk in Russia because that's where she was deported to. That's all we ever heard.

I'd always hoped she would survive. She was such a strong person, and she was relatively young, and very capable, but the odds were just impossible. It was very hard to come to terms with when you've always had that hope. And, of course, we had no grave really, no parting, no end, no funeral. It's that sort of faint feeling in the air of hope, and that hope suddenly fading.

Later, when Hella went back to Quakenbrück, we decided to erect a memorial stone in the cemetery because she has no grave. And on this stone we wrote: 'That her death is our mode and reason for life' – what happened to her, we would strive, as far as we could, that such a thing would never happen again.

Of course, you look at the world and, unfortunately, we're just very small individuals in a large pond. But I hope we both have done our best. Quite often in actions I ask myself: am I doing the right thing, am I hurting someone in what I'm doing? That doesn't mean I'm always a good person. I have my weaknesses, the same as everyone else. But it does serve as a reminder when this has happened to you.

ALEXANDER GORDON

From the moment I left Germany to go to England, my mother was sitting in No Man's Land in the camp. I got letters from her quite often, until the war broke out. I still have them all.

Eventually, my Aunt Judith bribed some officials and got my mother out of the camp into Grodno, Poland, which was later occupied by the Russians. After the Germans marched in, I never heard another thing. Total silence. I think if she survived the bombardment, she was probably arrested and sent to Auschwitz or another camp.

Alexander Gordon's mother in Zbaszyn, 1938

At the end of the war, I tried to find out what happened, but whatever family was left in Poland all disappeared. I was the last one in the family to get out.

VERA GISSING

When the war started, and all correspondence with our parents ceased, Eva tried to keep up my hopes that we would be reunited. She wrote to me almost every week.

At the Czech school we were better informed about what was happening at home and I worried a great deal. But Eva never lost hope we would be reunited with our parents. As the end of the war drew near, and we were all waiting with hope and fear for news of our parents, she and I were in constant contact.

I was the first child at the school to hear that my mother had actually survived the war. She sent a four-line letter to some business acquaintances of Father's in Stockholm. First Eva, then I received a telegram from them, which said: 'Congratulations, both your parents alive and well.'

It was the happiest moment in our lives. But it was a tragic mistake. They mistook my mother's and my aunt's signature for my mother's and father's signature. When the lists of the survivors of Belsen came to our school, I found both Mother's and Aunty Berta's names on the list with the numbers which had been tattooed on their arms, exactly the same, except for the last digit, so I knew it was them and no one else. But Father's name was not there, and I began to worry that perhaps he had not survived. Again, though, I felt so fortunate that God had given me back my mother.

I enlisted in the first transport of children to go back to Czechoslovakia, which the government arranged for those of us who were in Britain without parents.

I was at Aunty Margery's saying goodbye when I received a letter from Eva. She always was a terrible scribbler. This letter was written in an immaculately tidy handwriting, and as soon as I started reading it, I knew she was leading to something grave.

She broke the news to me very gently, very carefully, that though Mother had survived the liberation of Belsen by the British army, she died of typhus two days after the end of the war, and therefore we were never going to see her again. That was the most cruel blow fate could have dealt us. To have her given to us, and then to have her taken away so cruelly, was something that took an awful long time to come to terms with. I don't think I ever will.

A few days later we received a letter from an unknown woman telling us that her husband was convinced that my father had been shot on a death march from one

Eva and Vera's parents, Irma and Karel Diamant, taken after the girls' departure

concentration camp to another in December 1944.

The Rainfords and Aunty Margery both offered to adopt me, but I wanted to go home. There was no question of my staying in England.

When I was repatriated to Czechoslovakia in August 1945, on our airplane sat about fourteen friends of mine from our school, and each one of us was an orphan. And so was nearly every child who came on those Kindertransports from Prague.

At the airport I was met by Aunt Berta, who was the only survivor of our family. She buried not only my mother in Belsen, but our two cousins who were due to come out on 3 September 1939. All three died of typhus after the liberation of Belsen.

My aunt was so thin – just skin and bones, and her eyes were pools of indescribable sadness. As she hugged me and I hugged her frail body, I vowed that I would try to bring some happiness and laughter into her life.

Later, in my hometown, I was given my most precious possession, a letter from Mother to say goodbye, written on the eve of her deportation. When I read the letter, I cried to my aunt, 'I should have been with her. I shouldn't have let her go through all this suffering on her own.' And my aunt said, 'How dare you say that! Don't you realize that the knowledge that you were in safety was the only consolation, the only happiness that she and your father shared to the end?'

EVA HAYMAN

I remember I was nursing in the children's ward, joking with the kids and laughing. I was called to the telephone and there was a telegram for me at my friend's house. I asked her would she read it. Over the telephone I heard: 'Your parents were gravely ill. There was no hope. Wait for further news. Berta.'

I probably didn't quite take in that my parents were dead, so I went back to the ward and carried on making beds until one of the little boys said to me, 'Why aren't you laughing this time?'

That's when I burst into tears and ran out. I remember going out in the garden and just lying on the lawn. I didn't want to be with anybody. It was such a shock. Suddenly the future which we'd always painted wasn't there. There was no future. There was just an emptiness. And I realized that I had to let Vera know, in case she hadn't heard yet.

I was lying there, trying to compose a letter to her in my head. That was the hardest task, to tell her. Soon after that, I can't remember how it happened, I got a holiday and I spent a week with Vera at the Czech school before they were repatriated. By then, of course, my sister was seventeen, I was twenty-one, and I didn't have to look after her any

Telegram to
Eva Hayman,
1945

more. We were equal, and friends, and we could cry together and comfort each other.

But when I heard the telegram, that's when I finished writing in the diary I wrote for my parents. The last paragraph in it was:

Today this journal ends, for my dearest mother and father know it all. Now they're aware of each thought in my head, each word, every deed.

Rest in peace, my dearest, may happiness surround you in the domain where suffering can't reach you. Be joyful about us, but do not cry with us. Our lives will be dedicated to the memory of you. By the moon and the stars, for ever will my love soar to you, wherever you are.

And that is where the English journal finished.

Last Letter from Vera and Eva's Mother / January 1943

My dearest children,

My life belonged to you, and you and your dear father were the happiness of my life. If only this letter were not to say goodbye, if only fate, which has treated me so cruelly, would once more allow me to be reunited with you and the one we all so dearly love, if only we could resume our life together, life filled with joy and love . . .

When I was sixteen years old I met your father. Never did I think that one person could give so much love and happiness. My life turned into the most joyful dream, the most wonderful fairy tale. When we were married on 12 December 1920, I was the happiest person alive. Four perfect years went by and then you arrived, Evicko, who are nineteen years old today, to whom I should like to say so many beautiful things, but to whom – and to my dear Veruska – I am now writing this sad letter, yet hoping that one day I may be able to tell you everything, to hold you close to my anguished heart.

On 13 November, two days after your father's birthday, I was numbed by the cruel blow which fate dealt me – and you – my dearest children, on that day . . .

They took away father, your good, kind father who took such good care of us, whose only wish was your happiness, who so hoped to be reunited with you one day, who so looked forward to that day; he lived for you, he had faith in you, and he believed – so very very much . . .

For six weeks he was kept at the county court in Boleslav, where the Gestapo had taken him, then he was transferred to the Little Fortress in Terezin.

On the 12th of this month it will be my turn to leave. Since the beginning of the month I have been sharing my home with the Goldschmidt boys from next door. Their father is in the same prison as yours; their mother died a year ago, and so I shall now go with them. I am not afraid of going, for I shall meet your grandfather again, and Aunty Berta, Mila and Karel; the others have gone on to Poland. I fear nothing, but I am filled with anxiety and endless pain. Your father and I wanted to live, work and suffer together, and now they have torn us apart. I promise you, my dear children, that I shall be brave, that the thought of you and of our dearest one will be my strength and that I shall not give up – but will fate allow me to see happier days? . . .

This letter will be given to you; always hold these friends in high esteem and never forget their goodness.

And now, my dear children, on behalf of your father and myself, I wish you – not only for the new year, not only for Eva's birthday, but for the rest of your life . . . Be happy, be brave. We gave you love, we gave you the foundations of life, we wanted to give you more, so much more . . . How I wish that fate would make up to you all it has refused us, how I hope that your life will flow smoothly, filled with joy and happiness. Remember your home and us, but do not grieve. Your whole life lies before you, life which you will build at the side of your husbands. I give my blessings to them and to your children; I shall be watching over you from Heaven, and praying for your happiness.

I embrace you and I bless you,

Your mamika.

INGE SADAN

After about two years of not hearing from our parents, life sort of stretched on endlessly, but suddenly we heard that our parents had reached Spain. That was a neutral country and they could start writing letters again. Of course, they were concerned: how are we doing? We lied and wrote beautiful letters – everything was fine. It really is amazing how much you can fabricate in twenty-five words, how many lies – good lies.

Our letters kept them going on their way, because life was very hard in Europe, even in neutral countries. When they reached Portugal, we continued to send them glowing reports of how wonderful life was in England for us. It must have made them very happy how well everything was going. We began to believe it ourselves, even.

Then, in January 1944, we received a telegram. The telegram said: 'Arriving Friday, 4.45. Engelhard.' That was all. We saw from the telegram it was from London. So, suddenly, they were arriving after five years.

Unfortunately, 4.45 was the train that my school friends were coming back on as well. I knew that since the whole village also was aware they were coming, they would all be at the station. My schoolfriends would see me and my brother and sister meeting our parents for the first time in five years . . . It was a tremendous ordeal.

We went down to the station to wait, and I couldn't cope with it. So I went back home saying, 'I'm going home. I'm going to put the kettle on. They'll need a cup of tea.' I mean, how English can you get?

I waited, and waited, and waited. It took ages, like a year, but it might have been half an hour. And suddenly there's my brother and sister with this elderly couple, with suitcases and bags, coming up the path.

Bertha and Inge's parents, Moshe and Rosa Engelhard, England, 1944

I remember rushing down to meet them. I knew they were my parents, but it wasn't the same parents I'd left. They were much older and they were worn-out, and, obviously, we weren't the same children that they'd sent off. Suddenly I realized I couldn't say anything except their names, 'Mutti' and 'Papa', or I couldn't speak to them because I'd forgotten all my German, and they hadn't learned much English.

We just stood there looking at each other. It was such a traumatic moment. It was wonderful, and yet it was terrible. Then they came up to the house and, in true English fashion, I made the cup of tea.

BERTHA LEVERTON

It was sad for Inge because she couldn't speak German any more. My brother spoke it with difficulty. I was the only one who could communicate with our parents.

We children had all three decided that once our parents were here, everything would be fine. They would take us away and we'd start a new life. And they would never be told of what we had suffered.

I'm afraid I was the traitor, though, and I broke the promise that we'd made to each other because that first night my mother slept in my bed and she dragged all the story out of me. All night we talked.

In the morning it was my job to make the tea and to bring it to Aunty Vera and Uncle Billy in bed. And I was exhausted. I just couldn't get up. They called, 'Tea!' and my mother, who could only speak a sentence or two of English, got out of bed and went into their room. She said, 'You make tea. No more my child make your tea.'

Then the storm broke. I don't know how my father did it without speaking English, but he went to the village telephone and he summoned the Refugee Committee in Manchester. I never heard from the Refugee Committee, but my father found it on the telephone without speaking English. And he said, 'You come immediately.' He realized that it was going to come to blows if they didn't take us away. They came and there was a tremendous scene and they took us away.

I remember the very words of the Refugee Committee lady, very lady-like, and she said to my parents in German, 'Either Bertha is the biggest liar or the biggest fool.' My mother turned around and said to her, 'I wish she would be a liar.' My mother thought I was very foolish. What my mother didn't realize, and my father never realized, and we never talked about, was that I could have left – I earned more than enough money to support Theo, Inge and myself – but Uncle Billy and Aunty Vera were not going to let Inge go. They told me many times, 'You go if you want to. We can't stop you.' (I was just on the point of being twenty-one.) 'But we'll never let Inge go.' And I realized I couldn't leave her there. She was fourteen then and in danger, not only for the housework that she would have to do, but in danger of Uncle Billy. And I couldn't risk a thing like that.

So I stayed. My mother reproached me, 'How is it that you stayed such a fool? You said you were earning money, couldn't you have gone?' We never told. That is one thing our parents never got to know, the reason I couldn't leave my sister behind.

INGE SADAN

My father went with me to school. He heard that my French teacher was from Germany and her mother ran a hostel and that's where I stayed until the term ended.

I left Uncle Billy and Aunty Vera's that morning and never went back. My brother was sent to another hostel in Manchester and my parents made for Birmingham where we had two male cousins. I left the hostel on the 4th day of the 4th month of 1944 to join my parents in Birmingham, where I started a new life.

I remember arriving about midday on a Thursday or Friday. My mother had been cooking for the Sabbath and she gave me something to eat. It was gefilte fish – the first time I'd had gefilte fish for at least five years. I wanted more, and I said, 'I want another piece.' I couldn't speak to my mother in German, but she understood pretty well. And she said, 'No, no, there's more.' So then I had chopped liver – all a sort of preview of the Sabbath meal. I had chopped liver and I wanted more. 'No, no, there's more to come.' So I had soup, noodle soup. Then there was meat and potatoes, and apple compote – it was all these old tastes coming back to me. Had anybody taken me to the Ritz or anywhere else any other time in my life, it would never have tasted as good as that meal. That was my best meal ever; it was just heaven.

Here I had my parents again, and I'd had this wonderful meal; still it was very difficult to get back into being a family again. Our parents wanted us to be a family straight away, as we had been in Germany, but we'd had so many different experiences in the five years we'd been apart. They were running away while we were more or less safe, but we had bombing and they didn't. It took a long time for us even to talk about the different experiences we had, apart from the language, because it took me about six months to relearn some German.

A normal teenager is mixed up. I was twenty times worse than a normal teenager. I was very shy. I wouldn't mix with people, except at school. Socially, I was a misfit, and that worried my father very much. He forced me to go to youth groups. That was another thing, he and my mother were religious, and we, of course, hadn't kept any religious observances for years.

Although it was very difficult in the beginning, we did manage it. After about a year I felt part of the family again. Once my parents came, I didn't lie any more, I didn't steal any more, which really should give hope to people. I always feel if you're stressed, you react in certain ways that will end once the stress has gone. So there is hope for humanity, I would say. You can get to be a decent person again, even if you've done things that weren't so commendable.

ROBERT SUGAR

The first time I heard that any of my parents survived was the beginning of 1945. I got a letter from an American airman in Italy, who had crashed or been forced down behind Russian lines, in Hungary. There he met a number of survivors, among them my mother, and she gave him a letter that she had survived. At that time she did not know yet whether my father had survived.

After my mother went back to Vienna to get my father to move, they fled to Budapest because Hungary was still neutral then. My mother sent emissaries back to Vienna to get my grandmother to walk across the border, but my grandmother had varicose veins and never made it out. She was deported on the twenty-third transport to Minsk.

In Budapest my father was immediately drafted into Hungarian forced labour. For the first few years it wasn't too bad because the Nazis hadn't fully taken over yet. But all that changed towards the end of the war. Typically, though, my mother tore off the yellow badge and refused to be deported. She just said, 'I'm not going.' She went underground.

My father was with the Jewish forced-labour battalion, which was massacred at the Hungarian-Austrian border. While my mother escaped by pure daring, he just escaped by luck. It was the middle of winter, his feet were frozen, and he hobbled back to Budapest on frozen feet.

So now I get this letter from my mother, and once again, I'm different. Everyone else's parents, not a word, and here my mother has survived. By now I wanted to share the fate of the others, although I couldn't admit that to myself.

I had gone through a serious period of mourning. I'd lain in bed one night and said, if only I could see my mother once more in my life. I just let myself go. By the time the news came she had survived, I had already done my mourning. At that point I was enjoying my youth so much, my freedom, I couldn't admit the monstrous idea to myself that I wanted to stay the way I was. I didn't really want to rejoin a family again.

But once again, it's ambivalent because I was very proud of my mother. I was proud that I belonged to an indestructible race.

In 1947 she showed up in Belfast, on her way to America. It took her from 1945 to 1947 to get all the papers. And she arrived ten times more elegant than anybody in Northern Ireland. She had Hungarian leather bags and all the fancy stuff that hadn't reached Ireland yet.

At that time I wanted to stay in Belfast. Northern Ireland just suited me. I liked the pace of life on the island. You don't have to become king of the world to live there. I went up to the Belfast Committee and

I said, 'Listen, could you help my parents get out from Hungary?' But they were finished with the refugee business, and they said, in so many words, 'Nothing doing, kid, we're through with refugees.' All of us who had relatives elsewhere were told to get going. The Belfast Jewish Committee had done enough, and now it's time to say goodbye. Although a small community, they had saved hundreds of Jews, but they wanted to go back to their old life.

So I left Northern Ireland. My friend Gert helped me carry the bags to the bus. If I would have dared, I would have wept, but we were not allowed to weep because we were not only Zionists, but British, and we Jews couldn't show any weakness to anyone. We were told, 'You can't show any weakness. You cannot cry.'

I couldn't have said it at the time, 'I love this place', but it became such a reality in my life. I loved our farm, the countryside, that location. And here I was going again. I was never really that interested in going to America. But I did.

KURT FUCHEL

After the war ended, my parents called or wrote, I'm not sure which, and told us where they were. They were hidden by some extremely wonderful people in the south of France and I was told that they were alive and that someday I would probably have to go back and live with them. I think I was horrified by that idea.

Uncle Percy persuaded my parents to wait until I finished the English school certificate at age sixteen, and also they needed time to re-establish themselves. After all, when the war ended, they were in a small village, owning nothing except the clothes on their back. So they moved to Toulouse and got a place to live. My father got a job and eventually, in 1947, they were ready for me.

I didn't want to, but the Cohens took me to Paris, where I was to meet my parents. I remember standing outside the hotel, and I saw in the distance my parents approach. I couldn't look at them directly, so I looked at their reflection in the window of a shop as they walked towards me. And I felt a very, very strong emotion. It was a sense of elation, of love – I suddenly felt it and fought it. But I knew it was them.

Kurt Fuchel,
age 18, with
mother and
father,
Toulouse,
France, 1949

We went to dinner in a restaurant, and I remember it was difficult because I didn't speak German or French, and they spoke very little English. I had the Cohens on one side, my parents on the other. I felt caught in the middle. I didn't want to get too close to either at that moment.

When it came time to say goodbye to the Cohens, I realized for the first time, I think, consciously, that they had loved me, especially Percy, because he was in tears, and I'd never seen him cry before. It was a realization which has stuck with me.

My parents let go of a seven-year-old and got back a sixteen-year-old. My mother, especially, wanted to carry on where she'd left off. But a sixteen-year-old doesn't like to be treated like a seven-year-old.

My mother was terribly afraid of anything happening to me: I shouldn't go out alone, I shouldn't do anything risky. Of course, what I wanted to do at sixteen was to get to know some girls. And it wasn't easy because how do you get to know a girl when you're desperately shy and you don't speak the language? So it was a very difficult time for me.

Of course, I'm very lucky. I realize this: whereas most of the *Kinder* never saw their parents again, I not only had mine back, but another set of parents as well. What more could one ask for?

MARIAM COHEN

We went over to Paris to take Kurt to his parents. We met at this restaurant. Kurt's father, who was more demonstrative than the mother, put his hand through Kurt's curls. And Kurt gave him a wallop. My husband said, 'Don't you ever do that again, Kurt. Your father is showing you his affection.'

Then we had to leave him. Kurt was terribly upset. You can imagine. I remember him looking back. It was very, very sad. He didn't want to go. He didn't know them. But, I mean, what could you do? He was their son, and they wanted him. They'd lived to get him back. You can understand that. What they'd been through was dreadful.

LORY CAHN

At the time I was liberated, which was 15 April 1945, I was in Bergen-Belsen. I only stayed at Auschwitz six to eight weeks. After that I was transferred to Buchenwald, then to Dachau, then to Kurzbach, then taken on a march to Gross-Rosen. We finally came to Bergen-Belsen at the beginning of 1945. It was excruciatingly cold and there was snow on the ground.

We were all quite sick and worn out. I was deathly ill. Bergen-Belsen was just about the worst. Every time we went to stand outside, we smelled bodies. People were dying by the hundreds.

One morning we heard a lot of noise and hollering. We said something must be happening. The English army was coming in to liberate us. Everybody was running out, but I was too sick to move. I crawled halfway out on my hands and knees, but I couldn't go any further. I lay there and I prayed to God. Suddenly, there was a soldier in front of me, asking if he could help.

It was a month before my twentieth birthday. After four years and eight concentration camps I weighed 58 pounds. To put that in perspective, when my son was six years old, he weighed 60 pounds.

The soldiers tried to be good to us and they gave us chocolate and chicken soup, instead of bread and something dry or something to drink. That was a disaster. People were dying by the second from the rich food.

A couple of days later, they were sending soldiers around to compile lists. We were liberated by the English army, but they had a contingent of all the other armies: French, Russian and American.

One day this soldier came and asked everybody in my barrack to give our name and where we came from. He asked our nationality, and when he heard that I spoke German, he spoke German to me. I was fascinated. He was from Germany, but he was with the Americans. I saw him maybe once or twice, but only very, very briefly.

They took me to a hospital, where I met quite a few people I had known before, including a couple of people from Breslau. We all asked, 'What's happened to us?' It was just too, too unbelievable to grasp. I never gave a thought about my mother, my father or anything. That only came a little bit later. My mind needed to be reborn, and I needed to get a little stronger to even think.

After a month of still being in the camp, they moved us because the camp was so infected they had to burn it down. People who were well enough to travel came to the camp looking for others. We were told we could take a bus to the next city, Hanover, where you could go and register your name so the rest of the world could find out who survived and how to find you.

I think I was one of the very first ones to go. I was not that strong, but I wanted to find out if I could get any information. We arrived at a regular house and there were a lot of elderly men standing outside.

As we walked inside, I noticed a little man some distance away, and I said, 'Oh, my God, that's my father.' Then I realized, no, no, that's not my father, but he lived with my father in the same building in Theresienstadt.

I went to talk to him. I said, 'Do you know who I am?'

He said, 'Yes, you're Louis's daughter. You don't look too good, but that's who you are.' He looked fine. He had just come from Theresienstadt.

I said, 'Theresienstadt? Do you know what happened to my parents?'

'Yes, your father is in Theresienstadt.'

I said, 'What do you mean, he's in Theresienstadt? How can that be?'

'Well, Theresienstadt stayed the way it was all along.'

'Well, how about my mother?'

'Oh, your mother, they took her three months before to Auschwitz. She went into the gas chamber.'

If he had told me I'd just won a million dollars, it would have affected me the same way. I didn't cry a tear. It was as if I heard it but it didn't mean anything to me, anything whatsoever. I was so numb that later on, when I thought of it, I felt ashamed of myself that I had absolutely no reaction to it.

But I was so thrilled to hear my father was alive. I couldn't believe it because he was always the one who was sick, and I couldn't believe that he survived and my mother didn't.

This man told me there was a bus that went to Theresienstadt once a week. I talked to the bus driver, who said he could ask for my father there. At the last minute, I thought, no, maybe this isn't good enough. My father might not believe him. The bus driver gave me a little piece of paper and I scribbled my name on it, so my father would see my handwriting. I didn't write anything – only my name.

The bus driver told me when he was going and how many days later he'd come back. He said, 'We'll get here about five, six in the morning.'

I said, 'Well, I'll try to be there waiting.'

The day before they were due to come back, I went into town with the bus. I could have asked the people working there if they had a place for me to stay, but I was so innocent and so unworldly – I didn't know anything. It was like I was born again.

I sat on the street all night long, waiting for my father to come. I was so scared. I had no watch. I didn't know the time. The bus finally came, and I was so excited. I stood up and I looked into the bus. There were a lot of people coming out. And little by little, a few more. Everybody came out but my father.

I said to the bus driver, 'Why didn't you bring my father?'

He said, 'I'm sorry to tell you but they told me in the office that two or three days before I returned, your father went on a bus to Berlin.'

I said, 'Oh, my God, how am I ever going to find my father in Berlin?' Where we were was like from here to China because there was no transportation. There was nothing. It was terrible.

I went back to Bergen-Belsen. A couple of weeks went by and I started to get a little stronger. I met two guys who had been walking around looking for family. They had gone through quite a bit of Germany, and they had come across a little town in Bavaria, in which they might stay, which was not damaged at all. They went to the city hall and were told to speak to the Americans in charge, at the American military installation. The officers there said, 'We would only be too happy to have some Jewish people moving in.' They asked my girlfriend and me if we would go with them.

It took us a couple of days to get there. We stopped along the road and begged for food, and we slept with the animals on farms. Two or three nights we slept with the pigs – it stank like crazy, but it was nice and warm. Eventually we reached the town and got to a very nice house. It was the first time in my new life that I walked into a completely furnished house, with beds and nobody there but these two guys, and my girlfriend and me. We couldn't believe it. It was late at night, we were exhausted, we went to bed.

The next morning we got up and there was nothing to eat. A couple of soldiers came and brought us food. They spoke German – they were all originally from Germany, Jewish boys – and they said tonight was Rosh Hashanah,* which we hadn't realized. They said they would return that night with some food, and if there were enough people maybe we could say a prayer or two. We said fine. We were in such a daze, we didn't know what was happening. It was like we were living in a dream world.

Evening came, and I was very unhappy. I had left the very few things I'd had on the back of an army truck that had given us a ride to this town, and now I had nothing to wear except what I had on. My feet were very swollen and I had to take my shoes off. It didn't matter much that I had nothing else to wear, but I remember thinking at the time, I wish I had a pair of shoes on.

Then the soldiers all walked in, and they introduced themselves. One of them was Walter Cahn. I said, 'We've met before.' He had taken my information in Bergen-Belsen, just after liberation. After all this it was unreal to run into somebody you knew just by chance again. And this man Walter turned out to be the man who would be my husband.

Walter was also the person who helped me find my father through the Red Cross and Military Intelligence. It took almost eight months to find him and another four before we could get together again and he could come to where I lived at the time. It was an unbelievable reunion. The last time I'd seen him was in 1942, and it seemed like it was a hundred years.

He told me that at the very, very end, just before Theresienstadt was liberated, a few people were given a chance to go to Switzerland. My parents were among them. A week or two before they were to

* The Jewish festival of New Year.

leave, they deported my mother. My father wasn't aware of it at the time because they were lodged in separate areas.

When he heard about her deportation, he said, 'Isn't there anything that can be done because we were selected to go to Switzerland? Can you look at the papers?' But it was too late. They asked my father whether he wanted to go, but he said, no, he didn't want to go because he thought for sure they'd come for him, and he would be reunited with my mother, through death.

NORBERT WOLLHEIM

In Auschwitz we all lived from morning till night with the pressure to save our lives. In the morning you didn't know if you would still be around in the evening. And in the evening you didn't know if you'd still be alive the next day.

Survival is an accident. You cannot ask a soldier who comes out of battle, 'Why were your comrades, left and right, killed, and you survived?' You have no explanation for that. It's an accident.

Certainly, I would say, the fact that I was able to work as a welder in Auschwitz after a while helped me. As a welder I worked under a roof and was not exposed to the elements, and that was very impor-

Norbert Wollheim (*right*) with Rabbi Leo Baeck, 1950s

tant. But this is not the whole answer. The answer is, it's an accident.

At the moment of liberation, we were very happy, but on the other hand, really very sad because I realized that I was one of the last who had survived, that all the others who had gone with me to Auschwitz or had been taken to Auschwitz would never return. My then wife, my child, my sister, my parents and, all in all, approximately seventy aunts, uncles, cousins . . .

There were usually around a thousand people on the trains to Auschwitz. At the end of the war I tried to find out how many had survived from the train on which I was deported. I could only find six or seven, myself included.

Eva Hayman with husband and children, New Zealand, 1957

Chapter Eleven

LIVING WITH THE PAST

'It's strange that it's only six years out of a long life,
and those six years will affect the rest of your life.'

EVA HAYMAN

HEDY EPSTEIN

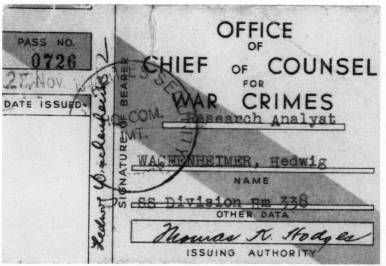

Hedy Epstein's interpreter's pass for the Nuremberg trials, 1946

In July 1945, I went back to Germany to work for the American government. When the train stopped for the first time in Germany, there were children on the platform begging for candy, chewing gum, whatever. There were people on the train, just like me, who were refugees from Germany or Austria and had been in England during the war, and some of them gave these children whatever they had with them. I just became absolutely livid: how dare you give these Nazis whatever you have with you? I was totally unaware until that moment how much I hated Germans. And some of those so-called Nazis were maybe five years old, ten years old, certainly not Nazis.

Hedy Epstein (*centre rear*), age 22, interpreter at the Nuremberg trials

But that hatred for the German population stayed with me for many, many years – for way too long.

One of the reasons I went back to Germany was to look for my parents. The most sensible place to go would have been Kippenheim, but I didn't go back until August 1947. I think on some level I knew my parents didn't survive, but as long as I didn't go back to Kippenheim, I could still say, well, maybe they're back in Kippenheim. I know it doesn't really make a lot of sense, but I think it was my survival mechanism. I just wasn't ready yet to accept the fact that I no longer had parents, that I hadn't had parents for a long time.

Hedy Epstein's parents, Ella and Hugo Wachenheimer, 1938

In August 1947, I finally summoned up enough courage to go back to Kippenheim because I knew I wouldn't be staying in Germany much longer. I arrived at the railroad station, and as I walked towards the village, with every step my fear increased. I felt that I was back in the 1930s, in the Nazi period, and someone might recognize me, know that I'm Jewish.

When I walked past the house where I used to live, I didn't dare look at it. I just gave it a quick glance out of the corner of my eyes. I went to the village hall, not knowing who was there, but I was wearing my American uniform that had been given to me for security reasons, and I felt that might give me some protection because they might think I'm an American. I was quickly shown to the mayor. He examined my identification papers and I told him that I used to live here with my parents and that I wanted to go back to where we had lived, but that I was afraid to go there alone, and would he accompany me. He readily agreed to do that.

By the time we arrived at my home, which was just a few steps away, I decided I didn't want to go inside. I wanted to remember it the way it was in my childhood, even if my memory was faulty. So even then, it was still difficult to face the truth.

In 1956 I received two letters from a French organization, advising me that my parents had been sent to Auschwitz. Soon after that I had a recurring dream. I'd dream it once, twice a week, but when I woke up I never knew what I'd dreamt. I just knew it was this awful, awful dream again. I'd be extremely agitated and upset, and I wasn't able to go back to sleep.

Then some time during the 1960s, I had that dream again and, maybe for the first time, I spoke out loud, and I said, 'It's not my fault. I didn't do it.' My husband woke me up and said, 'You didn't do anything, you're just dreaming.' Perhaps because he woke me up in the middle of the dream, for the first time I knew what I was dreaming. I dreamt that I was back in Kippenheim, and that I was putting my parents on a train, and I knew full well where the train was going, that it was going to a concentration camp, and that they were going to their death.

I immediately understood the dream: this is because of my guilt feelings because I survived. After that, I didn't have this dream any more.

In September 1980, I finally decided to go back to Europe and to visit the various camps where my parents had been. The last camp that I visited was Auschwitz. When I stood on the spot where the cattle cars arrived, and where the selection was made by Dr Mengele and his cohorts, I finally accepted the fact that my parents and other family members did not survive.

I didn't really grieve even then. I don't know even how to put it into words. It wasn't grief, just a terrible, terrible pain, and I wanted to get away from Auschwitz. There wasn't a bird. There wasn't a fly. There was no vegetation. Except around the crematoria. There was an abundance of goldenrod there. I'd never seen goldenrod so high, and I know what fertilized it.

Hedy Epstein, London, 1999

The autobiography I wrote is called *Remembering Is Not Enough** and I certainly do my share of remembering, but remembering also has to have a present and a future perspective. You can't just stop at remembering.

I don't think I ever made a conscious decision to devote myself to human rights and social-justice issues. Someone helped me. I can't pay back or thank some of the people who helped me, but I can do something for other people. Nobody can do everything, but if each and every one of us does his or her share, then maybe someday we'll have peace in this world. I'd like to live that long.

LORY CAHN

Many times, even while I was in camp, I thought about it: what would have happened if my father hadn't pulled me out of the Kindertransport? I wasn't concerned so much about what happened to me, but would I have been able to help my mother and father through the awful ordeal we all had to go through? I would have never, ever

* The book is in German and its title is *Erinnern Ist Nicht Genug*.

mentioned that to my father again, 'Why did you do that?' Because I think I would have done him very wrong. Being a mother, I can fully understand what it would mean if this is what I would have had to go through with my child – God forbid.

Once I saw my father again, I was so thrilled to be with him, and to hold him, and have him hold me, and to hug me and kiss me. My father was always very, very loving – big hugs and kisses. He was a very strong-willed person, and apparently, I must have inherited that from him. My main concern was always, 'Let me be strong, and let me try to make it. I made it that far – I want to make it to the end, regardless of what the end was.'

In 1947 I left Germany for the United States and married Walter Cahn. My father remained in Germany, and I was always very, very anxious to see him again. My husband wanted me to visit in 1960, but then the Berlin Wall went up and we weren't able to go. It was 1962 before I was able to visit him again. We didn't have any money at the time, and things were tough. Walter decided he couldn't go; he had to work. I went with my son. I was corresponding with my father, and he was extremely anxious to see me and to meet his one and only grandson.

When I arrived in Germany at the airport, I suddenly thought, oh, God, I should have never come back to this place – this is Germany, and I felt pretty bad. If it wasn't for my son holding on to my hand, I think I would have turned around and said, 'To hell with it, let's go back home again: why did I have to come here?'

But I knew I wanted to see my dad, and we got there the next day, and it was an unbelievable reunion. The best thing that could have happened to him was to finally see his grandson and to have me again.

The first day, I walked out with my father on the street. People talked to him and I kept thinking, why is he so friendly with these people? These are Germans. These are the ones who've done all this to us.

Little by little, I said, 'What am I going to do? Am I going to hate everything that has to do with Germans? I don't think that's right. My father lives here. I shouldn't feel that way.'

I wanted to ask my father whether he would ever consider coming to the United States, but I realized later it would have been totally impossible because he was too ill. At that time he was a little bit older, and not too well, but still going strong. I was fortunate to visit my father with my husband and son two or three more times. He died in 1972, leaving behind a second wife who had been very, very good to him.

One day after one of my trips, a group of friends asked me how I felt going back to Germany. I realized that if I wanted to hate everything that had to do with the Germans, I would not be able

Lory Cahn,
Los Angeles,
1999

to live a normal life, and definitely not a happy life.

Thank God, I have the most wonderful husband in the world, and a wonderful, happy marriage, even though a lot of tragedy has happened to my family. I would not have been able to live that way if I would have had nothing but hate for the Germans.

You can't hate everything that happened then. For years and years I talked about this, in the universities, and in schools, and in any organization that contacted me. I was always giving speeches – nobody should ever, ever forget what they have done to us. But I don't want to hate for the rest of my life.

LORRAINE ALLARD

I still have dreams, and certain things come back: I don't know what age I am, but life is quite normal. Whatever we're doing is an everyday happening. I could be sitting in the living room with my parents, or having a meal, carrying on a normal conversation. And then I wake up and say, 'I'm not there in that room. I'm not with them.'

We had a garden in Fürth, which was about ten minutes' walk from where we lived, and my father always had to be persuaded to go. When I was tiny I remember him piggy-backing me sometimes. Mother used to walk behind and say, 'You'll hurt yourself. Drop her! She's too heavy.'

I dream about this again. We're going to the garden and my father is carrying me on his back. And this is when I wake up. There's never anything terrible in the dream, except the fact that I'm living with my parents, as if they were just alive next to me, but I wake up and they're not. And as old as I am, I'm still sobbing because I realize it was a dream.

Lorraine Allard with grandchildren (*left to right*), Jonathan, Georgina Lore and Andrew, London, 1999

I now look at my fourteen-year-old grandson, and I think, this is the age when I lost my parents, home, country. Still, a lot has been made up to me from where I lost out. I had a hard time until I met my lovely husband – my second husband. We've been married over thirty-seven years. And I have a lovely son from my first marriage. He is a consultant rheumatologist. He's got all the degrees anybody could have. He is very active, and very successful, has three lovely children. I feel I'm a very lucky person because there are other people who've gone through an awful lot and haven't ended up like this.

I have a second cousin here, and she says, 'Anything you haven't had, you've got now.' Which is so true. And I'm very grateful and very proud of the whole family.

EVA HAYMAN

It's strange that it's only six years out of a long life, and those six years will affect the rest of your life.

Vera Gissing
(*left*) and Eva
Hayman,
England,
1999

I ceased to be a child when I boarded that train in Prague. I never was a child again after that. Even at school, whatever I participated in, whether it was games or anything else which I enjoyed, if I was happy, I would have this guilty feeling at the back of me, 'Well, my parents might be unhappy, and I am happy.'

Any time there is any change now, big or small, I find it very difficult to cope with it. I fear the same thing I felt when I got on to that train. I can talk to myself as much as I like, telling myself I'm foolish; it doesn't alter it. The same kind of fear builds up. That's one inheritance I have from those six years.

My experience of coming to England made me grateful for life, but also guilty for being alive. Here I was alive, and my parents were dead. I didn't suffer, and they had suffered. It didn't seem fair that I should be here.

On the other hand, whether I wanted it or not, as a nurse I had a tool to help other people with a different kind of suffering. So I thought maybe there is a reason why I survived. I had to have a reason why I survived because I didn't want to have survived.

I don't think I ever lost my strength, but for a long time the confusion in my head and heart was profound. When I was married and had children – to be a mother and have a family of my own – then I suddenly felt a new sense of belonging.

URSULA ROSENFELD

When I was younger and wanted to integrate, I used to feel rather sad. I wanted to belong. As a child, I didn't want to be different. I wanted somewhere to find roots and feel I belonged. In the later years of my life, I feel that I've been accepted. Nobody's ever said to me, 'Well, you weren't born in this country.' I was as entirely accepted as everyone else. And I gradually felt that I had somewhere I belonged.

I abhor nationalism as such, but I like the British way of life. Contrary to what other people think, I think British people are very warm. They've been very good to us. I've made a lot of very good friends. Britain is a society that does accept people from outside and, in fact, is a much more cosmopolitan community than we always give it credit for.

For instance, about twenty-five years ago I was appointed a magistrate in Manchester by the City of Manchester, which is quite an honour. And in 1971, my husband Peter and I were away in Geneva when we got a telegram saying that the Queen had in her mind to honour him with the MBE for his work in adult industrial education in this country. Our first reaction was to refuse it because we don't really believe in a class society where people have great distinctions. Peter also felt he hadn't done anything special – he had just done his job. But then we felt that, perhaps, it was an honour towards people who'd come to this country – Peter was born in Berlin and came here as a refugee too. So he did accept it.

We went to the palace to meet the Queen, and he got his distinction, which was quite an amazing event. Two of our children went along because, unfortunately, they only allowed us two children. Not many people in this country have four children these days. That was quite a difficult job, to decide which of them to take along with us.

Peter and Ursula Rosenfeld, Wedding Day, near London, 1 June 1946

Ursula
Rosenfeld
with her
husband and
children,
1963

When I look back now, strangely, I see a similarity between my fierce defence of the British way of life and my father's fierce defence of the German way of life, his belief in the German people, his inability to believe ill of them. I know wrong things have been done in this country, but I continue to defend the British way. I have a French friend who often calls me up and says, 'I know you see no ill in this because you're too English.' Perhaps it's a subconscious thing. My father probably wanted to belong and be part of the community in the same way that I want to belong.

INGE SADAN

I notice that my children have suffered from the five years I spent as a refugee in England. There are all sorts of feelings and reactions peculiar to the children of the Kindertransport: anxiety if you don't meet the person you're supposed to meet at that time or at that place, a general feeling of having been abandoned, of having to fight for everything.

When I go anywhere, I never leave my children with a sad look on my face. I'm always smiling because I made my mother smile and pretend to be happy when we went. I couldn't bear the thought of crying.

Once when we were going back to Israel from England, just after the Yom Kippur War, my mother cried as we left the house. She was so upset that she'd cried that she and my father rushed to the airport just to say goodbye with a smile. Shortly afterwards, my mother died. That was the last time I saw her.

All in all I think I lead a pretty normal life now, but I have no roots, and that bothers me. I think that's why I'm a very avid gardener. I get my roots through gardening, and also through my grand-children, who are so rooted in the country of their birth – which is Israel – that that's where my roots are beginning to grow.

I myself haven't got the same roots, although I love Israel, and will always live there as far as I know. I *chose* to go there. That's tremendously important. All the Israeli *Kinder* who went there, over a thousand of them, *chose*. They weren't pushed, they weren't sent, they weren't separated any more.

Inge Sadan (*left*) and Bertha Leverton, 1975

To be a refugee is the most horrible feeling because you lose your family, you lose your home, you're also without an identity. Suddenly you're a nothing. You are just reliant on other people's good nature and help and understanding. That's why I always have a soft spot for anybody who's in trouble. Living in Israel, I feel for the new immigrant. I feel for the Russians, and the Ethiopians, and anybody who's new, especially if they come without their families. Then, you know, if I can do anything, I do it. I just wish that people would learn, especially now with Kosovo and the Yugoslav experience, and in Africa. I wish God had made people more tolerant and understanding.

ROBERT SUGAR

After the harsh way we were treated as children, it always surprises me when people treat you properly. 'This waitress was so nice, let's tip her fifty bucks.' I mean I don't, but I am always surprised that others treat me as if I were just part of the human race. That may be a personal thing.

The younger you were, though, the more unforgiving you are of

Robert Sugar, New York, 1999

your parents. You may say, oh, they were so brave and saved you, but they really abandoned you.

We were four friends, very close friends. We called ourselves The Four Musketeers, right? And the only serious conversation we ever had, we all agreed, if it ever happens again, we will not send away our children, we will stay together no matter what. That's what we said.

Later on, as we grew older, we mitigated it, we said: if it ever happens again, we promise to take each other's children in, we will not send them to strangers. Then we were already being political. But when we were little, we said we will not send the children away. I attest to that.

BERTHA LEVERTON

One evening I was watching a boring television programme and my eyes were wandering around the room and they fell on the photographs of my lovely grandchildren. One of them was exactly the same age I was when I left Germany. I looked at the photograph and thought to myself, you, your brother, your sister, your cousins in Israel, you have no inkling of what your grandma went through at your age. At that time we didn't talk about our experiences. My grandchildren knew I'd come from Germany, they knew little bits of the story, but they never really knew what we went through.

Well, I'm a very impulsive person, so I jumped up, went to the telephone, and phoned up the only friend I'd kept in touch with from my school-days. I said, 'Ilse, I'm going to make a get-together, a reunion of the *Kinder* from fifty years ago. Do you realize it's forty-nine years we've been in this country and nowhere in the *Jewish Chronicle* or anywhere in the press is any mention of the Kindertransport?'

I didn't really know much about the transports. I didn't know how many children had arrived. I didn't know how many hostels there were. It was just a feeling that I wanted to see some of my friends again. And she said, 'Yes, that's not a bad idea. We should do something for next year.'

So I got started. I thought I'd hire the synagogue hall two doors away from where I lived, and if I was lucky, I'd get a hundred people together. But as the news got out, people began to write in from all over. By the time I got cold feet, I didn't realize what I'd started. It was absolutely the right time for a reunion, because any earlier we were busy making a living and bringing up our children. Nobody wanted to think back. It was too raw, too soon. Now the time was right and the idea struck a chord.

Within a year we had our fiftieth anniversary reunion in London, in June 1989. It made a tremendous impact on everybody; it was very moving, very special. That's when I founded ROK, Reunion of Kindertransport. After the reunion we carried on. I'm very proud of the fact that this is probably one of the few organizations in the world that cuts across religion, politics, income, education. We all call each other by our first names – even the millionaires. And we have given back to the countries who have given us refuge and shelter. We have not only taken, we have returned the things we received by way of education and support.

The ROK has been a tremendous getting-together and exchanging of views and life stories. It's been very important to realize there are others like ourselves. A lot of the *Kinder* had been isolated; they hadn't realized how many of us there were. But there's been a determination in all of us to make good, to prove Hitler wrong, and through our children and grandchildren, and future generations, to show that we have survived.

CHARLOTTE LEVY

All those I know who have escaped the Holocaust and started a new life have done well. The deeply shaking and uprooting experience had ploughed us and brought more strength to the surface than we had attributed to ourselves. This has been the Jewish fate and experience all through history.

Hitler could take all our material possessions, our money, our jobs and our homes, but he could not touch what we had in our heads and hearts and these were the assets with which we could build a new life for ourselves and our children.

FRANZI GROSZMANN

It was certainly difficult coming from Vienna to England. You were suddenly thrown out of your life. You were there to do what had been done for you before. And we really didn't know how to do it.

Franzi Groszmann, Lore Segal and her grandson, Benjamin, New York, 1999

But I'm always amused by these kinds of things, that one can do things which one isn't used to. Everything that has happened to me was easier because I can take things as they are. I do not ask for very much in life. What has to be done, I can do – not always very pleasantly, not very nicely, but I do it, and I don't very much suffer. I get cross about it. I get funny about it. But in the end I can do it.

You just take whatever comes to you. Just take it and do. Don't complain. Don't sit down and cry. When Lore had to leave Vienna for England, there was no crying at home, neither my husband nor I. Lore didn't see it, at least, when I cried.

LORE SEGAL

I am dazzled, from the point of view of the writer, by having had the experience of the English class system from the inside. Who else has the unbelievable good fortune to live with the Jewish manufacturer, the English working-class union man, railroad stoker, a munitions factory worker, the milkman, the Anglo-Indian Victorian ladies? Whoever has the sheer advantage of not studying this from the outside, but being a helpless member from the inside of these families? Seems to me it was a gift. It didn't seem so at the time.

JACK HELLMAN

We were two years in England, then we emigrated to the United States. My parents had an affidavit from my mother's brother and they wanted to be reunited with my sister and my mother's brother. The quota from Britain to America was slightly different than it was from Germany to America, so when our number came up, we went.

I was tremendously sad to leave. I was very heartbroken to start all over again in a new place, where I knew nobody. Those years in England were the happiest of my youth. Nobody had a farthing more than anyone else. There was no caste system. We were all equal.

My parents, too, I never saw them as happy in the United States as they were those two years in England.

Jack Hellman, New York, 1999

KURT FUCHEL

It took time after our reunion, but I certainly rebuilt a relationship with my parents. I felt my old love returning for both of them. Eventually, in 1956, our quota number for the United States came up and we had to decide: were we going or not? We decided yes.

By this time, I was a Frenchman and felt at home in France. I had served in the French army, even been an officer briefly. But I realized that if it didn't work out in the States, we could always come back, where this was a one-time opportunity.

So we went to New York. Whereas travel has been associated with a lot of pain in my life, there was also a lot of excitement. Coming to America was an adventure. I remember the excitement of the trip on a French liner, the luxury of it. And I remember coming early one morning into the harbour and seeing the Statue of Liberty. It was emotional for me, and it still is. Of course, when I arrived in New York, the biggest factor of all was that I spoke the language! I could make conversation with a girl!

I treasure my English past, and my French past. I cannot have much sympathy for my Austrian past. Norwich is my home town, but I love New York. I still stay very close, by mail, with the Cohens. I've always kept in touch with them. Unfortunately, too many years went by during which I didn't see them, and in the meantime, Percy died. He was only fifty-eight when he died suddenly of a heart attack, and I had not got back to see him.

This saddened me immensely. I stayed in touch with John and Mariam. We exchanged cards, letters, presents, but the thrust was to get on with one's life, and this I did. Sadly, Mariam is the only one of my four parents who survives. I still stay very close to her because I feel she's a very important part of my family. I telephone her every couple of weeks or so. We don't talk very long – she's not very talkative – but she always says that she loves me and God bless. I call John also. I have a dual family, and it's fine now.

Mariam Cohen and Kurt Fuchel, Norwich, England, 1999

The stability of living eight years with the Cohens benefited me in many ways, gave me a rosy view of life instead of a jaded one. I do tend to see the bright side in things, and the funny side. But the ambiguity of being attached to two families, instead of only one, also affected me. I sometimes have a hard time committing 100 per cent, because I realize I'm torn between two sets of people.

MARIAM COHEN

Kurt has kept in touch with us all these years. He's been so affectionate. He comes to visit quite often. And when my sister married an American pilot, I went to the US. Kurt gave me a lovely time in New York. He took me all over the city. We took wonderful photographs from the top of the Empire State Building, and you could see all the way down. I've still got them all.

We took Kurt before the war because you felt you wanted to do something. I mean, there was not a lot we could do, was there, really? My mother, bless her, she took a little girl, Elizabeth, whose family used to phone every Friday night from Vienna. One Friday night, there was no phone call, and poor little girl, she knew what it was. She sat in that little grandmother's chair and she covered her head with a shawl, and she just sobbed and sobbed and sobbed. And we had to get the minister to come and try to comfort her, but she knew what had happened.

Man's inhumanity to man is unbelievable.

NICHOLAS WINTON

I don't know why the British rescued these children and other countries didn't. Perhaps it is because there is a very fundamental tradition in England of general charity work, which doesn't exist in other countries.

I don't know what people in America do when they retire at fifty-five or sixty, but normally you'll find here if somebody retires at that age, he'll be doing something other than playing golf and bridge. It's a tradition. I've been retired now for as long as I've worked, certainly over thirty years. Goodness knows what I would have done with those thirty years if I hadn't done charity work. And I've enjoyed it.

I don't look back much on that period of the Kindertransport. It was a job that I did and it was a job which was completed as far as I could complete it. There was nothing else to be done. Maybe a lot more could have been done, but much more time would have been needed, much more help would have been needed from other countries, much more money would have been needed, much more organization.

We may say the same thing in a few years' time about what's happening now in Yugoslavia. Nobody learns anything, that's the only thing that history teaches us.

VERA GISSING

When you think of the world today, when you think of the suffering, for instance what is happening in Kosovo now, the ethnic cleansing, the thousands and thousands of children who have been separated from their parents, or have been orphaned, and the people who are trying to get those children into safe havens of other countries, it's like looking into a mirror, seeing the past repeat itself.

I wrote my autobiography, *Pearls of Childhood*, in honour of Mother and Father, not just as a tribute to them, but to my foster-family and all the other families who took us in, and the kindness of the British people in general. It's also a tribute to all the millions who perished in the camps. By keeping their memory alive, and by marrying the experiences of the past to the atrocities which are happening now, I hope to make young people and grown-ups think more about the future.

ALEXANDER GORDON

Alexander Gordon, New York, 1999

People ask themselves, 'What is the purpose of your life? What are you doing here in this world?'

In 1938 I escaped the deportation to Poland. I got out of Germany on the Kindertransport. I was sent to Australia on a ship, and the ship was torpedoed – but it didn't go down. I got back to England and was in the army.

Why all these coincidences? I've come to one conclusion: I was meant to survive, not because of myself, but so that we Jews would survive and I would bring up another generation and they would live. And I look at my children, and my grandchildren, and I know there was a purpose to my life.

At the beginning of the war, I was very mad and disappointed in England. But then you realize that England was fighting for its life and defending itself against Hitler. As time has passed, I consider England my home. I didn't leave England because I didn't like it. The only reason I left was because I was all by myself.

I was looking for a family from the moment I was born until I came to America. The only relatives I ever knew were my mother and my brother; my father I don't remember. My mother had gone. My brother was in Israel. The rest of the family was in America. So I wanted to come to America.

But England is in me. England is my second mother; always I will regard it as such.

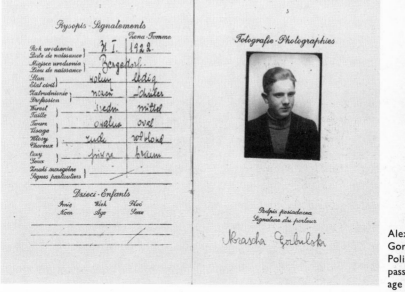

Alexander Gordon's Polish passport, age 16, 1938

Sylva Avramovici, age 10

IN MEMORY OF SYLVA AVRAMOVICI OPPENHEIMER 1928–1993

By Deborah Oppenheimer

I loved my mother dearly. As a child I believed that I was the centre of her universe, that she had only ever been my mother, that she had no life before my brother, sister and I entered her world. But my mother was hiding a profound grief from her own childhood and I made a silent pact to absorb it.

My mother rarely told stories about her childhood home, family, friends, escapades, school, celebrations, journeys, or any of the insignificant details that offer intimacy. Scarce were the emotional mementos and family photographs that might prove she had a past. I tried a few times to learn her story, but she would start crying, then I would start crying, and I'd retreat – out of love for my mother. Her grief was vast and deep. My brother, sister and I understood not to ask questions.

In 1939, shortly after her eleventh birthday, in a desperate act of love, my mother's parents placed her alone on a train and sent her from Germany to safety with strangers in England. She never saw them again. In the frenzy of war, she was transferred to a succession of placements that were incapable of providing love and nurturing. She cried herself to sleep every night for two years, longing for her parents who, unbeknownst to her, perished in a concentration camp. She discovered their names on a posted list at the end of the war.

My grandparents were one-dimensional solemn black-and-white portraits in a silver frame in the living room. As far back as I can remember, they were always there but never referred to. I knew virtually nothing about them. For me, they didn't exist.

Over the years we heard scattered fragments of my mother's life.

Sylva's parents, Avram and Alta Basia Avramovici, Chemnitz, Germany, 1941

We knew she had been on the Kindertransport. She lived with a Lord and Lady in a castle in England. And then there were the Fields, a British family that had briefly taken her in after an appeal in their synagogue. My mother stayed in touch with Milly Field and her older sister, Freda Nathan, for her entire life. We were particularly close to Milly's daughter, Rosalind, and her son, Roger. As a newborn, Rosalind was treated by my mother as her own personal baby doll. No one could pry the infant out of her arms.

My mother told me about letters that her parents had written to her in England, which she carried inside her shoe. One day during an air raid, she hastily destroyed many of the letters for fear of endangering her parents, only to discover the raid was a false alarm.

My mother, Sylva Avramovici Oppenheimer, was beautiful – thick black hair, porcelain skin, deep red lipstick, a radiant smile. I thought she looked like a movie star. She was honest, generous, elegant, refined, devoted to her family and loyal to the friends she kept a lifetime.

My father, Eric Oppenheimer, also escaped Germany, just before the Anschluss. He came with his parents and sister and a container of furniture and linens, past the Statue of Liberty, to Washington Heights. Still a teenager, he later enlisted in the United States Army and went back to Germany as an interpreter. One act of his military service was to participate in the liberation of Nordhausen, which he painfully captured in photographs. These photographs were always hidden from us.

My parents met shortly after my mother arrived in the United States in 1947, sponsored by her mother's surviving sister. She was nineteen years old and had, by then, lost her parents, her home, her education and her childhood. She contracted scarlet fever and went to a convalescent home to recover. There she met my father's cousin, Inge Oppenheimer, who was recovering from the aftermath of her concentration camp experience. They became friends, Inge brought

Sylva to meet Eric, and by mutual report, my father 'pushed' my mother around the basement, stepping on her toes, in his notion of dancing. He fell instantly and hopelessly in love. My mother always said how beautiful he made her feel.

She got a job at Longines watch company. My father was attending Columbia University. At the end of their day, they'd meet, riding the train just to be together for a little while.

My mother walked down the aisle of her wedding in a borrowed wedding gown, under an abbreviated name more easily pronounced than the one she had been given. Her marriage to my father provided the first real love that she had known since she left her parents.

My parents' common experience in Hitler's Germany allowed them to share their lives without ever discussing their losses. They wanted to put the Holocaust behind them and start a new life. They often said America took them in, 'America's been very good to us.' The student protests in the 1960s and 1970s were an ongoing source of friction between us. I didn't understand their blind patriotism; they disapproved of my teenage rebellion.

My parents were never apart. The only time my mother ever travelled without my father was to attend Roger Field's wedding in London in 1976. She fretted over what to wear and how she looked, and she fussed and primped for days before leaving. We realized my mother was deeply determined to prove to her English family that the immigrant girl had made good.

My parents didn't want to perpetuate the German culture. They did not teach us German. They boycotted German products and wouldn't think of buying a German car. Yet we grew up on German nursery rhymes, children's songs and books. German friends and relatives were always around. My father's parents visited every Sunday. And whenever my parents didn't want us to understand, or were angry with us, they spoke in German. In a house of three children, there was a lot of German spoken.

German music, Viennese waltzes and yodelling songs filled the air. We ate German recipes at my father's parents' house around the German dining set on German porcelain with German linens, holding German silverware the German way. We were raised with strict German precision, obedience and decorum. For first-generation Americans, we turned out awfully German.

As an adolescent, whenever I introduced my friends to my parents, they'd always ask where my parents came from. Yet I couldn't hear their accent, and neither could my brother or sister. It didn't occur to us to mention the Kindertransport. None of our contemporaries had ever heard of it.

One year, my father felt drawn to visit Germany. He hadn't been back since the war; he wanted to visit his grandfather's grave and show my mother where he was born. My mother went under extreme protest. Just as Americans wanted to know where my parents were from, the Germans were curious where my parents had learned their German. My parents chose not to reveal their origins. They had no love or trust for the Germans they encountered.

My mother and father worked with my grandparents six days a week, in the family hardware store. My mother would count the day's receipts and I'd see the numbers quietly cross her lips in German. More than the unheard accent, more than anything else, her calculations in German were so automatic that I understood deep down, my mother was German first.

My father had a heart attack in his forties and, as a passionate recreational pilot, was required to have a chest x-ray every year to renew his licence. Otherwise, he would have avoided the doctor. My mother protectively accompanied him but was infrequently examined herself. She had a fear of radiation. In 1990, she asked for a routine physical. She had no symptoms and no warnings.

The x-rays discovered a spot on my mother's lungs, in spite of never having smoked or even held a cigarette. An operation revealed that the cancer had metastasized to the lymph nodes. The surgeon explained the details to my father, sister and me late one night in the waiting room at Mt Sinai Hospital. There were tiny dots of blood on his gown which I'm sure he thought we wouldn't notice. I couldn't comprehend the words he was saying. I became a panic-stricken child.

I had never experienced a catastrophic illness. Aware of the preciousness of time, I became desperate to learn my mother's stories. I spent much of her illness in hope and denial, praying that she would recover, but I believed her past was a lifeline to her immortality.

A couple of times I tried to ask questions about her parents and childhood, but I didn't know where to begin. We would dissolve in tears, but, unlike when I was a child, I now felt a tremendous responsibility. I was convinced the grief of her past was contributing to her illness, and I worried deeply about the psychological and physical pain I could cause. I believed I was opening a Pandora's box that my mother didn't have the tools to close. I didn't want to cause her harm. When a good friend of hers chastised me, I felt as if I'd been unfair and selfish.

We did have respites. I have fond memories of climbing into her hospital bed and laughing together. When she was well, we took overnight girl trips with my sister. One night we crashed a stranger's wedding, even jumping on the *Hava Nagila* line snaking around the hotel's ballroom. We grabbed hold of strangers, did our bouncing steps, and got out undetected. We laughed so hard we cried.

One time after my mother's worst episode, when she suffered a seizure and disorientation and wasn't herself, a resident came to visit and check her progress in the hospital. My sister and I were joking in the background, behaving rambunctiously. My mother turned and gave us *the look*. With the purse of her lips or the squint of an eye, she could discipline us without a word. The resident called us outside to ask our thoughts about her mental state. Without hesitating, having just been given *the look*, we told him the mother we knew and loved was back to her old form.

Before her death, my mother gave me the present she had gotten from her parents on her eleventh birthday, her only possession from childhood. I'd asked her for the Mont Blanc pen and pencil set in a worn red leather case, with the name of her hometown stamped on the pen. When I unzipped the lid of the case, there was my mother's name, proudly written in her girlish handwriting. No gift could have been more meaningful to me. It was tangible proof of her childhood.

My brother called to tell me that our mother had died on 16 December 1993, at the age of sixty-five. To the end, she was heroic, she never lost her dignity, she never became bitter or complained. She grew from her illness and, while witnessing her strength, we all grew from it, too.

We mourned her, surrounded by family and friends. Roger Field and his wife, whose wedding she so eagerly attended in London, sat shiva with us. Her foster-mother had visited just weeks before.

Some time after my mother's death, my father discovered a hidden stack of letters in a drawer, written every day by my mother's parents to her in England after her departure. No one, not even my father, knew the letters existed.

It was shocking to touch letters my grandparents had held, written on tissue-thin stationery, the handwriting in elegant fountain pen. My mother's first cousin translated them, explaining references to other family members. Terms of endearment, 'my little mouse', made my grandparents come alive for the first time. I was thrilled my mother had been so deeply loved, but now her loss seemed that much greater and more painful.

Letter to Sylva from her 'Mutti'

There were other nicknames, family gossip, trivialities, and attempts at normalcy and parenting from afar. They asked how the trip had been, admonished her to 'be obedient, be a good little girl', they shielded her from their troubles. When she broke her birthday pen, her parents patiently explained that the pen was very expensive, that she should be careful with it, but she could return it to them in Germany and they'd have it fixed. War broke out before she sent it.

I had never thought about my grandparents – who they were or what they were like. Now I could conceive them as individuals, but I didn't know what to call them. How odd to have a relationship with people for whom I had no name. I recognized in their words, the love and strict discipline with which I had been reared, the devotion to family with which I had been instilled.

There is a Yiddish word *beschert*, meaning *meant to be*. In October 1995, I attended a dinner for a friend's father-in-law, an event honouring him for his philanthropy. I didn't realize, until that night, that he was a Kindertransport survivor. Nearly five minutes of archival footage on the Kindertransport were shown. I desperately peered into the faces, searching for my mother, wondering if I would recognize her young features. Later, when a speaker asked all the *Kinder* to stand, three tables of grey-haired men and women rose. I thought I was seeing an apparition. 'They live, they exist.' I had never before seen another *Kind*. It was overwhelming.

I always had an emotional awareness of the Kindertransport, but I never knew its history. I decided to learn everything that I could. In March 1998, I heard that there was a Kindertransport reunion scheduled for London in June 1999, the sixtieth and possibly last. Many of the *Kinder* were now in their seventies, their parents, foster-parents and rescuers easily twenty years beyond. I realized the clock was ticking and I was determined to preserve the stories, many of which had already been lost.

I received an application for the reunion, geared towards the *Kinder*. With the meagre information I had about my mother's past, there was little I could complete. Certainly, I knew my mother's maiden name, birthplace and birthdate, but I guessed (wrongly, I later discovered) the date of her departure, using the dates on my grand-parents' letters. I filled in the residences Hackney Hostel and Cockley Cley from the addresses on the envelopes. I attached a note apologizing for my ignorance and sent it to a post office box in New York.

I was given the name of Kurt Goldberger, President of the Kinder-transport Association Inc., who ironically lived twenty minutes from my parents' home. One day, I dialled his number. His wife, Margarete Goldberger, answered the phone and asked who was calling. When she heard my name, Margarete said, 'I know exactly who you are. I was at Hackney Hostel and Cockley Cley with your mother.'

Margarete Goldberger spent the next hour regaling me with stories of her and my mother's childhood – the cruel hostel matron, the names of other girls, a near-hit by a bomb that grazed Hackney

Hostel, evacuation to Cockley Cley Hall, Lady Roberts's kindness, and more. She promised photographs and invited me to join the girls at a Cockley Cley reunion the next summer, to coincide with the Sixtieth, hosted by the grandniece and grandson of Lord and Lady Roberts.

Sylva (*left*) and Margarete (*third from right*) with girls of Hackney Hostel, 1939

A timeline of my mother's life was emerging. I bombarded my mother's two surviving first cousins with questions about the family. I accidentally discovered there was a third lost cousin who had survived three concentration camps and was still alive somewhere. After much searching and stumbling, I found him in Canada, living under a new name, Rudy Roden, which he had adopted after the Holocaust.

Rudy had last spoken to my mother in the 1940s. He hadn't known how to reach her; he didn't know she had children; he didn't know she had passed away. His parents are referred to in my grandparents' letters and one is posted from their home in Prague. My mother was Rudy's favourite cousin and he had been thinking he would like to find her. He flew out to meet me. My family now extends to his children and grandchildren.

In December 1999, on the sixtieth anniversary of the first departure of the Kindertransport, Kevin Fagan, a journalist at the *San Francisco Chronicle*, commemorated the event with an article that included interviews with several *Kinder*. Contacted by a young woman eager to learn more about her mother's experience, Kevin referred her to me, although he and I had never spoken. He had heard about my efforts from the small but organized Kindertransport community.

The woman called my office, I offered to tell her what I had learned. She wanted to know my mother's maiden name. When I answered, she burst out crying, 'My mother shared a bed with yours at Cockley Cley!'

Her mother, who desires anonymity, lived in the gamekeeper's cottage at Cockley Cley with my mother for several months. In subsequent letters and on the phone, she told vivid stories of a fairy tale-like thatched cottage with a small window, and pegs on the wall to hold their ribbons and dresses (she said she coveted my mother's pretty clothes). She and my mother shared a mattress stuffed with twigs and leaves that had to be kneaded at night before they slept. They also shared a notched candle, by which they rationed their nightly reading. She had three years of diaries, and she carefully hand-wrote each entry that referred to my mother. She sent photographs, many of which I hadn't seen before, and we began an ongoing correspondence.

In June 1999, I went to the reunion at Cockley Cley Hall and visited the gamekeeper's cottage. I met other women who had lived in the Hall as girls, who remembered every detail of the life they had lived. They took me down corridors, up back staircases, into their dorm-style bedroom. Most of the girls had lost their parents. All had silently cried themselves to sleep. None of them ever shared their grief. They explained crying was contagious.

My father, brother and sister watched curiously as I unravelled the mysteries of our mother's life. My father came with me the first time I met Kurt and Margarete Goldberger to hear the early stories. After that, my father would call to tell me of lectures he attended, people he'd met, who might have some bearing on the Kindertransport. He found one of our *Kinder*, Jack Hellman, who is distantly related, after a *beschert* visit one day. A conversation he had with his cousin, Frank Cripps, and his wife Lucy, led to our discovery of Lory Cahn.

My sister attended the historic Sixtieth Reunion with me. We visited my mother's foster-mother, who gave us the name of another woman with whom my mother had briefly found shelter. My sister and I met the woman who, sadly, could provide no dates, no circumstances, no photographs and no memories of my mother's stay. She could, however, in an instant, locate and give to us the shoe trees my mother had left behind sixty years ago, stamped with my mother's hometown, signed by the now-familiar hand.

I journeyed to her birthplace in Chemnitz, an industrial town near Dresden. A representative of the mayor's office and the Jewish Community researched my family tree, providing copies of the ancient city register, with handwritten entries of births, deaths, marriages and business activities. Everyone had an entry except my mother. She was born after the city converted to an index card system, stored during the war in a facility that was bombed.

They compiled addresses – my mother's home, my grandparents' factory, my grandparents' newlywed apartment, my great-grandfather's home and, most disturbingly, the Jewish house to which my grandparents were relegated after their apartment was confiscated. The date my grandfather lost his business was also included. It occurred just before my mother's departure from Germany.

My mother's home was converted to a doctor's office in the 1950s. The staff let me in. I walked the worn tile floor in the building's entryway, slid my hand on the old wrought-iron banister. I searched without success for any indication that the apartment ever housed a family. I consoled myself that the windows looked out upon buildings unchanged. I walked in the backyard and traced a path through a garden I imagined my mother played in. It had the same rhododendrons and geraniums I'd grown up with back home. The city was filled with flowers and foliage my mother had duplicated in our garden. I wondered if it provided her with the same familiarity it now gave me.

In the padlocked Jewish cemetery, I found my great-grandmother Sabine's overgrown gravestone, with dates indicating her death just prior to my mother's birth. In observance of Jewish custom, Sabine was the inspiration for my mother's name; grandchildren born after my mother's death continue this tradition.

I told the woman from the Jewish Community about a favourite kindergarten picture I had of my mother. She wondered if the teacher was the daughter of a prominent Rabbi, both of whom perished in the Holocaust. She ran to get pictures of an old Montessori class. There was my mother in a different pose from the same day – another addition to my growing collection.

Sylva (*third from right*), in kindergarten, Chemnitz, Germany

I visited the Jewish house in which my grandparents spent their final days in Chemnitz. It overlooked the train station from which they surely sent their daughter and were later deported. I wandered the old terminal, now padlocked and decaying.

I visited the site of my great-grandfather's house. The records indicated it had been bombed. As I stood before the vacant lot, I slowly realized it was bordered by the wall of a building with the faded brick outline of my great-grandfather's modest peaked home, long since ripped away.

I began to understand the desperation that compelled my grandparents to send my mother away, and the circumstances that trapped them there. Once home, I reread their letters, attaching new meaning to each turn of phrase. I found photographs of my grandparents with deportation dates indicated on the reverse side. I don't know what my mother knew. I still don't know where my grandparents died.

The search for my mother's story kept her close to me. I can't account for all her placements, but in piecing together the details of her life, I began to understand what shaped her, and gained insight into who I had become. Friends worried the search might be depressing. I found it cathartic, uplifting and inspirational.

I didn't want the images of my mother to be from the final days of her illness. Now I could see her as a child, a young adult, and a young woman. I came to know her parents, her grandparents, her cousins, aunts and uncles.

Sylva Oppenheimer with her daughter, Deborah

There is a terrific irony to my search. If my mother had told her stories, I would never have felt the need for this quest. Now there's so much I want to talk to her about. I wish I could ask questions. I wish I could introduce her to the people I've come to know and love.

The *Kinder* accepted me. They heard my name and my mother's story and embraced me as their own. They have begun to speak of their experience. My mother could not, yet pieces of my mother and grandparents are illuminated in all their stories. I finally understood my mother's silence when one *Kind*, Eva Hayman, confessed her desire not to transfer any of her anguish to her children. 'By protecting them, I underestimated their love and their strength.'

The *Kinder* are completely familiar to me. I've grown up on their accents and their losses. They are my grandparents, my parents, my relatives, and my parents' friends. They've entrusted me with their memories, letters, photographs and keepsakes. It has brought out the best in all of us.

This is my tribute to my mother. I have found a relationship with her and my grandparents that is profound, nurturing and comforting. They guide me daily. Though in life she could not accompany me, in death I have no doubt she is at peace and enormously proud.

POSTSCRIPT

After the war, the children of the Kindertransport dispersed to all parts of the globe. Although the majority settled in England, many others chose to join relatives in the United States or Canada or to start life afresh in the new state of Israel; a few even returned to the countries which they had fled. Wherever they decided to build their lives as adults, almost all determined to 'put the past behind them'.

In their later years – often when their grandchildren reached the same age at which they had been forced to leave their homes and families – many began to reflect on the painful separation and uprooting of their youth. The fifty-year Reunion of Kindertransport organized by Bertha Leverton contributed to this re-examination of the past and made many *Kinder* aware, for the first time, of how many others had shared the same traumatic experiences as children. The desire to reclaim their past, to celebrate their successes, and to communicate their stories to grandchildren and future generations, has encouraged many in their later years to write down or recount their personal histories on videotape.

In searching for the witnesses for our film and book, we have read through a great number of diaries and memoirs, published and unpublished, read numerous transcripts provided by the United States Holocaust Memorial Museum and other Holocaust institutions, and hundreds of letters from parents and children. We've also viewed dozens of testimonies, many of them taped by the Survivors of the Shoah Visual History Foundation in countries throughout the world. In addition, we conducted our own interviews with *Kinder* from North America, Europe, New Zealand, Australia, South Africa and Israel and also searched as widely as possible for the few parents, foster-parents and organizers of the transports who are still alive.

No film, or book, can possibly present the complete range of experience of a rescue operation which saved over 10,000 lives. But in selecting the witnesses who speak here, we have tried to represent what we consider the most essential aspects of the Kindertransport. We chose our subjects not only for their diversity, but also for their willingness to confront the pain and trauma of their childhood. Even in their seventies, many were still struggling to make sense of their refugee experiences and to integrate their past and present in an effort to construct a meaningful narrative of their lives. As painful as it was to face their losses, many of them have found the giving of testimony itself healing, often enabling them to see themselves and their histories in a new perspective, or to discover things about themselves that they have never voiced before. As filmmakers, we feel privileged that they have been willing to share their stories with us; and in editing their interviews, we have tried to preserve, as much as possible, the individuality and spontaneity of their voices.

Sadly, one of the men who bears witness in this book, Norbert Wollheim, died five weeks after our interview with him at his home in Queens, New York. Norbert's willingness to postpone his own flight from Germany in order to save the lives of thousands of Jewish children exemplified the spirit of the Kindertransport. Although his sacrifice resulted in his own internment in Auschwitz and the death of his wife and three-year-old son, he never stopped believing in the principal creed of his Youth Movement – that it is not enough to live only for yourself. In 1951 he sued I. G. Farben, one of Germany's largest manufacturers, for back pay for the two years of slave labour he spent at Auschwitz building a synthetic-rubber plant. His suit opened the way for a settlement with Farben that established a fund of $6.43 million to compensate other Jewish labourers. While starting a new family, and a career as an accountant, in the United States, he continued to pursue survivors' claims and remained an active spokesman for the Holocaust community throughout his life.

More than sixty years have now passed since the Kindertransport, and the sense of mortality weighs heavily on a great many of the participants. Several who speak in these pages saw their interviews as a last opportunity to tell their stories to a larger world. We are grateful for their sharing them with us. Their words are a testament to their resilience and their humanity.

THE WITNESSES

The Kinder

Lorraine Allard (née Lore Sulzbacher) was born in Fürth, Bavaria, Germany, and came to Lincoln, England, at the age of fourteen. She lived with the same foster-family until the age of eighteen when she joined the ATS (Auxiliary Territorial Service) and drove staff cars during the war. After VE day, she learned that both her parents had perished at Auschwitz. She presently lives with her husband in London. *(See pp. 21, 57, 89, 122, 153–65, 167, 181, 215, 219, 246.)*

Lory Cahn (née Lory Grüenberger) was born in Breslau, when it was still part of Germany. At fourteen she was slated to leave for England on the Kindertransport but, at the last moment, her father could not bear to part with her. At the end of 1941, she and her parents were deported to Theresienstadt, where she was confined for a year and a half before being separated from her parents and sent to Auschwitz. For the rest of the war she was transferred from one concentration camp to another until she was liberated at Bergen-Belsen, weighing fifty-eight pounds. She currently resides with her husband in Pennsylvania. *(See pp. 23, 61, 108, 191, 235, 244.)*

Hedy Epstein (née Hedy Wachenheimer) grew up in Kippenheim, a small town near Freiburg, Germany. She was fourteen when she came to London, where she lived with two different foster-families. After the war she returned to Germany as an employee of the US government in order to search for her parents, both of whom she later discovered were murdered at Auschwitz. A German memoir of her experiences, *Erinnern Ist Nicht Genug* (Remembering is Not Enough), was published in Germany. Her home is in Missouri. *(See pp. 36, 68, 91, 111, 132, 178, 190, 241.)*

Kurt Fuchel (né Kurt Füchsl) was born in Vienna, Austria, where he lived until the age of seven, when his parents sent him to Norwich, England, on the Kindertransport. He was taken in by the family of Percy and Mariam Cohen and stayed with them until the age of sixteen. His parents escaped from Austria to the south of France and were sheltered by French families during the war. In 1947, Kurt was reunited with his parents in France where the family continued to live until 1956 when they emigrated to the United States. A past president of the Kindertransport Association Inc. (KTA), Kurt resides with his wife in New York. *(See pp. 49, 66, 126, 181, 199, 233, 255.)*

Vera Gissing (née Vera Diamant) the younger sister of Eva Hayman, both of whom were rescued by Nicholas Winton, was born in Čelákovice, Czechoslovakia. Vera was almost eleven when she arrived in England, where she lived with two different families before she joined the Czech school in Wales. Although both her parents died in the Holocaust, she returned to Prague after the war to set up home with her one surviving aunt. In 1949, she emigrated back to England, where she continues to live. Her book, *Pearls of Childhood*, is based on her childhood diaries. *(See pp. 53, 95, 110, 129, 182, 202, 223, 258.)*

Alexander Gordon (né Abrascha Gorbulski) was placed in a Jewish orphanage in Hamburg at the age of seven where he remained until he graduated high school. Afterwards he went to work on a farm to prepare for immigration to Palestine. Following Kristallnacht he was one of the first to leave Germany on the Kindertransport. Since he was sixteen when he arrived in England, he was arrested in June 1940 when the British government ordered the internment of refugees between the ages of sixteen and seventy from enemy countries. Two weeks later he was shipped to Australia on the HMT *Dunera* and interned there for over a year until he volunteered to join the Pioneer Corps and returned to England. He served in Britain, France, Belgium and Germany until the end of 1947, when he emigrated to the United States. He now lives in New Jersey. *(See pp. 43, 58, 83, 107, 113, 140, 185, 223, 258.)*

Eva Hayman (née Eva Diamant)   was fifteen years old when she left Czechoslovakia with her younger sister, Vera. She spent two years in an English boarding school before taking up nursing. Her wartime memoir, *By the Moon and the Stars*, is based on her diaries which she started writing in June 1939, her last day in Czechoslovakia, and finished in July 1945, the day she learned of the death of her parents. She resides in New Zealand, where she has lived for the last forty-three years. *(See pp. 54, 94, 109, 117, 131, 204, 225, 247.)*

Jack Hellman (né Hans Joachim Hellmann)   was sent off to boarding school in Frankfurt when he was nine to avoid the anti-Semitism he experienced daily in Tann, the German village where he was born. After Kristallnacht, the house mother of the school wrote to Baron James de Rothschild asking if he would take in twenty-six children as well as her husband, herself and two daughters. The Baron agreed and Jack and his schoolmates left Germany on the Kindertransport. Once in England he also prevailed upon Baron Rothschild to provide a work permit for his father. His parents arrived in England on the day Hitler invaded Poland and remained there for two years until the family was able to emigrate to New York, where Jack Hellman continues to live. *(See pp. 33, 62, 86, 105, 139, 177, 255.)*

Bertha Leverton (née Bertha Engelhard)   is the oldest of three children from a Polish-Jewish family in Munich, Germany. She had her sixteenth birthday at Dovercourt Camp, shortly after she arrived in England with her brother Theo. A family in Coventry took her in to be their maid. Eventually, the family also took in her brother and younger sister, Inge, who had been in Germany up until that time. Bertha conceived and organized the Fiftieth Anniversary Reunion of Kindertransport in 1989 and also compiled and co-edited a collection of 250 remembrances of the transports, *I Came Alone*. She was a principal organizer of the 1999 Sixtieth Anniversary Reunion in London, where she lives. *(See pp. 40, 63, 87, 103, 145, 168, 209, 229, 252.)*

Ursula Rosenfeld (née Ursula Ellen Simon)   lost her father on Kristallnacht when he was arrested by the SS and murdered at Buchenwald. Shortly afterwards, her mother sent thirteen-year-old Ursula and her older sister, Hella, from Quackenbrück – the small town where they had been raised – to an orphanage in Hamburg. The girls remained there until they left for England the following year and were taken in by a widow in Brighton. Ursula's mother did not survive the war, and Ursula has remained in England, where she was appointed a magistrate for her adopted city of Manchester. *(See pp. 26, 73, 92, 109, 114, 127, 213, 222, 249.)*

Inge Sadan (née Inge Engelhard)   came from Munich to Coventry, England, at the age of nine when her elder sister Bertha managed to convince the family she was living with to act as her sponsor. Inge and her older brother and sister spent five difficult years with their foster-family until their parents arrived in England in 1944. Inge lives in Jerusalem, Israel, where she co-organized a 1994 reunion and edited a book of Israeli *Kinder* reminiscences called *No Longer a Stranger*. *(See pp. 42, 103, 169, 207, 228, 230, 250.)*

Lore Segal (née Lore Groszmann)   was ten when Hitler marched into Austria. Nine months later she was on the first Kindertransport to leave Vienna. At Dovercourt Camp she wrote letters to relatives that eventually reached the Refugee Committee in London and helped to get her parents a domestic service visa. They arrived in Liverpool in time for her eleventh birthday. Lore Segal's novel, *Other People's Houses*, recounts her experience as a refugee child living with five different British families during the war. She lives in New York in the same apartment building as her mother, Franzi Groszmann. *(See pp. 46, 59, 81, 99, 114, 141, 171, 211, 221, 254.)*

Robert Sugar   was eight years old when he left Vienna. He was sent to a Jewish refugee hostel in Belfast, Northern Ireland, from where he was sent to the refugee farming settlement near Millisle, in County Down. After the war, which both his parents survived, Robert emigrated to New York in 1947 to join his mother. A graphic designer and author, Robert still lives in New York and has written extensive educational material on Jewish history as well as designed visual exhibits for the KTA, on whose executive board he serves. *(See pp. 51, 66, 86, 106, 135, 210, 231, 251.)*

The Parents

Mariam Cohen is a foster-parent who took Kurt Fuchel into her family during the war. Her husband, Percy, died in 1963. She still lives in Norwich and enjoys regular visits from Kurt. *(See pp. 124, 201, 234, 257)*.

Franzi Groszmann followed her daughter Lore Segal from Vienna to England where she and her husband worked as a domestic couple during the war. At the age of ninety-five, she still has breakfast with her daughter every day. Recently she celebrated the birth of her second great-grandson. *(See pp. 81, 102, 145, 175, 254.)*

Charlotte Levy sent her son Hans to live in England with the Schlesinger family at the age of nine. A few months after the death of her husband, she was able to escape from Leipzig herself and make her way to England with her infant daughter. She is now 100 years old and lives with her sister in a retirement home in New Jersey. (See pp. 30, 59, 84, 105, 183, 253.)

The Rescuers

Nicholas Winton was a 29-year-old London stockbroker when he journeyed to Prague in December 1938. The desperation he encountered in the camps of refugees – the thousands of Jews, dissidents and Communists who had fled the Sudetenland in the aftermath of the Munich Agreement – prompted him to try to save their children when he returned to London. In the nine months before the war he was able to bring 664 Czech children to England. Although his wartime heroics have never been officially recognized in Britain, in 1983 he was honoured with an MBE for his services to the community. In Czechoslovakia he was awarded the Freedom of the City of Prague in 1992. He was recently awarded the service Above Self Award by Rotary International for exemplary humanitarian service, the only British recipient among 150 honorees. *(See pp. 78, 148, 182, 257.)*

Norbert Wollheim was twenty-five years old when he began organizing the Kindertransports in Berlin. An escort for several of the transports, he returned each time to Germany to continue his work, which ended with the outbreak of the war. In 1943 he and his wife and three-year-old son were deported to Auschwitz. He was the only one of seventy relatives to survive. He died in November 1998 at the age of eighty-five. *(See pp. 31, 65, 77, 99, 112, 119, 197, 239.)*

ADDITIONAL READING

Abraham-Podietz, Eva, and Fox, Anne, *Ten Thousand Children: True Stories Told by Children Who Escaped the Holocaust on the Kindertransport* (Behrman House, Springfield, NJ, 1998).

Bader, Alfred, *Adventures of a Chemist Collector* (Weidenfeld & Nicolson, London, 1995).

Bartrop, Paul R., with Eisen, Gabrielle, *The Dunera Affair* (Schwartz & Wilkinson, Melbourne, 1990).

Baumel, Judith Tydor, *Unfulfilled Promise – Rescue and Resettlement of Jewish Refugee Children* (Denali Press, Alaska, 1990).

Bentwich, Norman, *They Found Refuge* (The Cresset Press, London, 1956).

Blend, Martha, *A Child Alone* (Vallentine Mitchell & Co., London, 1995).

Breitman, Richard, and Kraut, Alan M., *American Refugee Policy And European Jewry, 1933–1945* (Indiana University Press, Bloomington, 1987).

Drucker, Olga Levy, *Kindertransport* (Henry Holt & Co., New York, 1995).

Eden, Thea Feliks, *A Transported Life: Memories of Kindertransport* (Herbooks, Santa Cruz, 1995).

Epstein, Hedy, *Erinnern Ist Nicht Genug* (Unrast Verlag, Germany, 1999).

Gershon, Karen, *We Came as Children* (Gollancz, London, 1966).

Gershon, Karen, *A Lesser Child* (Dufour Editions, Inc., Chester Springs, PA, 1994).

Gillman, Peter & Leni, *Collar the Lot: How Britain Interned and Expelled its Wartime Refugees* (Quartet Books Ltd, London, 1980).

Gissing, Vera, *Pearls of Childhood* (St Martin's Press, New York, 1988).

Göpfert, Rebekka, *Der Judische Kindertransport Von Deutschland Nach England* (Campus Verlag, Frankfurt/New York, 1997).

Gottlieb, Amy, *Men of Vision* (Weidenfeld & Nicolson, London, 1998).

Grunberger, Richard, *The 12 Year Reich: A Social History of Nazi Germany 1933–1945* (Da Capo Press, New York, 1995).

Hayman, Eva, *By the Moon and the Stars* (Random Century New Zealand Ltd, 1992).

House of Commons Official Report, *Parliamentary Debates, Fifth Series, Volume 341* (H.M. Stationery Office, London, 1938).

House of Lords Official Report, *Parliamentary Debates, House of Lords, Volume III, No. 16, Wednesday 14 December, 1938* (H.M. Stationery Office, London, 1938).

Jacoby, Ingrid, *My Darling Diary, a Wartime Journal from 1937–1944* (United Writers, Cornwall, 1998).

Kaplan, Marion, *Between Dignity and Despair: Jewish Life in Nazi Germany* (Oxford University Press, New York, 1998).

Kushner, Tony, *The Holocaust and the Liberal Imagination: A Socital and Cultural History* (Blackwell, Oxford, 1994).

Leapman, Michael, *Witnesses to War* (Penguin Books, London, 1998).

Leverton, Bertha, and Lowensohn, Shmuel, *I Came Alone, Stories of the Kindertransport* (The Book Guild Ltd, Sussex, 1990).

London, Louise, *Whitehall and the Jews 1933–1948* (Cambridge University Press, Cambridge, 2000).

Patkin, Benzion, *The Dunera Internees* (Cassell Australia Ltd, Melbourne, 1979).

Pearl, Cyril, *The Dunera Scandal* (Angus & Robertson, Sydney, 1983).

Sadan, Inge, *No Longer a Stranger* (Inge Sadan, Jerusalem, 1999).

Samuel, Diane, *Kindertransport* (full-length play) (Plume, 1995).

Segal, Lore, *Other People's Houses* (The New Press, New York, 1994).

Selo, Laura, *Three Lives in Transit* (Excalibur Press, London, 1992).

Sherman, A.J., *Island Refuge: Britain and Refugees from the Third Reich* (Frank Cass Publications, Essex, 1994).

Sim, Dorrith, *In My Pocket* (Harcourt Press, Orlando, 1997).

Turner, Barry, . . . *And the Policeman Smiled* (Bloomsbury, London, 1990).

Wasserstein, Bernard, *Britain and the Jews of Europe, 1939–1945* (Books International, Israel, 1999).

Whiteman, Dorit, *The Uprooted: A Hitler Legacy* (Perseus Books, Cambridge, MA, 1993).

Wijsmuller-Meijer, Truus, *Geen Tud Voor Tranen* (No Time for Tears) (P.N. Van Kampen & Zoon N.V., Amsterdam, 1962).

Zeller, Frederic, *When Time Ran Out: Coming of Age in the Third Reich* (Permanent Press, Sag Harbor, NY, 1996).

Zurndorfer, Hannele, *The Ninth of November* (Quartet Books Ltd, London, 1983).

Additional Resources

Kindertransport Association, Inc. (KTA)
www.kindertransport.org

Kindertransport UK
Association of Jewish Refugees (AJR)
1 Hampstead Gate
1a Frognal, London NW3 6AL
Tel: 44 (0)20 7431 1821
        44 (0)20 7431 6161
Fax: 44 (0)20 7431 8454
kt@ajr.org.uk

Reunion of Kindertransport Israel
POB 71105
Jerusalem 91079
Israel
Attn: Inge Sadan
Tel/Fax: 972 (0)2 5634026

Dunera News
Hay-Tatura Association
87 Clow Street
Dandenong
Victoria 3175
Australia
dunera@netlink.com.au

Survivors of the Shoah Visual History Foundation
Tel: 818-777-4673
www.vhf.org

United States Holocaust Memorial Museum
100 Raoul Wallenberg Place SW
Washington, DC 20024
Tel: 202-488-0400
www.ushmm.org

Into the Arms of Strangers: Stories of the Kindertransport
www.intothearmsofstrangers.com

Kindertransport Journey: Memory into History
KTA Visual Exhibit
Designed and produced by Robert Sugar

ACKNOWLEDGMENTS
By Mark Jonathan Harris and Deborah Oppenheimer

Our deepest gratitude to the *Kinder*, who inspired us with their eloquence, strength, modesty and generosity. We thank you for the privilege of hearing your stories.

We also wish to honour the parents of the 10,000 children whose lives were saved by the Kindertransport. Their love and courage is beyond comprehension.

This book would not have been possible without the benevolence and trust of the Kindertransport community and their families, who have shared their most personal stories and their irreplaceable mementos. Special thanks to the Kindertransport Association, Inc. and Kurt and Margarete Goldberger.

We are indebted to our documentary film team, whose gifts and talents inspired and challenged us: Judi Dench, Kate Amend, Don Lenzer, Lee Holdridge, Gary Rydstrom, Corrinne Collett, Alicia Dwyer, Bill Russell, Zanna Williams, Lou Fusaro, Jeff Victor, Peter Miller, Ned Hallick, Teri Dorman and Edith Lowell.

We are profoundly grateful to all our friends at Time Warner and Warner Bros., particularly Gerald Levin, Barry Meyer and Bruce Rosenblum, whose compassion, generosity and leap of faith granted this project life and ensured that these stories would not be lost.

We offer our heartfelt thanks to Bill Swainson and Karen Rinaldi at Bloomsbury Publishing for their faith and confidence and their guidance in shaping the stories contained within these pages. Pascal Cariss's skilful editing respected and preserved our witnesses' voices.

Warmest thanks to Lord Richard Attenborough and David Cesarani, whose knowledge and experience have enriched our understanding of this period.

Barbara Lowenstein's initiative and determination set this book in motion. Many thanks to her and to Norman Kurz of Lowenstein Associates and Mary Bruton of Abner Stein for their perseverance.

We owe a deep debt of gratitude to Tom Distler of Brooks & Distler for his meticulous concern for our best interests and for his trusted counsel.

The United States Holocaust Memorial Museum has been an enormous help throughout this entire project. Not only did they generously open their incomparable resources to us, but they have continuously supported us with their creativity and professionalism. Special thanks to Dr David Marwell, Raye Farr, Susan Snyder, Genya Markon, Brett Werb, Chris Sims and William F. Meineke, Jr.

We would like to thank the other Holocaust museums and film and photo archives throughout the world that assisted us, particularly the Survivors of the Shoah Visual History Foundation, whose extraordinary collection provided invaluable research information.

Our grateful appreciation to all the family, friends and colleagues whom we cannot name individually, but who contributed through their love and understanding.

By Deborah Oppenheimer

I have been graced with the friendship of Cayce Callaway, and her boundless encouragement, imagination and sense of humour.

Loving gratitude to Jacqueline Véissid, for her tireless research and dedication.

I treasure Bruce Helford for his understanding, resourcefulness and generosity.

I am deeply indebted to Robert Egami for his determination and insights.

Humble thanks to Brenda Teague for her moral support and loyalty.

A very special thanks to Patrick Perkins for all he has taught me about love and family.

I am grateful for the support and love of Jamie Lee Curtis.

The wisdom and guidance of Tom Fontana have been a cherished gift.

My father, Eric Oppenheimer, has given me the standards, love and work ethic that have sustained this project. I am fortunate to have in my brother, Alan Oppenheimer, and my sister, Wendy Martorella, loved ones with whom I share my history and my memories.

Most of all, loving thanks to my mother, Sylva Sabine Avramovici Oppenheimer, for her inspiration and her legacy.

PICTURE CREDITS

Lorraine Allard, *p.21, p.152, p.158, p.198, p.218*

Bettman/CORBIS, *p.142, p.146*

Miki Kratsman/Bettman/CORBIS *p.80*

Bildarchiv Preussischer Kulturbesitz, Berlin, *Frontispiece, p.35, p.38, p.58, p.64, p.69, p.70, p.122, p.181*

Lory Cahn, *p.23, p.193*

Mariam Cohen, *p.124, p.200*

Hedy Epstein, *p.91, p.241, p.242*

Herbert Friedman *p.90*

Kurt Fuchel, *p.50, p.67, p.126, p.234*

Vera Gissing, *p.224*

Margarete Goldberger *p.268*

Alexander Gordon, *p.43, p.76, p.189, p.223, p.259*

Eva Hayman, *p.54, p.205, p.226, p.240*

Jack Hellman, *p.34, p.87*

Hulton Getty/Liaison, *p.104, p.121, p.185, p.209*

Institute of Contemporary History and the Wiener Library Ltd., *p.116, p.120*

Jewish Chronicle, p.52, p.125

Leo Baeck Institute, *p.239*

Bertha Leverton, *p.41, p.147, p.229*

Charlotte Levy, *p.85*

Henry Lowenstein, *p.100*

National Archives, *p.56, p.148, p.150*

The National Trust – Waddesdon Manor, *p.139, p.177*

Sylva Oppenheimer courtesy of the Oppenheimer family *p.260, p.262, p.266, p.271, p.272*

Ursula Rosenfeld, *p.27, p.74, p.93, p.109, p.249, p.250*

Inge Sadan, *p.170, p.251*

Lore Segal, *p.82, p.98, p.166, p.173*

Michael Steinberg *p.107*

Robert Sugar, *p.51, p.137, p.138*

INTO THE ARMS OF STRANGERS

UCLA Film and Television Archive, p.20
United States Holocaust Memorial Museum, *p.75*
Warner Bros. Pictures (photos by Cayce Callaway) *p.244, p.246,*
  p.247, p.248, p.252, p.254, p.255, p.256, p.258
AP/Wide World Photos *p.118, p.129*
Nicholas Winton, *p.79*

A NOTE ON THE AUTHORS

Mark Jonathan Harris is a two-time Academy Award winner, most recently for the 1997 Best Feature-Length Documentary, *The Long Way Home*. He is a professor and former Chair of the Production Department of the USC School of Cinema/Television. He is also a journalist and author of five award-winning children's novels.

Deborah Oppenheimer, whose mother came to England on the Kindertransport, is the president of Mohawk Productions, a production company at Warner Bros.

A NOTE ON THE TYPE

The text of this book is set in Linotype Sabon, named after the type founder, Jacques Sabon. It was designed by Jan Tschichold and jointly developed by Linotype, Monotype and Stempel, in response to a need for a typeface to be available in identical form for mechanical hot metal composition and hand composition using foundry type.

Tschichold based his design for Sabon roman on a fount engraved by Garamond, and Sabon italic on a fount by Granjon. It was first used in 1966 and has proved an enduring modern classic.